MADAGASCAR

Land Of the Man-Eating Tree

By Chase Salmon Osborn, LL.D.

HELIOGRAPH

INCORPORATED

Somerville, MA
USA

AUTHOR'S DEDICATION

Dedicated to the London Missionary Society
and the Christian Missionaries
Who Have Labored Sacrificially in Madagascar

PUBLISHING INFORMATION

Originally published in 1924 by the Republic Publishing Company, Inc., New York.

This publication © 2012 by Heliograph, Inc., Somerville, MA. ISBN: 978-1-930658-71-4.

This publication contains the complete, unabridged text of the original publication, using the original's spelling and punctuation, although we did introduce additional paragraph breaks for readability. We scanned and reset the text into a two column format: the original book was over 400 pages in length.

We reproduce the photographs in their originally published sizes, slightly cropped. We apologize for their poor quality, but our copies were all ex-library and had seen heavy use.

Set in Minion Pro and **Mostra Nuova**.

Cover, Layout, and Production By Matthew Goodman.

Heliograph, Incorporated
26 Porter Street
Somerville, MA 02143 USA
www.heliograph.com
info@heliograph.com

TABLE OF CONTENTS

Isagoge 1

I   The Land of the Man-Eating Tree 1

II   The Making of the Island 4

III   The Great Rift Valley of Africa 7

IV   Aborigines of Madagascar 9

V   Early Inhabitants 13

VI   Races and Peoples of Madagascar 14

VII   Ancient Accounts of Madagascar 18

VIII The Bunkoing of Benjamin Franklin 19

IX   Yankees Fight in Madagascar 20

X   Americans in Madagascar 22

XI   Madagascar's Robinson Crusoe—Robert Drury 24

XII   Captain Kidd and a Pirate Republic in Madagascar 27

XIII A Rare Letter From Dr. David Livingstone 31

XIV High Emprise of a United States Army Surgeon 33

XV   Missionary Work in Madagascar 35

XVI The French Campaign of Conquest 37

XVII Seizing People by Wholesale One Kind of Enslavement 39

XVIII Gallieni as Governor of Madagascar 40

XIX From The French Official Standpoint 43

XX   French Government in Madagascar 47

XXI Madagascar At The French Exposition 48

XXII Malagasy Native History 49

XXIII Morals, Marriage And Virtue 65

XXIV Trial by Ordeal Common Use of Deadly Poisons 66

XXV Malagasy Burial Customs 67

XXVI Malagasy Marriage Ceremony 69

XXVII Average Malagasy Conditions of Living 71

XXVIII Malagasy New Year Festival 73

XXIX Traditions and Folk Lore and Life Among the Natives 77

XXX Embryos, Silkworms and Locusts as Food 94

XXXI Infanticide Not Uncommon 95

XXXII The Burial of a King 97

XXXIII Sepulchers of the Malagasies 99

XXXIV Hunting Wild Cattle 101

XXXV Some Malagasy Games 103

XXXVI Musical Instruments and Music 104

XXXVII Modes of Travel and Transportation 105

XXXVIII What They Know of America 108

XXXIX Minerals of Madagascar 110

XL   Animal Life 113

XLI Topography, Soil and Climate of Madagascar 116

XLII Flora of Madagascar 119

XLIII Madagascar a Complete World in Miniature 123

XLIV Farewell 124

MAPS AND ILLUSTRATIONS

ANCIENT MAP OF MADAGASCAR v

MODERN MAP OF MADAGASCAR vi

NOSIVALA RIVER FALLS, ON THE EAST COAST 5

IKOPA RIVER NEAR TANANARIVO 6

ANKARATRA RANGE 7

RIVER NEAR VATOMANDRY 8

BARA, BARA-MENAHARAKA, TANALA & SAKALAVA 15

ANTISAKA MAN & WIFE, ZARAMANAMPY WOMAN & CHILD 17

TANALA WOMEN & SERGEANT IN COLONIAL ARMY & HIS FAMILY 17

ANCIENT GATE IN THE WALLS OF TANANARIVO 18

SPRING AT THE EDGE OF THE CITY 19

AMBOSITRA, 150 MILES SOUTH OF TANANARIVO 25

VATOMANDRY, EAST COAST 25

ROMAN CATHOLIC CATHEDRAL, ANTANANARIVO 29

CHURCH OF AMBOHIPOTSY, ANTANANARIVO L.M.S. MEMORIAL CHURCH 35

RADAMA II, RANAVALONA I, RANAVALONA II, RANAVALONA III 37

FRENCH GOVERNMENT TRAINING SCHOOL 41

NATIVE POTTER'S SHOP 41

ROFIA PLANTATION & NATIVE SPINNING ROFIA FIBRE 49

PLAYING FANARONA 50

HINDU MAGICIAN IN MADAGASCAR 51

FAT OXEN AT THE FAIR 52

MANIOC AND PATATES MARKET 53

NATIVE WORKING CATTLE 54

VILLAGE SMITHY 55

BETSIMISARAKAS DANCING 56

AT THE FAIR AT SOBIKY, BETSILEO 57

MAKING HATS FROM AHIBANO GRASS 64

SILKWORM COCOON ROOM 65

FESTAL DAYS: DANCING ON A FÊTE DAY 76

FESTAL DAYS: OPEN AIR THEATRE 77

CHILDREN PLAYING FAMPITAHA OR COMPETITION DANCE 79

THE GAME OF KINDRIANDRIANA OR "PLAYING HOUSE" 79

BLOOD BROTHERHOOD 81

MALAGASY PREVENTIVE MEDICINE 84

PRACTICING DIVINATION 85

MAKING A LAMBA FROM NATIVE SILK 92

LACE MAKING 93

AN ANCIENT TOMB IN THE FOREST 98

THE TOMB OF THE PRIME MINISTER, RAINIHARO 99

THE VALIHA 104

MUSICAL INSTRUMENTS 105

THE TRAVELLER'S TREE 121

P. de S. baftiano

Lago cerado

S. andrea

C. de S. antna

Tera de gada === S·LORENZO

Areafmopola

P. de S. aago

Encaido

MODERN MAP OF MADAGASCAR

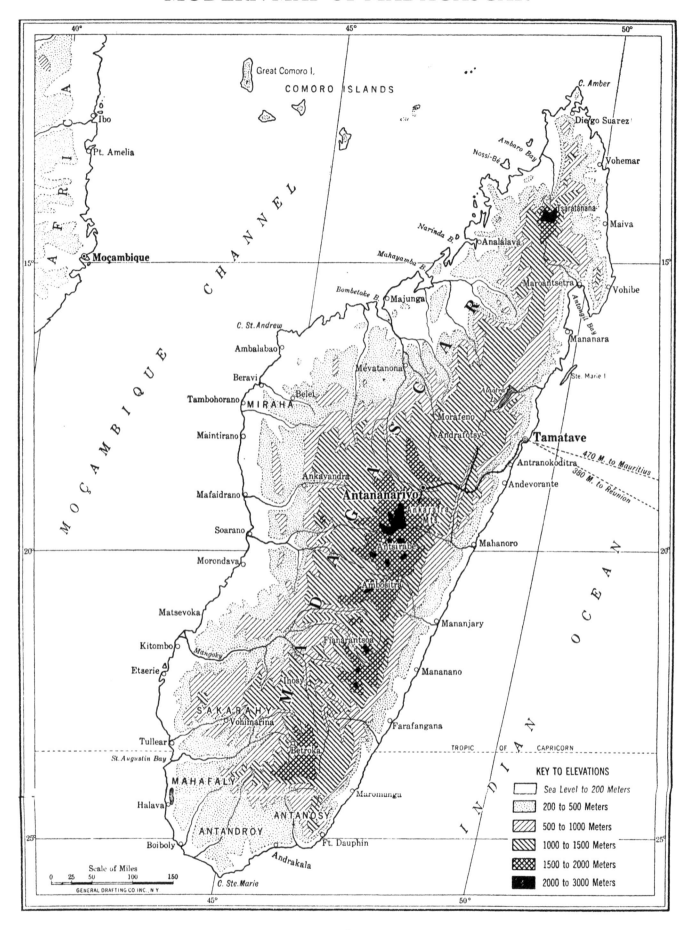

KEY TO ELEVATIONS

Sea Level to 200 Meters
200 to 500 Meters
500 to 1000 Meters
1000 to 1500 Meters
1500 to 2000 Meters
2000 to 3000 Meters

Scale of Miles
0   25   50   100   150

GENERAL DRAFTING CO INC., N.Y.

ISAGOGE

THIS is the first attempt on the part of any American to write a book about that strangest and most characteristic of all places, the Island of Madagascar. The two regions on earth least known to-day are Madagascar and New Guinea. There is more literature on New Guinea than on Madagascar. This is strange because Madagascar is worth while in every way and New Guinea has only certain phases of value and interest.

Although Madagascar has always been a theatre of dramatic human action, the literature on it is small and in the English tongue is confined to a few excellent books by British missionaries written from the standpoint of their own activities—to a small work by Captain Pasfield Oliver; to the war books of Knight and Burleigh; to the translation of the interesting account of Abbé Rochon, who lived two centuries ago; to the strange tale of Robert Drury, by some doubted, told more than an hundred years ago, and to a very few other works. The great French work by Grandidier is the most ambitious study of Madagascar. It is a monument to a master scientist.

Americans have played an interesting part in the Mozambique arena. The first and only pirate republic was founded in Madagascar. American whalers, as at the Falklands, raised the Stars and Stripes over a portion of the island and claimed it for the United States. Benjamin Franklin unwittingly abetted an expedition to harass the French there at the same time that he was endeavoring to secure the aid of France in the War of the Revolution. Madagascar was the theatre of some of the tales of the Arabian Nights. The roc was probably the æpyornis titans and the tale of Sinbad the Sailor and the Old Man of the Sea had Madagascar for its scene. The island gave quarters to The Cid and Captain Kid and Vasco da Gama and Flacourt and Bourdonnais. It was the Cerne of Pliny and the Minuthiasde of Ptolemy. Marco Polo reported impressively upon Madagascar.

When the French ruthlessly seized it in 1896 there were more Christian churches to the population in Antananarivo, the capital of Madagascar, than in Paris. That was within two years of the time when the Philippines fell into the lap of Uncle Sam.

There is a vast difference between the policy of this nation in the Philippines and that of the French in Madagascar. We are planning to grant independence to the Filipinos. Nothing is more remote from the French thought than to grant independence to the Malagasies. Not one Malagasy, it is said, served France willingly in the World War. Many Filipinos served in the army and the navy of the United States of America with love and loyalty and courage.

In order to get to Madagascar one sails on a French ship from Marseilles. There are some other ways of getting there, but they are few, irregular and indirect. I visited the Island for the purpose of studying it. Also I delved in the archives of Lisbon, Madrid, Amsterdam, Paris and London for particulars. In this work I gathered enough material for twenty ponderous tomes. To select some of the material for a modest book was my greatest task. It is submitted as it is with no apology and no vanity. I have travelled and studied in every country on the globe. To me the most strange and interesting is Madagascar. It is a thousand miles long, has an area of more than two hundred and thirty thousand square miles and a population estimated at between four and five millions of peaceful, industrious, capable natives.

CHAPTER I
THE LAND OF THE MAN-EATING TREE

MOST of the time I shall be honest in this book. All of the time I shall try to be honest. Because of this pledge I am going to tell you that the purpose of the title of this chapter is at once to enmesh your interest. Madagascar has been called "The Land of the Man-eating Tree," since prehistoric times as our vain and insufficient chronology goes. I do not know whether this tigerish tree really exists or whether the bloodcurdling stories about it are pure myth. It is enough for my purpose if its story focuses your interest upon one of the least known spots of the world.

Now you are, at the most modest estimate, of average intelligence. Please for a second consider how little you know about this second largest island on the globe—in fact nearly a continent. Only New Guinea is vaster in area than Madagascar, and size is not always a safe measuring standard of values.

But let us return to the man-eating tree. Why should there not be such a tree? There are insect-eating plants. The same tendency and mechanism in a tree would permit it to gorge a human being. In travelling from one end of Madagascar to the other a thousand miles and across the great island, many times traversing the nearly four hundred miles of breadth, I did not see a man-eating tree. But from all the peoples I met, including Hovas, Sakalavas, Sihanakas, Betsileos and others, I heard stories and myths about it. To be sure the missionaries say it does not exist, but they are not united in this opinion, despite the fact that it is properly their affair and responsibility to discredit and destroy anything and everything that fosters demonism and idolatry. No missionary told me that he had seen the devil tree, but several told me that they could not understand how all the tribes could believe so earnestly in it, and over hundreds of miles where intercourse has been both difficult and dangerous, unless there were some foundation for the belief. Again, it may be emphasized that while a man-eating tree is an unlikely thing it is not an impossibility. The upas tree is said to exhale a deadly poison; other vines and vegetation are so toxic that susceptible persons are affected who go near without even touching them; there are nettles that sting painfully and there are plants that entrap their live insect prey and consume it. The best known of the latter are the sarraceniaceæ. Sarracenia purpurea is the well-known pitcher plant or hunter's cup.

At the London Horticultural hall in England there is a plant that eats large insects and mice. Its principal prey are the latter. The mouse is attracted to it by a pungent odor that emanates from the blossom which incloses a perfect hole just big enough for the mouse to crawl into. After the mouse is inside the trap bristlelike antennæ infold it. Its struggles appear to render the Gorgonish things more active. Soon the mouse is dead. Then digestive fluids much like those of animal stomachs exude and the mouse is macerated, liquefied and appropriated. This extraordinary carnivorous plant is a native of tropical India. It has not been classified as belonging to any known botanical species.

The most lurid and dramatic description of the man-eating tree of Madagascar I have seen was written by a traveller named Carle Liche in a letter to Dr. Omelius Fredlowski, a Pole. This letter was published in several European scientific publications, was given popular circulation in Graefe and Walther's magazine, of Karlsruhe, and was first published in America by the New York World in 1880. Then it pursued its conquest of interest around the world and appeared in the South Australian Register. Dr. R. G. Jay, of Willungo, Australia, read this account at a soiree at the Willungo Institute. So much for the character of the reception given to this long-forgotten report of the arboreal monster. One of the first inquiries I made in Madagascar was about this tree. Of all the tales I heard none was better than the description in Liche's letter, and also Liche seemed to be better informed as to detail and to possess enough character to make his report impressive.

The letter of Liche to Dr. Fredlowski was written from Madagascar in 1878 as follows:

"The Mkodos, of Madagascar, are a very primitive race, going entirely naked, having only faint vestiges of tribal relations, and no religion beyond that of the awful reverence which they pay to the sacred tree. They dwell entirely in caves hollowed out of the limestone rocks in their hills, and are one of the smallest races, the men seldom exceeding fifty-six inches in height.

At the bottom of a valley (I had no barometer, but should not think it over four hundred feet above the level of the sea), and near its eastern extremity, we came to a deep tarn-like lake about a mile in diameter, the sluggish oily water of which overflowed into a tortuous reedy canal that went unwillingly into the recesses of a black forest composed of jungle below and palms above. A path diverging from its southern side struck boldly for the heart of the forbidding and seemingly impenetrable forest.

Hendrick led the way along this path, following closely, and behind me a curious rabble of Mkodos, men, women and children. Suddenly all the natives began to cry 'Tepe Tepe!' and Hendrick, stopping short, said, 'Look!' The sluggish canal-like stream here wound slowly by, and in a bare spot in its bend was the most singular of trees.

I have called it 'Crinoida,' because when its leaves are in action it bears a striking resemblance to that well-known fossil the crinoid lily-stone or St. Cuthbert's head. It was now at rest, however, and I will try to describe it to you. If you can imagine a pineapple eight feet high and thick in proportion resting upon its base and denuded of leaves, you will have a good idea of the trunk of the tree, which, however, was not the color of an anana, but a dark dingy brown, and apparently as hard as iron. From the apex of this truncated cone (at least two feet in diameter) eight leaves hung sheer to the ground, like doors swung back on their hinges. These leaves, which were joined at the top of the tree at regular intervals, were about eleven or twelve feet long, and shaped very much like the leaves of the American agave or century plant. They were two feet through at their thickest point and three feet wide, tapering to a sharp point that looked like a cow's horn, very convex on the outer (but now under surface), and on the under (now upper) surface slightly concave. This concave face was thickly set with strong thorny hooks like those on the head of the teazle. These leaves hanging thus limp and lifeless, dead green in color, had in appearance the massive strength of oak fibre. The apex of the cone was a round white concave figure like a smaller plate set within a larger one.

This was not a flower but a receptacle, and there exuded into it a clear treacly liquid, honey sweet, and possessed of violent intoxicating and soporific properties. From underneath the rim (so to speak) of the undermost plate a series of long hairy green tendrils stretched out in every direction towards the horizon. These were seven or eight feet long, and tapered from four inches to a half inch in diameter, yet they stretched out stiffly as iron rods. Above these (from between the upper and under cup) six white almost transparent palpi reared themselves towards the sky, twirling and twisting with a marvelous incessant motion, yet constantly reaching upwards. Thin as reeds and frail as quills, apparently they were yet five or six feet tall, and were so constantly and vigorously in motion, with such a subtle, sinuous, silent throbbing against the air, that they made me shudder in spite of myself, with their suggestion of

serpents flayed, yet dancing upon their tails.

The description I am giving you now is partly made up from a subsequent careful inspection of the plant. My observations on this occasion were suddenly interrupted by the natives, who had been shrieking around the tree with their shrill voices, and chanting what Hendrick told me were propitiatory hymns to the great tree devil.

With still wilder shrieks and chants they now surrounded one of the women, and urged her with the points of their javelins, until slowly, and with despairing face, she climbed up the stalk of the tree and stood on the summit of the cone, the palpi swirling all about her. 'Tsik! Tsik!' (Drink, drink!) cried the men. Stooping, she drank of the viscid fluid in the cup, rising instantly again, with wild frenzy in her face and convulsive cords in her limbs. But she did not jump down, as she seemed to intend to do.

Oh, no! The atrocious cannibal tree that had been so inert and dead came to sudden savage life. The slender delicate palpi, with the fury of starved serpents, quivered a moment over her head, then as if instinct with demoniac intelligence fastened upon her in sudden coils round and round her neck and arms; then while her awful screams and yet more awful laughter rose wildly to be instantly strangled down again into a gurgling moan, the tendrils one after another, like green serpents, with brutal energy and infernal rapidity, rose, retracted themselves, and wrapped her about in fold after fold, ever tightening with cruel swiftness and the savage tenacity of anacondas fastening upon their prey. It was the barbarity of the Laocoön without its beauty this strange horrible murder.

And now the great leaves slowly rose and stiffly, like the arms of a derrick, erected themselves in the air, approached one another and closed about the dead and hampered victim with the silent force of a hydraulic press and the ruthless purpose of a thumb screw. A moment more, and while I could see the bases of these great levers pressing more tightly towards each other, from their interstices there trickled down the stalk of the tree great streams of the viscid honey-like fluid mingled horribly with the blood and oozing viscera of the victim. At sight of this the savage hordes around me, yelling madly, bounded forward, crowded to the tree, clasped it, and with cups, leaves, hands and tongues each one obtained enough of the liquor to send him mad and frantic. Then ensued a grotesque and indescribably hideous orgy, from which even while its convulsive madness was turning rapidly into delirium and insensibility, Hendrick dragged me hurriedly away into the recesses of the forest, hiding me from the dangerous brutes. May I never see such a sight again.

"The retracted leaves of the great tree kept their upright position during ten days, then when I came one morning they were prone again, the tendrils stretched, the palpi floating, and nothing but a white skull at the foot of the tree to remind me of the sacrifice that had taken place there. I climbed into a neighboring tree, and saw that all trace of the victim had disappeared and the cup was again supplied with the viscid fluid."

CHAPTER II
THE MAKING OF THE ISLAND

MOST of us are provincial in our horizons. This condition of mind and understanding undoubtedly makes for a kind of chauvinistic smugness and satisfaction. This provincialism is abnormal in New York, London, Paris and in all places where there are vast groupings of human beings. In a recent synthetic essay by George Ade this interesting trait of ordinary bimana is set forth splendidly and with grace and kindness. But I do not wish to refer to or qualify humanity by the adjective "ordinary," which has no legitimate place in language, because there is nothing ordinary in the universe or upon the earth; certainly humanity is never ordinary even if we sometimes in our indolence of comprehension lightly think it is. And what sheep we have always been and are; and what parrots, too, with neither fine wool nor ornate feathers. Let us try to think that this also is a good thing. The one makes for local loyalty and the other gives us those things that others supply that we have not the initiative nor inventiveness to get for ourselves.

Stevenson went to the South Seas to live and die and wrote fascinatingly of that region of mythical voluptuousness. I say mythical because it is so frightfully hot that no one but a native who doesn't know what voluptuous means could possibly have vitality enough to enjoy or sense or taste it there.

Melville, puritan that he was, with insufficient hemoglobin, wrote of Tahitiland as became a cold-blooded artist and purist who seemed scarcely to see or know the passions of nature that ferment under the South Sea sun. Louis Becke was the opposite of the good Melville and he wrote stuff so like reality that his "Ebbing of the Tide" was interdicted in such libraries as the one at Honolulu, though for my life I do not know why, because his writings are the most honest and artistic in atmosphere of any that have tried to mirror those dream islands of naked bronzes, drowsy perfumes and rhythmically swaying palms.

Now all these writers are as forgotten as temperate zone conventional virtue; mind you I say conventional. So along comes that clever fellow O'Brien to-day with blue-purple tales from those same almost valueless South Seas but seductive because they stimulate a kind of lazy eroticism such as old men retain. It is the same intellectual prostitution that demands the cheap sex novel. Not two decades have floated down the stream of time since Becke and the others. Yet O'Brien is greeted as one who plows new fields, and he does indeed plow very well, but the new thing is merely the new generation afflicted with the same old erotic mind-sloth. Gregarious as we are in thought as well as in grouping physically, we have no persistence of either knowledge or interest. There have been ten thousand vogues of the same kind since the world began, which accounts for the processions of frauds and reformers and for all the cleavages of interest and awakenings; even the so-called Dark Ages was only a period when man was most indolent intellectually.

So provincial are we that we called the great European war a world war when it was purely a war of the section called Christendom and was confined almost entirely to Europe, whose total area is only a quarter larger than the United States. Because of this provincialism we do not know or realize a lot of fine and worth-while things in our own land and over the world generally. It is not uncommon to hear it said that there is no hidden spot in the world; that the old earth is finished as far as exploration is concerned. This is not true. Quite a quarter of the globe is strange to civilized man. There are thousands of unknown square miles—yes, millions in Asia. Also in Australia, in South America, in Africa, and more than a million square miles in our own North America that are unexplored. In fact the weakest thing about life is that we do not know the world and each other as we should and must. When we learn of other lands and their peoples we shall come to have a new respect for their rights just as we wish, and, because we are strong, insist, that they shall respect ours. There is no spot so little known by Americans as Madagascar, although Americans opened the eyes of Madagascar to the world in much the same way that they did Japan's.

In several respects Madagascar is more singularly continental than any of the parts of the earth classified as such. More flora and more fauna are autochthonous than anywhere else in the world; more are to be found solely in Madagascar than are peculiar to any other land. Biologists do not agree as to why this is true. They are all dealing in conjecture and no one can go much further than he is carried by intelligent guess work. It is agreed that Madagascar must once have been attached to the African mainland and yet the island life is sufficiently dissimilar to cast a shadow of doubt even upon this commonly accepted conclusion.

The cataclysm that tore Madagascar and Africa asunder must have destroyed most of the life upon the island. A series of synchronous volcanic eruptions covering an area large enough to bring about striking diastrophic results could alone account for a cataclysm of such magnitude. The same earth-tearing force that sunk the Mozambique Channel which separates Madagascar from the mainland also produced another result of vastly greater proportions. I refer to the Great Rift valley in Africa. There is no American bibliography upon the subject of the Great Rift valley and comparatively little has been written about it at all and certainly nothing that is commensurate with its cosmic importance. Consider that it is the

NOSIVALA RIVER FALLS, ON THE EAST COAST

most extensive structural weakness in the earth's physical constitution and that to the viewer on the moon it would be more prominent visually than the heights and depressions on the moon's surface as seen from the earth; and more plainly to be seen from Mars than we can see the canals of Mars. Into this huge dent more than twenty Grand Canyons of the Colorado could be dropped and then it would not be filled. I am convinced that one and the same force caused the immeasurable subsidences of the Great Rift valley and the Mozambique channel.

Nor is all the evidence for this conclusion conjectural. Notable changes in the surface of the earth are caused by subsidence, erosion and upheaval. The diastrophic agency in this instance was intense and widespread volcanic action. Signs of this are discernible over long stretches in both Madagascar and Africa. It was an instance of hundreds of Mt. Pelées in simultaneous eruption. In the same manner the Mediterranean islands that were once a part of the mainland of Italy were cut off.

At the time of this cataclysm there were two and perhaps three parallel mountain ranges in Africa. What is now the imposing Ankaratra range in Madagascar was a coastal range in Africa and back of it and parallel were other mountains. All of these mountains were volcanic and many became active volcanoes. From one end of Madagascar to the other are tufa, scoriæ, and every kind of lava flow and detritus. The same thing is true in Africa, but the evidence has been more completely obscured

IKOPA RIVER NEAR TANANARIVO

by alluvial wear, wind grindings, insolation, the growth of vegetation and other common natural influences. Craters everywhere and crater lakes, some of the craters active and others smouldering like the largest of all known volcanoes, the huge Menengai, prove the existence once of long volcanic ramparts. These became violent at the same time. Trillions of cubic yards of material were ejected accompanied by steam, hot water and gases and all the characteristic phenomena of vulcanism. Cavernous voids were thus created in the interior of the globe. Crustal supports were removed and gravity did the rest. Thousands of miles of surface subsided. The result was the Mozambique channel and the Great Rift valley.

It may have been that the waters that once covered the Sahara desert drained into the Big Rift only to continue on down into the bowels of the earth and disappear. Into the chasm that is now the Mozambique channel the ocean poured its waters and Madagascar became an island. There are no human records left of the time, but there are myths that are difficult to separate from the cosmic stories told in all lands among all primitive peoples about the Creation and about destructive episodes by flood and fire. Some idea of when this fracture of a continent occurred can be had from interesting sources that have at least a certain historical significance. Solomon's temple was built about three thousand years ago. The gold for ornamentation was obtained from the long lost mines that were

reached by way of ancient Ophir. It is now known to a sufficient degree of probability that these mines were in Southern Rhodesia near the present site of the interesting little African outpost of Victoria. Extensive and important ruins have been discovered there in recent years and eminent engineers and archeologists and ethnologists have made careful studies of them.

That distinguished American mining engineer, John Hays Hammond, has said that those gold fields in the center of which are the majestic ruins called Great Zimbabwe, alone of all the ancient sources of gold could have supplied Hiram of Tyre with the untold amounts he furnished King Solomon. The whereabouts of these gold fields were lost to the knowledge of man at this time; not another record was made after the temple gold was procured. Excavations and examinations made by me incidentally and by others more thoroughly have resulted in finding workmen vulcanized at their crucibles, as in the gruesome exhumations at Pompeii; I have found gold in the crucibles just as it was left when the destroying gases asphyxiated the artisans. Here too were imposing temples, dwellings, large storerooms for treasure, fortresses built with all the engineering skill of the moderns and more than enough to prove that a people of remarkable intelligence and ability lived and wrought here. Everything at this spot and for miles around is covered with volcanic substances. The cause of their doom was the same dread force that rent Africa in twain. It not only caught and killed all of the inhabitants in the area affected but cut off the caravan route so completely that no word and no record remained of the mines and the miners. Most of the population of the portion that became Madagascar must have been destroyed, necessitating almost an entire repopulation by races not now found in Africa. Of this I shall write when I discuss the people of Madagascar.

This estimate of the date of the split is confirmed by important vestiges on the great island. At several places and particularly at Antsirabe in Madagascar are hot lime water springs. These deposit calcareous layers that by now amount to many feet in depth. In these deposits have been found from time to time skeletons of the pigmy hippopotamus and of that interesting extinct bird the æpyornis titans. By keeping track of the speed with which these deposits are laid down over a given known period and by measuring the depth at which the fossils were found a fairly accurate idea can be obtained as to when the animals were caught there. This coincides with the time of the probable destruction of Great Zimbabwe. By the way this Great Zimbabwe is the scene of Rider Haggard's "She." Haggard never visited the place. He wrote the story while he was engaged as a British government clerk at Pretoria.

It may be concluded that the cutting off of Madagascar occurred about 1000 B.C. The African race mostly destroyed at the time may have been the Bushmen. I know that the Bushmen descended to a plane where it is hard to identify them with the skilled artisans and worshippers of Astarte. Their congeners were to be found in Madagascar, as the rare Vazimbas reported as late as Flacourt's time, but of this hereafter.

CHAPTER III
THE GREAT RIFT VALLEY OF AFRICA

AS I have said in the last chapter there is much to indicate that the Great Rift valley was formed by the same forces and at the same time that the cataclysm occurred which tore away the great island. Africa was not only fractured at the central west but also at the north where it was almost cut off from its connection with Asia. The subsidences compensating for the volcanic robbery of the interior of the earth extended more than a quarter of the way around the earth. This huge trough is so big that it has been seen by few travellers; even some of marked distinction like Colonel Roosevelt have passed many parts of it without recognizing it, or observing anything unusual enough to refer to or comment upon. They could see mountain ranges that extruded and broke in upon the horizon. But when it came to troughs and visible intrusions they did not see them. I offer this as a lesson in observation.

An object may be too vast as well as too small to be observed without deliberate care. In the important

ANKARATRA RANGE

instance of the Great Rift valley there has never been a complete exploration by one person. It is only by careful coördination of the work of many that it is known in its entirety. The best exploration, most extensive, most comprehensive, in which the most danger was encountered and the most difficulties surmounted was done by Professor J. W. Gregory, of the British Museum, whose work was carried on under the auspices of that splendid institution. No American that I know of has done anything on the geology of the Rift except myself and although I have traversed its entire length my original contribution amounts to nothing. Upon returning from one of my trips to Africa I was invited to lecture before the National Geographic Society in Washington. I made extended reference there to the Great Rift valley and also before the Chicago Geographic Society and at a number of universities, only to be amazed at the lack of knowledge of the subject displayed in America. It would appear then to possess value beyond its possible connection with Madagascar.

The Great Rift valley is the wonder of all wonders upon the face of the earth. Despite this I wish to repeat by way of emphasis that it is popularly unknown. I have never heard it referred to in general or special conversation by any person. It has not been seen by anyone person in its entirety and seems to lie beyond the purlieus even of scientific knowledge and appreciation. The longest, deepest, widest, strangest and most awful crack or dent in the earth's surface, the disturbance that accompanied its creation may

RIVER NEAR VATOMANDRY

not have been compensated for yet and slips that are causing earthquakes to-day may perhaps be traced to influences that began then.

The Great Rift valley extends from a point in central Africa south of the Zambesi river far northward into Asia, a length of more than five thousand miles. There are thirty lakes in its floor of which twenty-nine are both dead and blind; no inlet, no outlet; just great and small stagnant, noisome sinks filled with poisonous animal and vegetable life and sublife. Victoria Nyanza, with the greatest area of any lake on earth, is in the Great Rift valley and is the only imprisoned lake that has an outlet and its flow is so sluggish that there is not a fouler body of water anywhere. Both the Dead Sea and the Red Sea are in this marvellous depression. In some places this indentation is hundreds of miles wide and thousands of feet deep. A partial idea of its size can be gained from the fact that Lake Victoria Nyanza is more than two hundred and fifty miles wide and long and it is easily embraced by the big chasm. Nor does it fill it. Once it may have done so as there are evidences of extensive coastal recessions and the shores are still advancing from evaporation and a greater discharge than inflow.

The floor of the Great Rift valley is formed of lava and from one end to the other there are volcanoes. Some of these are terrible in their activity while others, though warm, are for the time being quiescent. Still others are apparently moribund, but are to be suspected, as on occasion the most

harmless looking of volcanoes become tragic in renewed death struggles. We explored one of these craters called Menengai. It is near Lake Nakuru, also in the Rift, and is not only the largest crater in the floor but is perhaps the biggest on earth. Menengai resembles Kilauea, but is much larger. Where the Halemaumau or "House of Everlasting Fire" is in Kilauea there is a warm oval cone in Menengai like the beehive dome of an observatory. Kilauea is 9,000 feet in circumference and 1,000 feet deep. Menengai is nearly nine miles in diameter and 2,000 feet deep. The floor of Kilauea is fissured lava and hot. The floor of Menengai is carpeted with a dense jungle growth of trees, bushes and vines, the whole interwoven and matted with lianas until it can be penetrated only by vigorously wielding a jungle knife; incidentally it is the lair of lions and leopards and other ferocious carnivora. On the hot dome at the center not even the hardiest of tropical vegetation can live. Thus there is an interesting bald spot which furnishes an opening for limited observations. The crater walls are terraced from the bottom upward, telling the story of successive eruptions in ages gone by. Natives worship spirits of fire and smoke and other imaginary forces in the many caves in the walls and are said to make human sacrifices.

In a few places the Great Rift valley narrows so that one may see across it. At these spots the walls are as straight as though cut with a channeling machine. One may approach the verge and look down into the yawning mouths of volcanoes. I saw no compressed areas of colors as in the Grand Canyon of the Colorado, but there was no lack of tinting, from the most pronounced to delicate nuances that defied classification. Once I saw the clouds settle into the vast pit and it was as if I were on the other side of the sky or upon another planet looking down upon an opaque cushion of mist. The far-reaching effect of the titanic cosmic struggle that made this scar cannot be apprehended or measured in any way. Chains of volcanoes threw out the substances that were charged into their great guns, pyroclastics everywhere. The consequent settling of the surface must have influenced the entire earth and may even be still at work at this time. The most stupendous thing to be seen in Africa and on earth is the Great Rift valley.

CHAPTER IV
ABORIGINES OF MADAGASCAR

JUST as the creation of the Mozambique channel involves the causation of the Great Rift valley so does the treatment of the aborigines of Madagascar involve the story of the Bushmen whose origin and fate have been an ethnic mystery. They appear to have been a race of cave artists and in prehistoric times to have been cave dwellers as well. By their work in many parts of the world they can be traced and a good deal may be learned about them. They were the inhabitants of ancient Iberia. Down to a recent day the decorations of their cave walls were to be seen in the caverns of the peninsula now occupied by Portugal, Spain and portions of France.

The work is distinguished by enduring pigments and by accuracy and action in drawing and by rich imagination and faithfulness in design. So characteristic are the pictures wherever found that it is entirely safe to attribute them to the same source. These wonderful drawings, which are the best examples of prehistoric art in existence, are to be found in caves from the Spanish peninsula to distant regions in Africa and in Madagascar.

If there is any conclusion to be drawn from this fact it is that these peoples once lived in the parts where these vestiges are in evidence, that they were of the same family and were numerous and powerful. The mere character and quality and other similarities in their art is not all that identifies them. They are dolichocephalic, orthognathous, steatopygous, low in stature and the women are longinymphal. In Portugal they were the Aurignacians, in France the Cro-Magnons, in Spain the Basques, in Algeria and Tunisia the Berbers; in central Africa the pre-Bantus, in South Africa the Bushmen and Strand Loopers, in Madagascar the Vazimbas. All the way they are to be unmistakably traced by their drawings. There were frequent variations, but their art gives evidence of their purity as undisturbed and unvarying as the sculptures of Phidias were true to the perfect Greek.

Much indeed is known about them in Europe, but their progress to Africa and to Madagascar, in the latter case as marooned Africans, has not been followed by ethnic students who have concentrated upon the still more conjectural Aryan genesis and hegiras. Taylor says in his work on the Aryans that for this short, dark type the name Iberian may be adopted, although Rolleston uses the term Silurian. Because of competitive vanity in guessing other writers have imposed their own names, such as Euskarian, and anything that would conduce to advertising their efforts, until there is a confusion in nomenclature that would be distressing if anyone seriously cared. The Cro-Magnon appellation comes from the discovery of a skull in a sepulchral cavern at Perigord in France.

Before the arrival of the brachycephalic Ligurian race the Iberians ranged over the greater part of France. They lived in the valleys of the Seine, Oise and Marne and were related to the Aquitani, one of the three races that occupied Gaul in Cæsar's time. Then they moved into further seclusion in the Pyrenees and their traces in the caves along the Garonne are particularly numerous. Bold excursions were made into the British Isles and Taylor is convinced that they. may be seen to-day in the types of certain Welsh and Irish. But he says their affinities are dominantly African. First the Ligurians and then the Romans pushed them along until they were forced down into Portugal and thence across the Straits of Gibraltar into Africa. Some of them or their congeners may even have gone there before the Straits were formed. From the shores they spread to the interior of the continent and swept all before them because they were an ascending race of bold nomads and soon to take another step upward in the scale of achievement by settling and building permanently. It is not a long distance to go from art to architecture, only another fine and kindred art. When the cataclysm occurred that almost totally destroyed them in Africa they were at the apex of their development as shown by the majestic monuments at Great Zimbabwe which are unexcelled in the world by either pre- or protohistoric peoples.

In Madagascar they came to be known as the Vazimbas. If anything their average stature had declined, and they had lost some of their characteristics through miscegenation and other and lesser influences. This led to different names and in other ways they began to be obscured. The chief authority on this primitive people of Madagascar that were surely of this stock was the learned botanist, M. Commerson, who accompanied M. de Bougainville around the world on that famous scientific voyage that gave the world so many new things to know and enjoy, not the least of which is the beautiful flower that is called bougainvillæa in honor of the admiral. Commerson, after acquiring a knowledge of Mascarene flora in Mauritius, then known as the Isle of France, visited at the direction of M. Poivre the French settlement in South Madagascar in 1768. From the earlier work of Commerson, who had a scientific reputation to maintain, it was natural that his correspondents and publishers should put the most implicit confidence in his recorded observations.

A writer of the time gives a good account of the reception of his strange claims for the mysterious land that taxed the senses of those who saw with their own eyes, not to mention the bewilderment of those at home with their remote and inelastic minds. There is nothing so hard to get into the average mind as something that is foreign to any preconceived plans of comprehension. Always explorers who have reported the unusual have been doubted. And the stranger the thing recorded the less it has been believed. Marco Polo perhaps did more to introduce the Orient to Europe than any other person and his reward was a reputation as a modern father of liars equal to the oblique renown borne by Herodotus. Commerson was no exception, although he has been verified long ago. So marvellous were his reports that his contemporaries even pitied him and said the poisons of the new wonder world had turned his brain and its miasmas had given him a delirium akin to insanity.

The truth was that he was well within bounds because he described only coastal discoveries and was never in the interior. No early traveller is now credited more than Commerson. He declared Madagascar to be different in toto from any country in the world. In 1771, writing to his friend the astronomer Lalande, he says:

"Quel admirable pays que Madagascar. C'est à Madagascar que je puis annoncer aux naturalistes qu'est la terre de promission pour eux. C'est là que la nature semble s'être retirée comme dans un sanctuaire particulier pour y travailler sur d'autres modèles que sur ceux où elle est asservie ailleurs. Les formes les plus insolites, les plus merveilleuses s'y rencontrent à chaque pas.... Il faudroit en effet des Académies entieres pour parvenir à connaître les productions de cette île, si la moisson serait trop abondante pour une seule Académie."

The Abbé Rochon, who made a voyage to Madagascar and studied the island in 1767 and 1768 and whose observations and records are comparable in dignity and accuracy to the work of Abbé Huc in China, regrets that the accounts of Commerson's important discoveries, or so many of them, were lost or scattered after the death of this indefatigable explorer, who died just as the scientific world was on the verge of giving him the full credit that Rochon lived to see accorded. The Abbé was a personal friend of Commerson's and was an eyewitness to much of his arduous work. He reports that the devoted biologist spent entire nights in preparing specimens which he had worked all day in the vertical rays of a tropical sun to collect, in order to keep them from being ruined. Abbé Rochon is zealous and loyal in his approval and admiration of M. Commerson, whom no naturalist seems ever to have surpassed in devotion and scientific knowledge. I have thus introduced Commerson because he is one of the great authorities upon things Mascarene. It was his report that furnished the first authentic trace of the lost race of little people in Madagascar. Translated, his letter to Laland about them is as follows:

"I will now proceed to give a description of a really extraordinary people who inhabit the highest mountains of Madagascar. In this relation amateurs of the marvellous will be more pleased than they were when I reduced the stature of the fabled Patagonian giants or mythical Titans of the region of Magellan's Straits, which have only resided in the heated imagination of poets and sailors, though just how even the mind could become caloric down in that land of cold and fog I cannot say. These Madagascar dwarfs are only half men (demihommes) and they form the bulk of a considerable nation."

M. LeGentil, the French astronomer who visited the regions of the Indian Ocean in 1761 and 1769 for the purpose of observing two transits of Venus and whose mission did not give him the right to do so, nevertheless takes issue with Commerson and in no pleasant way asks if the latter may not have fabricated from the word Esquimaux the name Quimosse or Kimasse which he gives to the dwarfs and claims is "Madecasse."

Indicating how sensitively jealous the French scientists were in that time and how without foundation was the gratuitous criticism of LeGentil, S. Pasfield Oliver, late an officer in the British Royal Artillery, writes in 1891 that two of the most cultured and accurate observers of the London Missionary Society had just satisfied themselves of the truth of M. Commerson's reports. The missionaries referred to were the scholarly Messrs. Cousins and Pickersgill.

These little folk communicate by means of clicks instead of words, which is a marked peculiarity of the so-called Bushmen. In their mountain fastnesses of the Madagascar Ankaratras these wild children are able to keep away from those who would study them, and in consequence not much is known about them. They were most numerous in the cliffs on the borderland between the western Sakalava and the Rova, in a wooded country extending from Mojanga to Mahabo. They subsist on wild honey, eels and lemurs, according to Oliver, who states that they catch the lemurs in traps and keep them and fatten them; so they have some taste about what they consume. Oliver says that they are nearly as black as the Sakalava and that they make a network of cords (hósy) from which they are called Behosy. This interesting artillery man says the Behosy are not only so timid that they die from fright when they are caught, but that it is very hard to come up with them because they jump from tree to tree like monkeys. Going back to Commerson as the best observer I quote him as follows:

"The natural and distinguishing characteristics of these little people are that they are fair, or at least paler in color than all the known black tribes around them [in which he disagrees with the description of Oliver]; their arms are very long so that their hands can reach below their knees without bending their body; and as to their women, they are scarcely to be distinguished by their breasts, except when they are nursing their young; and even then we are assured that most of them have to make use of cow's milk in feeding their offspring, when newborn.

Intellectually the Quimos are equal to the cleverest of the Madecasses, who are a bright and canny people. Although not given to heavy work, the Quimos are sharp-witted and brave. Their activity and courage has permitted them to hold their own with many in greater numbers who have made war upon them. It appears that their boldness is in ratio double their size and as they occupy an inaccessible region they are not apt soon to be exterminated. They live upon rice, various kinds of fruits, roots and vegetables and rear a great number of oxen and sheep, the latter with fat tails. The Quimos do not communicate with the different Madecasse castes that surround them, living bounteously and independently to themselves.

When the strong tribes make war upon them they retire (as do the people of San Marino) to their strongholds and there make a stand. Usually they pay tribute of cattle and sheep and thus end the trouble for the time being. They call this making sacrifices to their big brothers who are not at all brotherly. Their arms are (the same as their forbears had in Africa), sagaye, a kind of assegai, and a blow gun with which they shoot poisoned darts with deadly skill. In my visit to Fort Dauphin in 1770 I had the good fortune to see through the courtesy of M. Le Comte Modave, the governor, a Quimos woman he had among his slaves. She was about thirty years old and three feet, seven inches tall, with color the palest shade (de la nuance la plus éclaircie) which I had seen among the inhabitants of Madagascar. Her form was perfect except her arms were too long and all I could see of her breasts were nipples. Just before she was to have been included in a cargo of slaves for export she escaped to the hills and was not recaptured."

Abbé Rochon gives the report upon the dwarfs of Count de Modave, French governor of Fort Dauphin, in the final volume of his Voyage aux

Indes Orientales, as follows:

"When I arrived at Fort Dauphin in September, 1768, a rather unsatisfactory memoir was handed to me which contained some particulars of a peculiar people called Quimos who inhabit the interior of the island in latitude 22, south. I had heard of them before and had read what Flacourt wrote about them. The memoir said they were dwarfs, lived in a society that had civil laws and were ruled by a chief. I sent an expedition to learn what might be ascertained inasmuch as M. Commerson credited their existence and Admiral Flacourt and Prof. LeGentil discredited it. Although our guides were cowardly and treacherous I learned enough to prove that the dwarfs are real. They are called Kimos or Quimos. The average stature of the men is three feet, five inches; they wear beards long and rounded; women are shorter than the men. They are squat (trapus), have long heads, color less swarthy (bazanée) than the other islanders; hair short and wooly. They know how to work in iron and steel and they fabricate their own assegais. When they discover that marauders are about to come they tie oxen to trees and put provisions and other gifts in the way of the invaders. If these do not propitiate them and cause them to turn back the Quimos prepare to fight and make a valiant and usually successful resistance. This policy is so well known that their enemies are content with levying tribute in this manner.

Chief Ramonja made two expeditions and was badly worsted by the pygmies both times. Upon several occasions the chiefs of the big natives tried to get me to undertake the extermination of the Quimos, referring to them as monkeys and saying they were only to be considered as wild animals. When I refused to do as they asked and appeared to urge them to go up against the dwarfs they were adroit in excuses that convinced me of their fear and respect."

Abbé Rochon gathered so much evidence in support of Commerson that he can only account for the contradictory conclusions of Flacourt and LeGentil on the ground of their lack of trained equipment for accurate observation and record.

Cairns of the Vazimba, prehistoric autochthones, are to be seen all over Madagascar from the bare downs to the mountain tops of the Ankaratra. There is some uncertainty as to whether these are the same people as the Quimos-Bushmen. Like everything else in the big island the people are unusual, difficult to classify and still harder to trace to their original source. Graves of the Vazimba are looked upon with awe and reverence by the inhabitants. The Malagasy do not know whether they are their descendants or not. They prefer to take the safe side in this respect and if they owe anything by way of ancestor worship they propose to cast an anchor to windward by paying it. I found them careful in interring to place the head toward the point of the compass from which their ancestors were believed to have come. This practice placed all the dead with the head towards Malaysia—to the northeast.

There was for centuries a close touch between Madagascar and Zanzibar in slave trading. This gave occasion for Swahili to influence the tongues spoken as it has impressed the entire east coast of Africa, in some such manner as pidgin English has corrupted all of the China coast, hobson-jobson the Indian littoral and chinook the Great Lake, Hudson Bay and north and west regions of North America. Words in both Quimos and Vazimba may be quite certainly traced to Swahili. The Arab slave traders held the Malagasy in low esteem as slaves because of their small size, but they repeatedly proclaim their superior intellect. Dr. Schweinfurth says that he found that all along the Zanzibar coast the small people of Madagascar were known as the Berikeemo—a word meaning two feet high.

In this connection it is interesting to note that Dr. Schweinfurth concludes that there was a zone extending clear across Africa in which the people were imperfectly and insufficiently developed and bore a close analogy to the dwarfs of Madagascar. Andrew Battel, of Leigh, in Essex, England, was sent as a prisoner by the Portuguese to Angola, where he remained for eighteen years from 1589 to 1607. He tells of a little folk no bigger when full grown than boys of twelve. There is a skeleton of an Akka dwarf in the South Kensington museum, sent there by Dr. Emin Pasha. Stanley's expedition encountered Dr. Schweinfurth's Akka in large numbers and as late as the seventeenth century a similar small people were reported to be serving at the court of the king of Loango. So much for the dwarfs of Madagascar and Africa. I have much more evidence and have seen these small folk with my own eyes both in Africa and Madagascar.

The wild people of Madagascar are fast disappearing and few remain to-day, which should not lessen interest in them as an index of what men have been and of the favor, as well as responsibility, bestowed by Providence upon those who are supposed to be more perfect. Oliver says that among the Betsimisaraka people of the east coast are heard endless stories of the Kalanoro, a kind of wild men of the woods, who are represented as very short, covered with hair, men with flowing beard and both sexes almost fire worshippers. I heard these stories, which are persistent and are given wide credence by the natives. I was told of an eyewitness to an occurrence that is in common report. When spending a night in the heart of deep forest he was awake, watching the fire that had burned to a bed of glowing coals, when suddenly one of the wild men appeared without stitch of clothing, sat down by the fire, rubbed his hands together in a manner of enjoyment and seemed perfectly happy. The brave but inhospitable Betsimisaraka grasped a stick, dug to the coals and sent the hot embers in a shower over the naked visitor, who ran precipitately, uttering frightful shrieks.

Another tale has it that in the middle of a black night campers were disturbed by the appearance of naked man who looked around and, finding some rice left in a cooking pot, went away and presently returned with a nude woman. It must have been a honeymoon couple, the natives say, because they caressed, made love and fed each other with their hands, and appeared to communicate by grimaces. When they were interrupted they ran away into the jungle.

Now and then these wild people are captured but always escape before they are seen by European observers who might better authenticate and describe them. M. Leguevel de Lacombe who accompanied the army of Radama I to the north in 1824, heard of wild people when going through the forests near the Mananara River in the vicinity of Antongil Bay. M. Ternaux Compans found an interesting letter in the Bibliotheque Nationale at Paris from the Abbé de Choisy to M. l'Abbé de Marins, which he had printed in the Recueil Historique. It is dated at San Jacob, Madagascar, and by many has been considered a satire upon the stories then rife of things that seemed too marvellous to be true.

To-day there are not so many wild people and the inhabitants are quite well known, which does not lessen in any degree the rich folk lore of the natives nor detract from the tribal, individual and general superstitions that prevail and are to be regarded as having been peculiar to primitive man in all ages and countries. No other part of the world presents such a juxtaposition of the wild and the tame; the bizarre and the common of myth and truth. Here may be observed the original thought-trends of mankind.

CHAPTER V
EARLY INHABITANTS

NOT very much is known about the first inhabitants of any land that has been peopled for many centuries. It is not a settled question where the white race had its origin. Consequently it is not surprising that the origin of peoples of Madagascar is a subject beset with uncertainty. The aborigines have disappeared, but the present inhabitants have occupied the island almost from the time of its separation from Africa. The differing types and dialects clearly indicate different sources and there are many things to show also that they came to the island at different periods.

Mr. James Cameron was connected with the London Missionary Society, the remarkable organization that has done more to civilize the island all other agencies combined. A short time before he died in 1876 he prepared an article an English magazine in which he sought to show that the Malagasy are of Jewish origin. His interesting paper was not impressive in its in thesis, but it contained much of incidental value. It was never published. I found it among the records of the L.M.S. in Madagascar. In his introduction Mr. Cameron refers to the common belief among those who have given the matter attention that the Malagasy or at least the Hovas came from the Malay Archipelago; and were followed by others from Arabia, Persia, the African East Coast, India, the South Seas and elsewhere. A comparison of the Hova tongue with the Polynesian dialects shows many genetic similarities. The other island dialects exhibit no such relationship. Among the Malagasy there are tribal differences, discrepancies in dialect, a varying folklore and mythology, dissimilar customs, nuances of color, and ethnical peculiarities. Some have straight and others have kinky hair and still others have curly hair. There are both dolichocephalic and brachycephalic heads, wide distinctions in action and thought-trends and tendencies, no common religion and few universal superstitions. In short, there are many signs leading to the conclusion that the present population came at different times and from widely different places.

The traces of Judaism that Mr. Cameron noticed are not confined to the Jews, but are rather common to all peoples. Not one of the tribes have the great Jewish nose which has followed that people during all time and is a sign of strength of a kind. Because the Biblical dispersion of the Jews there is tendency to see the start of all peoples from that. Nor is there acquisitiveness to a noticeable degree in any of the Malagasy. They are not as improvident as the American Indian, that most unselfish and short-sighted of all aborigines. In every way the Malagasy native is safe from anti-Hebrew offensives and offenses.

Apparently the source of the world's population will always be a matter of interesting conjecture; Madagascar with the rest. Nor is the question one of major importance compared with the question whether man is worthy to exist where he finds himself or justifies his presence anywhere upon the earth. Mr. Mencken is one of those who think and dare to say that nothing is right on this tenth-rate globule. But just why anybody should expect things to be other than they are here is not apparent. If were perfect here and now there would be no object in fooling around where we are with nothing purposeful to do and nowhere to go except to some

other place as miserably perfect as this is.

CHAPTER VI
RACES AND PEOPLES OF MADAGASCAR

THE interest in the study of man by man did not originate with Mr. Pope. It has ever been the subject of greatest fascination. I am more interested in any black man or yellow or even white man, the meanest and least interesting of all, perhaps, than I am in dogs, stars, flowers, rocks, sea, or sky or anything else. I like to watch children play for hours and the Negro in Africa and in America is the drollest creature that I know anything about; by which statement I intend praise, gratuitous as it may be.

Deniker is supposed to be an authority on the races of the world and I so thought him until I had a chance to check up on him in Madagascar and elsewhere. He says the races in the big island are the Hovas or Huves, the Sakalava and the Malagasies. Now the designation Malagasy cannot be applied specifically to any one of the peoples of Madagascar. It can be correctly applied only to all of them indifferently. It is true that the Hovas and the Sakalava are the most prominent and best organized and most distinctive of all the Malagasies. But there are almost countless other tribes who claim independence of them, and with a great deal of reason. However, there is much evidence of miscegenation in all the peoples, and they graduate most delicately into types of easily traceable similarity.

A most unusual and interesting fact, when it is remembered that Madagascar is a thousand miles long, is that all the peoples speak more or less the same tongue and with decidedly greater uniformity than do the people of England. This proves their intelligence, their long association and makes for a possible homogeneity that will be a blessing to them and help the French markedly in governing them, if it not permit unified revolution when some leader comes along and arouses them.

All the types of man in the world have a near or perfect counterpart in Madagascar except the white race. This also indicates long settlement and much association with many peoples. Both

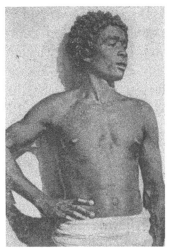

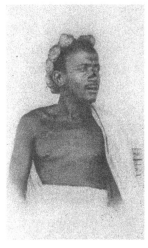

BARA   BARA-MENAHARAKA   TANALA   SAKALAVA

the morphological and the physiological somatic characters are present. There are true brachycephalic and equally perfect dolichocephalic skulls with every variation between. And there is every gradation of pigmentation except the white so-called which is never pure unless in the rare and unsightly albino. Personally the blackest Negro and the yellow Japanese and the bronze Samoans are more attractive than any albino.

Until man is clean as a matter of pride and principle that degree of pigmentation which permits the detection of dirt is the most desirable. It is not impossible that the source of all differences in pigmentation may be found to lie in the functioning of the ductless glands, and if so, science may easily solve the vexed question of racial equality which is bothering the vanity of the Japanese more than anybody else just now. When they come to know that if they can think well of themselves in terms of real merit, which is not a matter of color, and that everybody else will think well enough of them, there will be a secondary place for the really unimportant race equality subject. What we ought to strive for is to be the best kind of instrument we are rather than to cherish vain longings to be so much like others that we may be taken for them or thought their equals. We shall be their equals all right if we are.

This matter of skin color is engaging the world just now to a ridiculous degree. We have the yellow peril and they have the white peril and the funniest of all would be, if some folk not take themselves so seriously, Lothrop Stoddard's "Rising Tide of Color," which for pure human vanity has the Kaiser backed off the map. The poor jinx of Germany thought that the Teutons were the only people fit to rule, but "The Rising Tide of Color" klan regard all the white folks as quality, and are sure that the cursed old pill of the earth will go to Mexico as soon as there is a little more mixture in the blood of man. One has only think a little with the mind and not with the false social sense to say pooh to this rot. Just as if it made any difference what color the wrapper is on anything so long as it is not Sumatra.

The epidermis is formed of two cellular layers; the shallow horny ones that are freely exposed to the air and the layer of Malpighi underneath which contains granules of pigment in varying quantity. Sometimes the epidermis is modified to form either a mucous membrane, for instance on the lips, or a horny substance sometimes transparent, as the cornea of the eye, and sometimes translucent and more or less hard, as the nails. That the skin performs more functions than has been generally understood is coming to be realized now that the importance of the naked air bath is recognized.

It is known that failure of the ductless glands to function properly has a decided effect on pigmentation. The transplanting of some one or more of the known seven ductless glands or serums to be made from them might easily change the complexion without mixed marriage, which works, but is as apt to make a mongrel as a thoroughbred.

Already these serums are made by manufacturing chemists and wonderful things are being accomplished with them. They are variously stimulants or depressants or spasmodics and anti-spasmodics according to the application and the use and the result desired. Illustrating their remarkable power biologists and biological chemists who are studying life and have need of the egg in all its stages of development have learned that injections of therapeutic doses of the posterior lobe of the pituitary body sometimes causes a premature expulsion of the egg from the oviduct of birds. Very soon after this was discovered it was found that a somewhat larger dose could be relied upon to cause the immediate expulsion of the egg from any part of the oviductal tract. Before this it was almost impossible to get undeveloped eggs and then only by killing the mother bird. Now with pituitrin eggs can be had for study at any stage of development.

If this can be done and many other things no less remarkable is it too much to expect that the distribution and circulation of the color granules in the skin may be controlled and regulated so that there may be any color that the people of the world decide they wish, or no color at all? There are numerous examples of albino Negroes that have been made too white by glandular affections. Professor Louis Berman, biological chemist of Columbia University, says on page 286 of his treatise on "The Glands Regulating Personality," published October, 1921:

"Pigment deposit in the skin is controlled by the adrenal cortex. The reaction of the skin blood vessels to heat and humidity is controlled by the adrenal medulla."

Keith presents a good case for the view that the white man is an example of relative excess of the pituitary, thyroid, adrenal and gonad hormones. As for the adrenal status of the white man that great authority of his time, John Hunter, came to the conclusion one hundred and fifty years ago that the original color of man's skin was black. All the scientific knowledge gathered since that time supports this conclusion. Hunter discovered the interesting fact that pigment begins to collect

and thus darken the skin when the adrenal bodies become a seat of a destructive disease and from this he drew the proper inference that they had to do with clearing away pigment. Hence Caucasians owe their color or lack of it to some function of the adrenal glands and the Negro is black because the adrenal functioning is different.

Dr. Berman says that the Negro is subadrenal and the Mongolian is subthyroid. He adds that the relative deficiency of these internal secretions constitutes the essence of the white man's burden.

There is every reason for believing that the white man has more active ductless glands than the yellow and this being true all that is required to make the colored peoples white and have only a white race is to stimulate properly and regulate these mysterious glandular functionings. This is a job, but not a task impossible. A few hundreds are doing research work on the endless possibilities of glandular functioning. There should be and will be thousands engaged in this work.

When I set out to develop crudely the idea a world race all white might be brought about scientifically I had not read Berman and no approach to such an idea had been suggested to me by another. But it seems the thought is a near one after all and in reach of performance.

According to race the microscopic granules of pigment of a uniform brown are very unequally distributed to the nuclei of cells of the inner layer of the skin, producing external color from light yellow to black, depending on the thickness of the skin cover and the number of granules. It is this arrangement of pigment that colors the eyes and the hair and it ought not to be difficult to regulate once science starts proper research in this direction.

In Madagascar there may be found all shades, cranial angles, all shapes of the head and kinds of hair. There is not a more mixed population in any country in the world. The Hovas occupy the high table-land of Imerina from which comes their proper name, Anta-Imerina. Hova means free man, although not all of them have always been free. Most ethnologists pronounce them Indonesians with enough admixture of Malay to warrant the term Indo-Malays. Their skin is olive yellow,

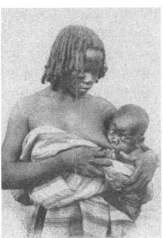

| ANTISAKA MAN & WIFE | ZARAMANAMPY WOMAN & CHILD | TANALA WOMEN | SERGEANT IN COLONIAL ARMY & HIS FAMILY |

their hair straight in some cases and quite wavy in others, the space between the eyes narrow as a rule, stature below the average and not much greater than the Japanese, head globular, as a compromise between brachycephalic and dolichocephalic, nose prominent and sharp. As the most numerous and the ruling population at the time of the French seizure they have been more closely studied than the Sakalava. They preserve many of the customs of the Indonesians, with their square houses on piles, sarong, instruments of music, fadi (taboo) in diet and habits, infanticide, polygamy, outrigger canoe, cylindrical forge bellows, form of sepulture, etc. The Hovas are tillers of the soil, shepherds and traders.

The Sakalavas are a perfect ethnic contrast: almost pure Abantu Negroes, shiny black, big and tall, head dolichocephalic, frizzy hair and flat nose. They are not nearly as civilized as the Hovas and are addicted to many old Negro practices of fetichism, voodoo, palaver and as also may be said of all the rest of the Malagasies, ruled by superstition. It is interesting to see how these two strong tribes grade together with the changes of type, color, and kind of hair as a result of ages of miscegenation. Grandidier thinks that the Hovas arrived in Madagascar not more than five or six centuries ago or perhaps at most eight centuries. It is a guess. It may be granted that they came since the island was split off from the mainland of Africa, although it is most likely that a considerable population survived the cataclysm that made the Mozambique breech.

The language of the island, astonishingly uniform, is of the nature of the Malayo-Polynesian with additions of Abantu, Arabic and traces of Hebrew dating from the early period of trade.

The presence of the Negro type in such numbers cannot reasonably be accounted for otherwise than that they survived the creation of the island. There are a million of them. When it is taken into consideration that they are notoriously not a seafaring people it cannot be concluded that they crossed the channel, narrow as it is. They have never been known to venture willingly out of sight of land and are not boat builders. There are too many to be accounted for as having come as slaves, so they must have been there all the time. Their habitat was farthest removed from the scene of the world quake and it is reasonable to conclude that they lived through it.

Nearest to the Hovas in type are the Betsileo, who live next to them on the south. Another prominent tribe are the Betsimisaraka and the Antambahoaka, a coast people who live north of the twentieth parallel south latitude. South of them are the Antaimoro, who have a tradition that they are Arabs. They are not so highly developed as the tribes I have mentioned, but they are an interesting people and are devoted to their clan and their land. If they go away to work, and many of them migrate temporarily, they always return if they live and if they die they are carried home for burial no matter how far it is. I have seen most gruesome and piteous processions of men

ANCIENT GATE IN THE WALLS OF TANANARIVO

carrying corpses home for hundreds of miles. When they go home they carry their relative or friend who has died at work. The awful smells, together with the sadness of it all, make an indelible impression that keeps one from ever forgetting the Antaimoro.

Also south of the twentieth parallel are the Antaifasinas, the Antaisaka, the Antanosi, all along the coast. In the interior are the Antsihanaakato, north of Imerina; the Bezanozano, nearly in the center of the island, and the Tanala, the Bara and the Antaisara in the south center. The Antaifasina, who number about 200,000, have close relationship with their warlike neighbors, the Antaisaka, and near the latter are the Vangaindrano. These tribes are all Mussulman in custom. It is of course true that whenever a chieftain became strong enough to lead he either contested the right of the ruling chief or took his following and trekked. If victorious he remained as ruler; if not he trekked and set up another tribe. This accounts for the tremendous tribal segregation in Madagascar.

The Bara are inland to the south of the Betsileo and side by side with the Antaisara, who are denominated true savages, whatever may be meant by that. It is perfectly plain that the Arabs have been among them and left their signs. Down around Fort Dauphin are the Antanosi. They too have gone far afield and are a rare mixture. They are a kind of link between the Hovas and the Sakalava and resemble the Betsimisaraka.

One of the most savage of all the tribes of Madagascar are the people of Antandroy. They store and eat cactus berries and fruits that their sterile land affords and like all the other Malagasies they are enough developed to be successful cattle raisers. There is no cannibalism in the island now so far as is known. At best only a superficial study has been made of the Madagascar tribes and not all of them have been listed or are known. I have not mentioned the Mahavelona, the Marovoay, the Onjatsy, the Zanakantitra, and many more that are closely akin to those I have referred to. Surely enough has been said to indicate to the reader that if he desires to study the little known people of the world plenty of opportunity can be found in Madagascar.

CHAPTER VII
ANCIENT ACCOUNTS OF MADAGASCAR

MARCO POLO called the island Madeigascar. There have been many names from the days of the Arabs and the Egyptians and the Phœnicians and wot not other ancients. More than one writer has conjectured that it is one of the theatres of the Arabian Nights and that the æpyornis is the roc of those classic tales. Ellis calls Madagascar the Great Britain of Africa, from its location across the Mozambique channel. It is many times the size of Great Britain, but its vital energy has been puny in comparison.

During the high days of the sailing trade to the Indies it was a common thing for ships to go through the Mozambique channel and provision at St. Augustine Bay on the southeast coast. Both Bartholomew Diaz and Vasco da Gama saw the island, but they do not mention it in the logs of their earlier voyages and in fact I have not been able to find even scanty allusion to it by the Europeans of the age of discovery until after the turn of 1500. The Portuguese credit its discovery to their national Lawrence Almeida and their early charts mark it as the isle of St. Lawrence. Tristan d'Acunha, whose name is perpetuated by the little coral group in the African ocean northwest of Cape Town, visited Madagascar some time about or a little before 1510. An early French name for Madagascar was Île Dauphine. Rochon thinks the Moors and Arabs called it Serandib, while others assert that Serandib was their name for Ceylon and that the Arab name for Madagascar was Serandah. Nobody seems to have been able to trace with any certainty the genesis of the name Madagascar. Natives to this time often refer to the island as Nosindambo, meaning the place of plenty of wild hogs.

The Malagasy are as proud of their island as the Chinese were of their Middle Kingdom and the Empire of the Seven Seas. They often use extravagant phrases in its praise, such as "All that is beautiful beneath the skies." Or they may say, "Thou that art in the midst of the vast waters."

An Englishman named Richard Boothby, engaged in the Indian trade, sailed to Madagascar in 1640 and wrote a book on it published in 1644. He was a close rival of the natives in appreciation. Boothby said that Madagascar was superior in every way to any of the colonies established in America, Asia or Africa by the English, French, Dutch, Spanish and Portuguese.

"It is likely to prove of far greater value to any Christian prince and nation that shall plant and settle a sure habitation therein than the West Indies are to the king and the kingdom of Spain," he wrote nearly three hundred years ago. Furthermore he says:

"It may well be compared to the Land of Canaan that flows with milk and honey; a little world of itself adjoining to no other land for many leagues. It is the chief paradise this day on earth. In further commendation thereof I will take the liberty of extolling it as Moses did, without offense, that same land of Canaan, of which it is the equal. It is a goodly land; a land in which rivers of sweet waters and fragrant fountains flow out of the valleys and the mountains; a land of wheat and barley, of vineyards and fig trees and pomegranates; a land wherein thou shalt eat without scarcity; neither shalt lack anything therein; a land whose stones are iron and out of whose mountains thou mayst dig brass."

Thus Osborne's Voyages quotes Boothby, page 634, Vol. II. Now of course there were neither barley nor wheat in Madagascar at that time, perhaps, but then were many other things of value to mankind which the generous Boothby does not mention. For it is a fact that there is not an area on earth where

SPRING AT THE EDGE OF THE CITY, A SOURCE OF WATER SUPPLY BEFORE THE DAYS OF MODERN WATERWORKS

there is as certain nourishment for man and beast as in Madagascar, taking one year with another and given a taste for anything and everything that is sustaining and wholesome. The very agencies that jeopardize certain staples there are themselves good to eat and wholesome.

So valorous are the natives and so unusual the tribal combinations that the island was not subjugated until a brief time ago and to-day the conditions of society in morals and justice and order are better than they are in France, the tutelary ruler.

It is a moot question whether it would not have been better for France to have submitted to Malagasy civilization than to have imposed her own with its head tax as a first object, direct and indirect.

CHAPTER VIII
THE BUNKOING OF BENJAMIN FRANKLIN

THIS is not an elegant phrase, but it exactly describes the case. We have in it an early precedent for what was done to Mr. Woodrow Wilson at Versailles. You will remember when Mr. Franklin went to France to obtain the assistance of France in our mutinous conduct towards George III. Incidentally we know now and I think we knew pretty well then that France could not have been prevented from fighting for us and with us at that time. Nevertheless we had to make a decent showing of beseechment in order that it might be charged up to us for future use. So over went Poor Richard and he did a good job of it. Citizen Franklin left his mark in salon and court and got away better than Citizen Genêt did later in this country.

Among the mistakenly gracious things Franklin did was to extend his friendship to a notorious French adventurer named Benyowski, whose ancestors had long before taken refuge in France during troublous times in Poland; so long before that he had become completely Gallicized. Benyowski had been for a time the French governor of as much of Madagascar as the French controlled. While thus employed he had been so incompetent and so dishonest that he was recalled in disgrace. This act occurred while Franklin was in France upon his mission and at a time when he was particularly anxious to please everybody in sight. It was naturally easy for Benyowski to ingratiate himself with the great American envoy at such a time.

He told the Doctor that he was a victim of political enemies and that all he needed was a chance to return to Madagascar in order to obtain evidence to vindicate himself. Dr. Franklin gave Benyowski, although he was a discredited and disgraced person, letters to the American government and also to wealthy American supporters of the revolutionary cause. Benyowski promised in return to equip a privateer and prey on the British. This was the successful bait that hooked Franklin. The result was not what the Frenchman represented nor what the American hoped for. Instead of doing what he said he would do Benyowski came to America, interested many on the strength of his credentials, secured a staunch Maine coast sloop, armed it, organized a Yankee crew and proceeded to Madagascar to make war upon the very same friendly power that Benjamin Franklin, George Washington and all of the colonials were courting.

Now this is an interesting story that does not appear in any American history, nor in any life of Franklin. There are, however, many proofs that it is true in the French archives and so prominent a person of that time as Abbé Rochon vouches for it in the following words: "He (Benyowski) insinuated himself into favor with Dr. Franklin; this fact is incontestable as I was an eyewitness of it, but I cannot reproach myself with having suffered that celebrated man to be ignorant of what I knew respecting this adventurer."

So it is true that Dr. Franklin was not only fooled, but he was fooled with his eyes wide open. Benyowski proceeded to Antongil Bay, the best known harbor of Madagascar. He told his Yankee crew that he was going there to prey upon British whalers. Many of them had sailed in Yankee whalers and to them the story was perfectly reasonable, as they knew that whaling vessels of all nations made Antongil a base. Nor does it appear to have been difficult for Benyowski to convert his adventurous crew to the idea of becoming masters of Madagascar with all the women, honors of government and loot that the eloquent Frenchman spread before their hungry eyes.

CHAPTER IX
YANKEES FIGHT IN MADAGASCAR

ONE of the very few accounts of Benyowski's adventurings is given by the Abbé Rochon. Inasmuch as I have referred to the Abbé a number of times it may be well briefly to introduce him. He was a member of the Academy of Sciences of Paris and St. Petersburg, Astronomer of the French Marine, Keeper of the King's Philosophical Cabinet, Inspector of Machines, Money, etc. From 1767 to 1769 he travelled and studied and carried out missions for the French government in Madagascar and the East Indies. The accounts of his travels and investigations rank in value and interest with the accounts of the travels in China of Abbé Huc. They are also comparable to the important Jesuit Relations of North America.

The facts of the operations of Benyowski after that gentleman sailed with his Yankee crew and vessel are given largely in the Abbé's own words. There is meager record of the events that occurred between the time when he sailed from the Colonies until he arrived in Mozambique waters. A lot of time was consumed in the voyage and there are unverified stories of piracy and privateering en route.

Finally, in early 1786, the French government got

word out to M. de Souillac, Governor of the Isle of France (now Mauritius) to be on the lookout for Benyowski and his crew. May 9, 1786, M. de Souillac sent the sloop of war *Louisa* after the pirate. Viscount de la Croix was in command of the sloop. The *Louisa* carried extra troops to the number of sixty men from the régiment of Pondicherry under M. Larcher, captain of Infantry. M. Mayeur, one of the men best informed on that part of the world, was also ordered to report to de la Croix and accompany him on the *Louisa*. They were alert and realized that they had a hard foe to deal with.

Benyowski invaded Agoncy, a native town to the north of Antongil, and seized all the ammunition in a large magazine where the local chief had stored it preparatory to warfare against a rival chieftain. De la Croix learned this and proceeded with dispatch and caution. He considered that his enemy was well prepared to give battle and he knew that Benyowski, no matter what flaws there were in his character, was not a coward.

The *Louisa* put into Foulepointe on Antongil Bay May 17, 1786, and provisioned. From there she sailed for Agoncy in quest of her quarry. She arrived there May 23, but de la Croix was not familiar with the uncharted waters and could not procure a pilot. This led him to stand out to sea again and come to anchor behind a cape to the eastward of Agoncy. Captain Larcher got ready to land his infantry for the purpose of reconnoitring. The coast seemed to be clear.

He manned his boats, took two cannon and pulled shoreward without molestation at first. Just as he was debarking a surprise volley was fired by some of Benyowski's skirmishers, who evidently were not in force, as they retired precipitately after firing, scarcely giving Larcher a chance to return their fire. Larcher shelled the woods and then landed without opposition. The terrain was examined and Benyowski's fort and settlement located. The route to the fort was beset by great difficulties. It was necessary to cross five marshes and a river that was unfordable. The river was spanned by a bridge ninety feet long. Benyowski had not destroyed this because he said it would permit the coming of an expedition of reprisal from Foulepointe, which he had recently

raided, and would admit of the repulse of this and the weakening of the Foulepointe garrison to such an extent that it would fall an easy victim.

He did not expect to be attacked so soon by French troops reinforced from another quarter. Larcher had crossed the bridge before he met any signs of further resistance. Soon after this his advance reported that a town could be seen and that they had counted fifty houses, one of which they judged to be Benyowski's because of its size and prominence, but that they could not see the fort because of some trees behind which the native guides that had been impressed said it was located.

The fort was soon sighted and reported to the main body with the intelligence that at least an hundred men could be seen hurrying with arms to the inner defenses. The fort was on a hill that commanded the surrounding country and was encompassed by high and sharp and stout palisades of the kind used by the French in the American Indian country. It was defended by two four-pounders and several swivels.

Benyowski opened the fight with a rifle volley, quickly followed by grape and cannister and in turn supported by the rifles. The Yankee riflemen did good execution, but the cannon fire went high and gave the French government regulars a chance to fill their ranks and continue their advance with a semblance of good order. When they got a little closer they returned the fire and as luck had it a ball struck Benyowski through the heart, killing him instantly and throwing his men into confusion. When Benyowski received his mortal wound he was in the act of applying a match to a cannon loaded with grape shot which would have repulsed the French, according to their own account.

The French report says that Benyowski had thrown a cordon around them and that they were about to suffer a rear attack when the killing of the rebel commander so disconcerted his forces that the French easily captured the fort and were in readiness to repulse the secondary attack. The few Americans who were captured were executed and the others made their way to the interior and some got aboard whalers at Antongil. It is stated but not verified that there are Yankee half-breeds on the island to this day who owe their existence to the defeat of Benyowski and the flying of the Americans to different parts of the hinterland, where they joined native tribes and remained to take wives and become a part of the mixed population. The fact of the existence of Connecticut blood in Madagascar is not difficult to prove, but it is more reasonable to trace it to whalers than to Benyawski's men. Thus ended the indirect and unintentional attempt of Benjamin Franklin to capture Madagascar. Americans have been dramatically concerned with the island since, as we shall see later.

As for Benyowski, he was a slippery rascal and the story of his lurid career would fill a big book. There is a lot of literature in French about him, but he is of interest to Americans only as the person who fooled Benjamin Franklin into making a filibustering expedition that failed.

CHAPTER X
AMERICANS IN MADAGASCAR

FEW indeed of our nationals to-day splendid as they are and alert and more human and less selfish than ever before, realize what is their heritage in adventure. More of the unknown, untravelled, untouched world has been opened and brought into vibrant connection with what we in almost humorous pride call the civilized lands by their ancestors than by anybody else. Whenever they go afield in any quest they have a brave past record to live up to. Nor is this strange. Those who first landed upon the frowning New England coast, who ascended the James, who threaded the St. Lawrence to the foot of Niagara and then assailed the deep forests, who turned southward and were not to be denied by savage or fever, who boiled their pails on the Wabash, Ohio, Mississippi and an hundred other streams, who traversed plain and mountain as braver men than the mythical heroes that dared the Symplegades, who bronzed their cheeks in the Great Lakes gales: these men and their women, too, were the pick of the earth.

Their gallant spawn covered the turbulent seas everywhere. They were up the Irrawaddy before any others, they were in the Indian Ocean after the treasure that had been for long the monopoly of the Moor, they were in the China trade with their swift clippers; by land and sea they went where others followed. So it was they awakened sleeping giants like Japan and stirred the world in all its parts. Restless souls that had known the wind-swept sky in every zone, it is not to be wondered that they were in Madagascar in the sixteen hundreds.

What were they doing there? Inasmuch as piracy in one form or another is still fashionable on both land and sea we need not blush at those early maraudings. They were after anything that could be turned into money and its equivalent. Colonial and British slavers hovered off the coast of Africa and did a smashing business in gold dust, ivory, spices and that cheapest of all commodities both then and now, human beings. It is officially recorded that in 1699 rice was taken from Madagascar to Charleston, South Carolina, and it is a fact that Carolina rice is the same as Madagascar rice; the best produced in the United States and not to be excelled in all the world.

Yankee whalers were the smartest and most numerous in Mozambique waters and the rocks of Antongil Bay display enduringly carved the names that are historic in New Bedford. Naturally they hobnobbed with the Malagasy and there are folk tales of their doings down to this very day, because hobnobbing is a Yankee specialty.

Madagascar waters were famous whaling grounds in that time just as they have come again to be to-day. Whalers believe that the whales of the Antarctic waters come northward at the proper time to have their young and to be relieved of their annual accumulation of barnacles in the fresher waters at the mouths of streams on the Madagascar and African coast.

There are many big whaling stations and rendering plants tributary to Madagascar waters to-day. But there isn't the romance about it that there used to be, or else I have undergone a change in sentiment and enthusiasm—and I do not believe I have. In the olden time when our Yankee fleet swarmed over the Indian Ocean there was hand harpooning and many a mighty tussle between man and leviathan; it was a leviathan then, but now it seems small because swift, daring, power whale boats as big as a whale are used and the harpoon is shot out of a big clumsy swivel gun on the bow. A bomb is attached to the big spear and when it explodes the whale is done for; it is not unlike dynamiting fish. I shot a whale an hundred feet long and somehow or other I was rather ashamed and found my only satisfaction in the fact that the Indian Ocean was so violent that morning that ours was the only boat in the Mozambique channel at the time; the others considered it too rough to venture forth. There are as many whales as ever in Madagascar waters and some think more, but the finds of ambergris have fallen off so markedly as to demand scientific explanation. In my opinion the reason is that the whalers are farther from the surface of the water than in the days of the small boat and do not see the floating treasure.

To this moment calico in Madagascar as in Africa is called Americani. Many of the names of prominent places on the island were given by Yankee skippers. It is a lot of fun and harmless for the men of the British outpost to try to tell how the Cape Codders made the names that have stuck in spite of everything. W. Clayton Bickersgill, a British vice consul in Madagascar in 1885, has this to say of the harbor of Bembatooka, on which the town of Mojanga is situated:

"Fancy the noblest anchorage in the island being introduced to all the white-sailed coquettes that come in from the ocean as "Bembatooka" while an imperious river sweeps through that bay with a title above reproach. And what of the harbor? How came it by the mongrel name it bears? Well, Bembatooka seems to be a relic of the pre-British charting period. In those days there were certain old sea dogs of Salem in Massachusetts who used to visit Madagascar in their voyages to Arabia and the East Coast of Africa. They were pioneers of the present American agencies in Tamatave and Mojanga (1885). The last named place had not, however, come into existence when the Yankees named the bay. Vessels making use of the harbor were accustomed to beat up into the inner bay and anchor within the point now named Amboaniho. Close by there was a Sakalava hamlet known as Fombitoka on account of a solitary Fomby or rotia

palm that grew in the neighborhood and which was used as a landmark. Fombitoka was known then to the skippers of Cape Cod. But these were not the men to be purists in respect of a Sakalava place name. The story is that one of them while spending an idle day with his charts as he was bowling across the Atlantic homeward bound tried to recollect the name of the lone palm port in Madagascar and could not. Whereupon he inquired of the mate, a person profuse in tobacco juice and profanity, who was not more ready in the matter of memory than his boss, but who calculated (mind you, kakalated) that the carpenter might know the name of the God-forsaken hole perhaps. So they summoned to the cuddy one Mr. Chips, who, being a funny man, had remembered the 'tooka' part of the place and from that they took a shot and put down 'Bembatooka' in capitals. It stuck like Yankee."

Our men were leaving their names and more than that everywhere in that time. It has been common to charge British and Confederate privateering with the destruction of our merchant marine. It is true that it left the ocean like a mist about the time of the sectional war between the States, but it was ready to leave on account of economic changes that by mere coincidence became operative at that time. It is not rash to assert that if the Yankee had wished to keep the sea no agency on earth at that time could have kept him off. He was the master of them all. There was more money on land than at sea and he discovered the fact together with the charm of land adventure. We had been a littoral people. Our thoughts had been on the coast and outward on foreign trade. Suddenly the American was introduced to a new world at home and the Civil War had a lot to do with the presentation.

Our commerce left the sea because we had a bigger and better market at home, better wages, better credit and no end of other advantages. Our people engaged wisely in the huge work of developing their own country, physically the richest on earth, and they had no time for anything so ordinary as foreign trade. From that day our foreign trade became an incident and it still is. We did not have to work to sell our surplus. The foreigners came and as good as begged it. We were so independent that we generally refused to make things the way the outsider wanted them; he could take them American fashion or leave them alone and he must pay cash for them and perhaps receive them in bad condition for lack of care in packing. On the other hand our home market was served better than any people of the world were ever taken care of. We are just now beginning to consider export business as it is thought of in countries where the foreign trade is of chief importance. All the government pap we can put in the nursing bottle will not put our ships on the seas again and keep them there unless we come somewhere near to competing in cost. This means as low wages as the others, as poor crews, as bad conditions in every way as obtain in the competing marines, or efficiency to offset them. That is what is wrong in the government shipping business today. The alternative is to let the cheap world do the cheap business. We have other things better to do.

CHAPTER XI
MADAGASCAR'S ROBINSON CRUSOE— ROBERT DRURY

MADAGASCAR has had a real Robinson Crusoe. It is proper to write real because Regent Lucius Hubbard of the University of Michigan has proved beyond a doubt that Defoe stole his story from the Dutch fiction of Sjouke Gabbés. The case of James Tanner, called the "White Indian," who was stolen in Kentucky by raiding Ojibways and lived thirty years as an Indian before he discovered he was a white man, and afterward became an Indian interpreter for the United States Government at Sault Ste. Marie, Michigan, is paralleled by that of Drury in a zone far removed and proves the validity of the saying that truth is stranger than any invention of the mind.

Drury was a boy on the English pirate *Degrave*, a 700-ton ship mounting fifty-two guns that passed the Downs February 19, 1701, on a voyage of adventure to the Indian seas. Captain Younge was the pirate chief. The *Degrave* was wrecked on the coast of Madagascar in 1702 and almost all hands except Drury were either drowned or murdered by the Malagasies. From Drury's stirring tale it is clear that the crew must have fallen into the hands of the Antaimoros, who are still wild and bloodthirsty savages. The boy was made a slave and had many hairbreadth escapes from death. Finally after fifteen years among the savages he was rescued and brought to England by a Captain William Macket in an East Indian trader. All England was thrilled by Drury's story and it was written by competent hands and first published in 1728. Four other editions followed: two in 1743, one in 1808 and the last in 1826. I have the edition of 1728 and the one of 1826.

This story of Drury is well told and is regarded as a work of authority on Madagascar so far as the observation of an ignorant but alert cabin boy could be. Drury not only tells in a fascinating manner all he saw, but gives his personal feelings as he lived the life of a slave among black wild tribesmen. So accustomed did he become to them and to their color that he took a handsome black wife and undertakes to say that he found her sweeter and more to his taste than any white woman could be. After his rescue Drury became a slave trader and sold hundreds of slaves in Virginia, requiring many voyages to Madagascar and Africa. The preface to the first edition is typical in all its composition and also gives a fair idea of the Drury adventure. It is here reproduced in full:

"As nothing is of a more amiable nature, so nothing makes a stronger and more lasting impression on the mind than truth; and whatever regard some may pay to a wittily-contrived and ingenious tale, the best that can be said of it is, that it is gay delusion, and an idle amusement exposed to view in the fairest and most advantageous light.

"The following historical narrative needs no such disguise or ornament to recommend it; for Captain W. Macket (who, by his certificate, has assured the public that he believed the account our author has given of his surprising adventures to be just and true) was not only a gentleman of an unblemished character in regard to his honor and veracity, but well known to be a man of too great a fortune and good sense to countenance and give a public sanction to a trivial fable, or imposition. Without doubt this gentleman, as well as the captains of

AMBOSITRA, 150 MILES SOUTH OF TANANARIVO

VATOMANDRY, EAST COAST

other ships, informed himself of a case so singular and surprising, for at Yong-old, where he took the author on board, William Purser, a native of Feraingher, was their linguist for some months; he spoke English well, and knew Mr. Drury there, and was an eyewitness to many of the most doubtful adventures here related for several years together.

"The captain after this went to Munnongaro, or Massaleege; there he saw Nicholas Dove, who was one of the boys shipwrecked in the *Degrave*, and saved in the massacre in Anterndroea; besides the opportunity he had of conversing with Mr. Drury in their voyage to the West Indies, and after to England. To this we may add, the second voyage Mr. Drury made was also in Captain Macket's service, though not in the ship under his command, he being a principal proprietor in Captain White's ship and cargo, as well as of his own and others. These circumstances were confirmed by the captain, who added, that he had seen others in his last voyage there, as well as natives who spoke English, and knew Drury, as some who were saved by flight with Captain Drummond and others, with this particular account, that this very Captain Drummond was the man Mr. Drury supposes him to be, and that he was killed at Tullea, seven leagues to the northward of Augustine bay, by one Lewes, a Jamaica Negro. Besides all this, and the captain's continued friendship to him to the last, even our author himself, though in a lower station of life, was well known to many persons of probity and worth now in London, who frequently

conversed with him while living, and who always esteemed him an innocent, inoffensive man free from all artifice and design. As this was the character he had amongst his friends and acquaintance, we think it would be needless, if not impertinent, to doubt of his veracity in the relation of anyone of his adventures, more especially after such substantial proofs for the truth hereof.

"It is probable that the account here given of the religion of the natives of Madagascar may by some be thought a mere fiction, and inserted with no other view than to advance some latitudinarian principles; but so widely distant is this from the real case that the most to be suspected part of the conversation between deaan (chief or petty king) Murnanzack and Mr. Drury, on divine topics, is real fact as here related; and the deaan's ludicrous reflections on Adam's rib, God's converse with mankind, and his creation of the world in six days, and his resting the seventh, etc., his taking these things for Drury's childish notions, and saying they were old women's stories, were delivered in that prince's own words. And if we consider the then circumstances of our author, that he was but fourteen years of age when he set out on this unfortunate voyage, his education at a grammar school, and in the principles of the established church; and that ever since his arrival in England and settlement in London, he has been firmly attached thereto, even to bigotry; it would be very weak and absurd to suppose him capable, or inclined to advance an imaginary conference with the dean upon so serious a topic, with no other motive than to favor free thinking, or natural religion, in opposition to that which was revealed, especially as they are points about which he scarcely ever concerned himself.

"In all those places where religion, or the origin of governments are casually mentioned, there are interspersed some occasional reflections, which are not, properly speaking, the author's, which is all the artifice made use of throughout the whole. It must be owned that topics so entertaining could not well be passed over, without making some proper and useful applications; yet no motive, how tempting soever, could prevail on the editor to alter any real fact, or add anyone single fiction of his own. Every transaction here related as like wise the character and conversation of every person introduced, are properly Mr. Drury's own.

"The religion of the natives of Madagascar, some authors will have to be Mahometanism; but without any manner of grounds for such a conclusion, since it has no resemblance of it in any other particulars, than in circumcision, and abstaining from their women at certain times, which were common to some eastern nations long before the Jews had it; or, indeed, where there is no reason to imagine that the name of the Jews was once so much as heard of.

"There are good grounds, on the other hand, to conjecture, that the Jews derived several of their religious ceremonies from them. For that their religion is much more ancient is plain from several reasons. First, from their regard to dreams, and divining by them, which by the Mosaic law, the Israelites were expressly forbidden. Secondly, from their shaving off their hair in mourning for their dead; whereas among the Jews the growth of it is strictly commanded, and is superstitiously observed to this day. Thirdly, from their sacrifices; as Moses commanded none but males to be sacrificed; so, on the contrary, cows are the greatest part of the Madagascar sacrifices, and are thought by these people to be the most acceptable oblations to their Supreme Deity. They have no burnt offerings except near their sepulchres, when occasionally opened, which, with the gums burnt with them, serve for a defence against all ill scents. Fourthly, but the most

notable reason of all is, that the owley, which these Madagascar people make use of for their divinations, and procure their unusual or extraordinary dreams with, is manifestly the ephod and teraphim, made use of by the Levite who lodged in Micah's house, as we read Judges xvii, and from which the Israelites could never be wholly brought off, though directly repugnant to the law of Moses, concerning which there seems to be no occasion for enlarging farther in this place.

"That the people of Madagascar did not derive their religion from any learned or polite nation is evident by their retaining no idea or remembrance of letters; nor their having a horse, or so necessary a machine as a wheel of any kind, either for carriage or use, which could never have been forgotten had they ever had them. That these Madagascar people came from Africa first seems most probable by their color; and perhaps from the Abyssines, or even from Egypt. The Virzimbers, indeed, by their wooly heads, must come from the more southern part of Africa. Deaan Tokeoffu told Captain Macket they had a tradition of their coming on the island many years ago in large canoes. But from wheresoever they came, it is manifest that their religion is the most ancient in the world, and not far from pure natural religion.

"We may reflect with pleasure on the devotion of these people, who address the Supreme Being on every occasion for His aid and assistance when in necessity or distress: and with true piety and hearts full of gratitude return Him their humble and unfeigned thanks for those blessings and benefits He confers upon them; yet have they no temples, no tabernacles, or groves for the public performance of their divine worship; neither have they solemn fasts, or festivals, or set days, or times, or priests to do it for them. But we may here observe, that as Melchizedeck was a king, and stiled the priest at the most high God (a phrase strictly correspondent to that of deaan Unghorray, the highest God) so it is the practice of the Madagascar kings, or lords, to be themselves the performers of all religious offices. Their mossees or prophets, indeed, directed the making their owleys of particular roots; or woods, having, as they tell them, magical properties agreeing to the spirits; as also that they must be made at proper times.

"There are two things in this history highly worthy of observation; that is, that there is a law among them against cursing a man's parents. What a reproach is this to countries called Christian where there is no law or punishment against even those who have the impudence and impiety not only of cursing others, but their own parents. The other is, that such is their regard and reverence to the most high God, that they swear not profanely; but such is the profaneness of even our Christian nation, that a man can hardly pass the streets (as Archbishop Tillotson observes) without having his ears grated and pierced with horrid and blasphemous oaths and curses, as are enough, if we were guilty of no other sin, to sink a nation. These give reputation to the general character of these people, that where the European or Mahometans have not corrupted them they are very innocent, moral, and courteous; and more so, with shame be it spoken, than most nations, who have all the advantages of a liberal and Christian education.

"There is yet one observation more, which, we hope, will not be thought improper here; which is, that our author's many deliverances are glorious and wonderful displays of the goodness and power of Divine Providence; and gave him, no doubt, an awaking sense of his obstinate disobedience to the will and entreaties of his tender parents' and friends, who so much and often pressed him to lay aside those wilful resolutions of his first voyage to the East Indies; wherein we may see the marks both of divine displeasure and goodness, the first in his shipwreck and slavery, the other in his delivery or release from thence. All which may serve as a lesson to the youth of future generations to beware, lest by their disobedience and obstinate forcing of themselves from the care of their parents or friends, they bring upon themselves those miseries and misfortunes which occasion a too late repentance.

"Much more might have been said upon this occasion, but as we have not room, we refer our readers to the perusal of the book itself; in which, we presume, they will not only find an entertaining, but profitable amusement."

"This is to certify that Robert Drury, fifteen years a slave in Madagascar, now living in London, was redeemed from thence, and brought into England, his native country, by myself. I esteem him an honest, industrious man, of good reputation, and do firmly believe that the account he gives of his strange and surprising adventures is genuine and authentic.
"WILLIAM MACKET.
"May 7, 1728."

CHAPTER XII
CAPTAIN KIDD AND A PIRATE REPUBLIC IN MADAGASCAR

THERE were pirates and slavers in the Indian seas before the mystic and fetching South Seas were heard of. And that region is much less touched now by civilization than the Pacific waters, although exploited thousands of years before them. Rochon tells many tales of the pirates in Madagascar and speculates intelligently upon the influence they may have had upon the natives of the great island. Johnson's "Voyages of the Pirates" has its scenes largely in the seas tributary to Madagascar and the records of the French East India Company are filled with dramatic brushes with the free gentry of the big seas.

The best known of the freebooters who made their headquarters in the Mozambique region and made in and out of the deep bays of Madagascar was Captain William Kid, also spelled Kidd. Kid was not a pirate at the outset. William the Third, King of England, gave a commission to Captain Kid to "command a stout ship of 30 guns and 80 men and go to the Malagasy seas in search of pirates, with full power to apprehend, seize and take them into custody together with all freebooters and sea rovers," who appear to have been distinguished from pirates at least by terminology.

At the time Madagascar was the worst nest of pirates in the world. The "fifteen men on a dead man's chest" would have figured as a typical social gathering. Kid was eager to sail after them and fitted out his command at once and named his ship *The Adventure*. Arriving in the Mozambique channel he cruised in and out without seeing any of his quarry—if he really wanted to see them. In any event he soon unfolded to his willing crew a plan of piracy that won for him a career of killing and robbing at sea that puts him in the first class of those luminous worthies that made sailing the ocean a hazard for several centuries and that finally brought Kid to the scaffold. He was caught red-handed and executed.

Kid and the English pirates did not attempt a settlement in Madagascar, but the French freebooters were more constructive. Misson and Caraccioli, the latter a Corsican, established a pirate town on the northeast coast of the island at Antongil Bay. Here they were joined by a Captain Tew, who was a superior sort of sea rover and the settlement grew into a dominion over a wide area and had an established farming support. There came to be a form of republican government that constituted the first pirate republic and the most considerable one of history. In volume II of Johnson's "History of the Pirates" is a full account of the republic. They called it Libertatia and built a pretentious capitol. Johnson says the laws were models of justice. From Libertatia for a long time they operated their pirate craft and were so successful that all grew rich. With wealth came immense power and their trade with the natives for slaves and semi-precious stones induced several of the adventurers to engage in the slave trade, and this took them to America.

On an early occasion in the history of Libertatia the pirates captured a Moorish ship on the way to Mecca with more than an hundred beautiful young women aboard. The Moorish masters of their harems had taken only their younger wives to entertain them on their pilgrimage. These women were distributed among the buccaneers and the result was a greater contentment and permanency than before. From this time on the colony grew until it reached its fullest development. Quite often they captured more prisoners than they could care for or could assimilate if they were Portuguese or other "foreigners." It was their custom to parole them and give them a ship and send them on their way. Although sworn to secrecy and not to fight against the pirates, the Portuguese forgot as soon as they were out of sight and if captured afterward they were made to walk the plank before all others.

Through these drifters the Portuguese government learned of the settlement and sent a fleet of five warships against Libertatia. One day a small dhow in which the pirates were teaching several Malagasies seamanship came into port in mad haste and reported themselves driven in by five tall ships heavily manned. Captain Misson was president of Libertatia at the time and happened to be in port. He at once took the measure of the greasers and his annals say they were driven off with sanguinary loss and the capture of two of the ships, which gives an idea of the formidable power of the pirates. Inasmuch as Abbé Rochon corroborates Misson there can be little doubt of the accuracy of the report.

No slaves were kept in Libertatia and all who reached that settlement and were permitted to remain were given their full liberty and were most loyal. At the same time the leaders of the colony were waxing wealthy in the slave trade with American colonists. Not infrequently Americans visited Libertatia and were so well pleased that several whalers settled there for a time but returned to New Bedford to die. The continual preying on the tribes for slaves provoked a war with the natives, who turned against the pirates the skill that the pirates had taught them in order to use them as marauders.

One of the speculations that legitimately grows out of the years of the existence of Libertatia before it was destroyed by long conflict with the Malagasies is as to the effect upon the quality of the slave population of America and the British West Indies the admixture of natives of Madagascar produced. A good many yellow negroes in the Southern states of America who are generally and carelessly rated as mulattoes may trace their source as Malagasies and some of them are quite pure in blood. As an average they are superior to the African but not as large physically.

For years the pirates were extremely popular in Madagascar among the natives, for they gave them firearms, rum, cloth, and taught them many things. Nor did they oppress or impress the natives near at hand and when the final wars came those Malagasies who were living near Libertatia fought for their neighbors with bravery. And to this day there are tales that have come to be almost myths of men who came from afar and treated the natives so well that their like had not been seen before or since. And there are stories of others who pretended to be legitimate traders who seized whatsoever they wished in the way of supplies and burned villages if they met with opposition and raped the women and made themselves so odious that they are classed with the slavers.

The fall of Libertatia was not the end of piratical activities in Madagascar waters. Other scattered settlements were formed and there was a kind of federation among them. Once more they grew strong and bolder than ever. They seized a large Portuguese man-of-war with Count Receira and the Archbishop of Goa on board.

Finally there was a concert of action against the pirates by England, France, Portugal and Holland. Most of them were rounded up in Antongil Bay and their ships burned. The plan the allies acted upon was to set a guard at the likely harbors and then send other ships of war to sea in pursuit. Sooner or later the pirates would be compelled to run in somewhere to revictual and get fresh water, and there they found an ambush and were entrapped.

In Voltaire's Histoire de Charles XII is an interesting reference to the Madagascar pirates. He says the pirates of the European and American seas were organized and were in Madagascar waters making a last stand against the lawful governments of the world. They wanted a leader to create a government of pirates, by pirates and for pirates. Charles XII had just retreated from his plunge into the Ukraine and the disastrous battle of Pultowa. His fortunes were desperate. His prime minister Gortz was ordered to treat with a deputation from the pirates who had been informed that they were welcome and would be heard and probably that an alliance could be formed.

As the ports of the world were closed to them they went in a Dutch vessel and were received by Baron Gortz at Gottenburgh. An arrangement was made by which the pirates were to subject themselves to the warring Swede and carry to him sixty war vessels laden with treasure, men and ammunition and arms.

ROMAN CATHOLIC CATHEDRAL, ANTANANARIVO

The negotiations with the corsairs were completed by Cronstrom, and Mendal for the King and Gortz. Before the arrival of the lawless armada Charles had enlisted the support of Cardinal Alberoni, who had governed Spain for his own glory at the expense of the people. Alberoni and Charles proved themselves equal to pirate chieftains by going back on the deal made by Gortz and by seizing the pirate ships and all the treasure. In fact it was the opportunity to do this that led Alberoni to join Charles.

Even after their ships were burned and they had been given a dose of their own medicine by Charles XII and Alberoni, the pirates went ashore in Madagascar and organized the natives against their enemies of the law. This they found to be satisfying in a way but unprofitable. So they hit upon a scheme that had in it all the possibilities of profit of their predatory life on the sea trade between Europe and India. This was to arrange to have the Malagasies sell to them the prisoners taken in the many wars that the tribes engaged in. If there was a lull in these wars the pirates stimulated them and soon did a swelling trade in human beings and in a safer way than ever, for they were not only pardoned by the Europeans whose nationals were in the slave business, but were actually encouraged and protected.

Thus America and England laid some of the foundation of their present wealth. Johnson tells of these activities and one sees in these pirates men of unusual constructive ingenuity in devilment. They were brave, too, and not only incited wars but got into the game themselves and caused the natives to think that the side that had white men was the one that always was victorious. This belief was capitalized most profitably. On one occasion the former pirates, who had now become statesmen, delivered a cargo of 600 slaves as their share of the booty from several native towns that they aided a chief to conquer. The chief agreed to give them even a greater share if they would continue to assist him and it came to be that if whites were seen in the warring ranks of this chieftain the opposition would at once become panic-stricken. The result was that this petty king became the master over all of the land of Methelge and the slave grabbers were given victims to the number of thousands.

An Englishman called Captain North is said to have been the most dramatic figure in these activities in Madagascar. He organized an army of natives with a sprinkling of renegade whites and won his reputation by capturing a fortified native town that had been looked upon as so nearly impregnable that it had not been attacked for a very long time. When North was a sea pirate he never attacked English or American ships, but confined himself to Moorish and Portuguese and Dutch. One fee from the Mongoro whom he led in battle was 100 slaves and 500 fat cattle.

There was much intermarriage between the pirates and the women of the island, or what passed as marriage. Some of the progeny became distinguished and are remembered for their prowess and service. One of these was Tamsimalo, who was the son of a notoriously bloodthirsty corsair by a native concubine. He took his mother's name and became a tribal king. He married among his mother's people and had several children. His daughter Betia was famous for her beauty and charm, and her name, which means "much affection" was given her after she reached the height of her womanly power as the greatest vampire princess of her time. The stories of her rule over men are voluminous and entertaining.

Tamsimalo saw to it that his son, whom he called John Harre, in memory of his pirate grandfather, succeeded him, but this son did not turn out well. One of the men whom Betia conquered and kept twisted about her fingers as long as she wished was Monsieur Grosse in the high employment of the French East India Company. He was sent by his company to found a settlement at St. Mary's. There he met Betia and fell in love with her. He showed so much attention to her that Betia's mother made war on him. But Betia was loyal and together they defeated the Dowager. Betia became the real ruler and kept Grosse by her side until he was caught in the act of robbing the graves of the old kings whose treasure in large amount had been buried with them. This was the most unpardonable of crimes because it incensed the gods and nothing could appease them but the death of the culprit. Betia tried to save her lover but that only incensed the natives, who rushed upon the French and killed them to a man. Betia had been kept informed by a trusty spy and escaped with Grosse to a secret cave. When the French authorities heard of the massacre at St. Mary's they sent a ship of war to punish the natives. This was late in 1754. The armed vessel blockaded the port of St. Mary's and bombarded the tribe there. A landing was effected and everything combustible was burned. Hundreds of Malagasies were drowned in trying to escape in canoes. Among those killed in this manner was the widow of Tamsimalo, who had instigated all the trouble.

It became necessary for either Betia or Grosse to go out of the cave in search of provisions and aid and to ascertain whether it would be possible for them to bring together a party of French and natives and renegades and set up a government. Betia was with child, but insisted that she would be safer than Grosse; and as he was a good deal of a sneak and a coward, as proven by his ghoulish efforts to get rich, he let her go. She was captured by the French and taken to the Isle of France. There she was tried for her life and partly because of her enceinte condition and additionally for the reason that she made eyes at the commandant she was given a clean bill and her freedom. It was decided to send her back to Madagascar and to use her talents in bringing peace and a better understanding between the natives. and the French. There had been much trade between the two before the sack of St. Mary's.

Accordingly Betia was accoutred as a queen and given costly presents of jewels and rich cloth. With her was sent a soldier named Bigorne, in the service of the French East India Company, who was desperately in love with her. Bigorne was the most accomplished linguist in the Indian service of the French. He was a natural intellectual and combined brains with a large and handsome physique of the sympathique variety that appeals to some women. Consequently he was as vain as a male guinea and easily believed Betia to be in love with him, an idea which she took care to encourage. She went back home and took him with her. Meantime her baby, a girl, was born and the French gave her a nursing retinue for it.

After giving Bigorne assistance in his agential work, so that he really made a record that improved his standing both with his employers and the French Government, Betia suddenly was reported missing and,the story was told that she had been kidnapped and killed by friends of her late enemy mother. This was a ruse, as she was so deeply in love with Grosse that she was willing to risk all for the sake of rejoining him. This she did and after three years she succeeded in surrounding herself with a sufficient following to start again in the business of government. Best of all she was fortunate enough to obtain possession of her little girl, whom she had apparently deserted.

No sooner had she obtained her child than the miserable Grosse started trouble by robbing some of the chiefs who were loyal to Betia. They were on the point of ambushing and killing both the princess and her cowardly paramour when they became convinced that Betia knew nothing of the craftiness of her partner. Nor did Grosse appreciate the fact that she had again saved his life, for he attempted to kill both Betia and their child. In this adventure he met a deserved death, and a portion of his heart was fed to dogs. Betia grew old as a queen of her people and is said to have retained her power over men to the last.

The full story of the pirates would make a large volume, for in the tributary waters of Madagascar they were bolder and flourished for more centuries than in any other part of the world before or since. They probably attacked the ships of Hiram of Tyre on their way to and from ancient Ophir a thousand years before the Christian era and kept up their marauding feats until late in the nineteenth century, a period of three thousand years.

There is room for more Treasure Island tales than a score of as fertile minds as that of Robert Louis Stevenson could produce, and the field is new and wholly unexploited by modern writers.

CHAPTER XIII
A RARE LETTER
FROM DR. DAVID LIVINGSTONE

WHILE in Madagascar I was told of a rare and most interesting letter written by that martyr to the missionary cause, Dr. David Livingstone, whose heart is in Westminster and whose bones are in the wilds of the Belgian Congo, Africa. It was written to a missionary of the London Missionary Society in Madagascar from Mohilla, one of the Comoro Islands, at a critical period in the career of Livingstone. Livingstone had just lost his wife, but was not cast down nor discouraged. He was concerned with affairs that surmounted all personal considerations. His reference to the queen of Mohilla is an interesting side light on the great missionary. Another touch is the pride of personal performance in piloting his ship, which was little more than a dhow, through the troublous seas of the nasty channel. He saw the effect of the battle between the *Monitor* and the *Merrimac* as clearly as the London *Times* stated it. But that he was human to a remarkable degree is shown by the reference to Lincoln and his associates as "these worthies" which was a clear reflection of the feeling of Britain against the North and the sympathy that existed for the South and its cause. But the letter speaks so interestingly for itself that it is here given in full. He was not so fortunate in obtaining an egg of the giant æpyornis as I was, for he secured only a few small pieces of shell, while I procured a very large and perfect egg, which is now in the museum of the University of Michigan at Ann Arbor. This is the letter and it is published for the first time in America; nor does it appear in any of the biographies of Livingstone:

"Mohilla Island, 25th of August, 1862.
"My dear Mr. Ellis:—

"Though there is not much probability of a letter reaching you from this out-of-the-way spot, yet the promise of the queen, who is a relative of Radama II, to forward it to Bambatouk by the first dhow going thither, and the value I myself put upon a letter when in somewhat similar circumstances, induce me to make the attempt at a word of salutation. In coming hither we ran close along a part of your western shore: and you in your most important and interesting work were brought vividly to my recollection. I need not say how earnestly I wished you health and prosperity, and God's abundant blessing.

"The queen here is said to be a cousin of Radama II—and she is under French protection—was made much of in view of probably being one day made use of as a claimant to the throne of Madagascar. We met Père Finasse here last year—you write the name Finez; but I suspect their hopes are now dimmed. She is married to an old stick of an Arab of Zanzibar, and has become a Mohammedan, which may be an improvement on the old ways of the Malagasee. Two of her subjects were opposed to the Arab husband's protective policy, and the French removed them to Mayotta, as prisoners of state. She is a nice little body, and as she admired the portrait of our queen the last time I was here, I took your book to show the pictures of the prince and princess. But in presence of the old husband she had to be a good Mohammedan, and not look at the image of any living being. I think that your people may thank the Supreme Ruler, who has guided the feet of the messengers of the Gospel of Christ to their shores, instead of the emissaries of soulcramping superstitions.

"A great deal of slave-trading goes on from the coast of Africa to Majama Bay, near Cape St. Andrew. The people here name the principal slave-port Menabay. It is carried on chiefly by Arab dhows; and if Radama II knew half the miseries inflicted on Africa by those who carry on the traffic, he would not hesitate to imitate Radama I in stopping the export of slaves, by at once forbidding their import into his dominions. This one great act of Radama I is always mentioned as the glory of his reign, and it will be quoted to his fame in all future generations. I would not dictate this measure, but I have no doubt that should his attention be drawn to the subject and information be obtained, his own sense of what is right will lead him to legislation such as will bless both Madagascar and Africa. Apart from all considerations of justice and mercy, it is impolitic to allow a traffic which tends to render labour unpopular. The Malagasee will rise in the scale of nations only by hard work. You may tell him if you think it proper, that while labouring to put a stop to this horrid traffic by pacific means, it will be a joy to my heart in Africa if he will cooperate in the same noble work in Madagascar.

"I got out a steamer at the beginning of this year for Lake Nyassa, whence there is an export annually of 19,000 slaves to Zanzibar alone. She is in pieces, and when we get up to the cataracts of the Shire we shall unscrew her, and carry her past; but we had to put her together first in the low Zambesi delta, and had great sickness in consequence. My dear wife, whom I never intended for that exposure, was the only victim of the fever and I now feel lonelier in the world than before. Much reduced by sickness and having a Johanna crew who wished to return home, we came away in the *Pioneer*, and found her a good little ship on the ocean. She rose on the huge waves from the south like a little duck. Need I say that I felt a little proud when, by the sole guidance of a land lubber like your servant, we lay to at three a.m. of 23rd, deeming ourselves seven or eight miles off Mohilla, and as day dawned found ourselves in sight of this, the first land we had seen since we left the Zambesi. You must excuse this little bit of boasting egotism. We go on to Johanna, and thence to Rovuma, being still very anxious to get an outlet for Lake Nyassa, away from our inveterate slave-dealing friends the Portuguese.

"Possibly you have later intelligence from Europe than we, but in case you have not, I may say that the war in America still goes on; that the slave question is coming at last prominently forward. The president offers to insure pecuniary compensation to any state that may abolish slavery. This may be only to secure the border states, which have but few slaves, to the Union. But the question has forced itself upon the government, and more must be done than these worthies imagine. An engagement between the iron-plated vessels—South and North—after pounding at each other for five hours, ended so differently from the fight of the Kilkenny cats that the *Times* declares that the whole British navy consists of only six ships, viz.: our iron-plated ones. Several wooden ships were destroyed by the southern iron-plated one, with the greatest ease, and we are now all activity in iron-plating men-of-war. In France religious questions excite the greatest interest of any. Thanks to the Pope for his obstinacy, the Italians made a demonstration against the poor old man's temporal sovereignty, and this causes many to search for light in spiritual matters. The Bible is recognized more and more widely as the cause of England's prosperity, and one pious Italian named Perfetti says that, having asked many true disciples what had led them to Jesus and to peace, he always received this answer, 'the Bible,' 'the writings of the Fathers,' or 'the Cross is the way of Light,' or pointing silently to heaven; 'but none ever referred to the priests, or the high dignitaries of the Church of Rome.'

"Very considerable changes are made for the better in education in Austria. Rev. Dr. Reed, of London, and Rev. Professor Cuningham, of the Free Church, are dead. Our good little queen bears up bravely against her heavy bereavement; and I cannot wish better for Radama and his queen than that they may be as much beloved for their virtues, as is our own beloved sovereign by us all. With good wishes, I am,

"Affectionately yours,
"David Livingstone.

"Can you get any of those famous big eggs? (Dinornis.) I got a small bit."

CHAPTER XIV
HIGH EMPRISE OF A
UNITED STATES ARMY SURGEON

Dr. J. Perrott Prince, a distinguished surgeon and soldier of the Union army in the Civil War of America, did all he could to keep the French out of Madagascar. The story of his life, I had it from his own lips, reads like pages from the history of the days when men went spiking up and down the earth with spear at tilting angle, spirit aflame and life as cheap as crested foam.

He was born February 7, 1838, at New Brunswick, just over the Maine border, whither his ancestors had fled during the hegira of American loyalists in 1783. He had in him the blood of the North that has made such remarkable men in the States and Canada.

Bluntly to tell his experiences in Madagascar without properly presenting him to your mind would be to rob the story of half its dramatic value. When the Civil War broke out (I should like to call it always the war of the sections just to please the soul of Marse Henry Watterson, but it is such a clumsy designation), young Prince, who had already made his home in Massachusetts, and had graduated at the Massachusetts Medical College, offered his services and was made an assistant army surgeon.

But he would forget his job in a fight and would grab the first gun dropped by a fallen soldier and go into battle. This was soon bound to get him into trouble on one side or the other, and sure enough he was captured at the battle of Gaines' Mill and sent to Libby prison. It was before the decision to make no exchange of prisoners and he was soon out and at it again. He was assigned to the staff of General Miles and as such attended Jefferson Davis professionally, after the capture and imprisonment at Fortress Monroe of the Confederate president. Dr. Prince was severely wounded at Gaines' Mill and got dysentery and a bronchial affection at Libby, both of which became chronic. He never got rid of the latter, but that did not lead him to lie around on a pension. When the war was over he was honorably discharged with the rank of brevet lieutenant colonel "for faithful services," but not until he had followed the army in its campaigns southwest, where he saw service against hostile Indians.

The peace of his Acadian birthplace evidently had not entered his soul, for he found life as a civilian in crowded places intolerable. So off he went to South Africa. The diamond discoveries in the Kimberley region were made not long after his arrival and he left Cape Town for the diamond fields. The Griquas resented the encroachments of the inrushing whites and broke out in open warfare. This was right to the desire of a man who liked better to give punches than pills and he organized Prince's Horse and went after the blacks. A young man named Cecil J. Rhodes applied to the doctor-soldier for service and as he seemed a likely fellow was made a second lieutenant.

One day when they were well into the enemy's country Rhodes could not be found. Colonel Prince thought he had been ambushed, but in four days he appeared and asked for a court-martial. He said the war was over and until he proved his story they thought him crazy. It seems that the idea came to Rhodes to go and see the Griqua king (McKenzie McDonald style) and have a talk with him. With Rhodes it was no sooner thought than done, so off he went and ended the war in a manner satisfactory to all concerned.

Nor was this the only time that Cecil Rhodes ended a native war by bravely acting upon his own initiative. By the time the Matabele broke out Rhodes had got to a place of prominence and authority. Nevertheless he made up his mind to go and see King Lobengula, ruler of the Matabeles and a brave and bloodthirsty fighter. When Rhodes announced his intention of seeing Lobengula without an escort all of his associates begged him not to do so and Dr. Prince eagerly sought to go with him and told him the story of the cowardly killing of the American General Canby by the Modocs, which had occurred only a short time before and under circumstances similar to those of the undertaking that Rhodes proposed. There was no deterring him and he saw Lobengula alone, although the Matabele had a strong guard. The Matabele war was ended at the conference.

So much for talking things over fairly even with a so-called savage.

Dr. Prince and Cecil Rhodes became fast friends and as personal and confidential physician to him the Doctor was closer to Rhodes than any other man that lived. So one day when the Empire Builder was damning Oom Paul Kruger more savagely than usual Dr. Prince asked Rhodes why he didn't "clean him' out." There and then the Jameson raid was planned. Rhodes said he thought the thing could easily be done if they had a bold spirit who would lead their forces. Prince told him he had a young red-blooded assistant he had recently brought out from London who could turn the trick. What happened is well known. When I told John Hays Hammond these facts, which I had from Dr. Prince personally before he died, he replied that he never had known before who was responsible for that infernal scrape which so nearly cost him his head.

When Dr. Prince's fame as a physician was at its height and honors were coming to him from America and Europe he received a summons to attend Queen Ranavalona of Madagascar. A royal tub was sent for his use and he sailed at once. But it may be a long voyage from Africa to Madagascar in a fairly good boat, as I have found, and it took the dhow that was carrying the Doctor so long to make the passage that the queen was dead when he arrived. He told me that this was a piece of excellent luck as Her Majesty had a fatal malady and was bound to die, and if she had passed away on his hands he was certain it would have cost him his head; at least several Malagasy medical men had been executed for failing to cure the queen, which I take to be a myth but which is not such a bad idea after all.

Something of even greater importance to the welfare of the island than the death of the queen was impending. The Malagasy government was expecting war with the French. There were signs of it in abundance. The French had looked upon Madagascar as their own ever since the days of Flacourt in the middle of the seventeenth century. The islanders were without arms and ammunition. Dr. Prince quickly learned this and proposed to supply them. An arrangement was made by which the Doctor was to get them a boat that could transport munitions of war to them and then could be transformed into a sort of fighting ship. He was to be paid in silver plate, moidores, doubloons, pieces of eight and jewels that had been accumulating secretly in the royal treasury for a century. They gave their new ally seven tons of treasure and he left for England at once.

Once there he got a spy to tell the French secret service just enough about the matter to fool them. His own spy kept track of him for the French and told them what was not going on. Dr. Prince bought a ship, loaded it with powder, shot, shells, guns and even some mines. Then he had his man inform the French that he intended to land at a point near the mouth of the Betsiboka river, the largest stream on the island. The French fleet hovered within striking distance of Mojanga while the Doctor sailed to the other side of the island and landed at a point between Foulepointe and Tamatave, a much better spot for the Malagasy. He arrived at the hour in the night agreed upon nearly a year before. The Madagascar government made poor use of what they got when the fighting came on as it did soon afterwards.

Dr. Prince had his treasure melted down in England and realized nearly double what he had figured on, due to the fact that there was considerable gold in the plate and the value of the jewels was greater than he had estimated. He was not much luckier than the Malagasy, for he lost it all and more in a filibustering expedition that he engaged in against Portuguese East Africa. He was a rare and restless American and was held in distinguished esteem in Durban, where he lived until his death in 1916. The world is not what it was and there will be few such lives as his in the future.

CHAPTER XV
MISSIONARY WORK IN MADAGASCAR

THERE is no part of the world where foreign missionary efforts, so called, have justified themselves and borne fruit as in Madagascar. And also in no portion of the globe have I met such high grade and devoted women and men in this service. The first missionary work done in the island was by

CHURCH OF AMBOHIPOTSY, ANTANANARIVO
L.M.S. MEMORIAL CHURCH

that mighty organization of God and the Church, the London Missionary Society. It was organized more than a century ago and if it is denominational at all it is Congregational.

The L. M. S., as it is called wherever it is known, began its labors in Madagascar in 1818. With an intermission of a few years, due to its expulsion from the country by a hostile pagan monarch, it has been active ever since. The women and men in its service from first to last have been of the highest character and moral equipment. They have died and have suffered at times worse than living death in the cause of the Master and of their unusual and unsurpassed organization. Their service has been as varied as it has been unselfish.

They have not only taught Christianity as a rule and philosophy of life and living, but have also trained the natives in educational directions, have developed better agricultural methods and, best of all, they have been the true and sympathetic friends of the masses of the tribes.

In return they have been rewarded by the faith and trust and consistent practice of those whom they have converted. During the years of persecution the Malagasies proved their devotion to their new faith and their courage in it by going to death by torture without a tremor or a whine. They were starved, beaten, enchained and thrown over cliffs to the dogs and not in a single instance did they cringe or purchase life and immunity, as they were offered opportunity to do, by renouncing their faith in the teachings that had been brought to them from over the seas. As much as anyone thing, this struck fear into the hearts of their persecutors, and the policy toward them was changed by a new ruler.

The yoke they bore was as heavy as the one borne by the early followers of Christ who for more than three centuries after the death of the Man of Nazareth kept alive the truths He taught until they builded them into the fabric of a Christian civilization which is indeed still imperfect, but which is working towards a rule of love and a law of justice and a habit of mercy.

I am reminded of the charges against the Chinese Christians that were poured into my ears during my first visit to China. My informants assured me that there was not one real Christian in all of China. They averred that the Chinese had gone to the missionaries to get what material benefits they could from them and nothing else; that they were merely "chow" Christians and would desert the Cause at any time they were confronted with danger or suffering or if their rations were cut off.

Then came the Boxer uprising and thousands of Chinese Christians died miserably and more thousands risked death by brave and loyal service not only to the missionaries but to foreigners generally. The siege of Pekin could not have been withstood if it had not been for the trustworthy Chinese Christians who risked all to carry food and information and serve the beleaguered in every possible way. So it was in Madagascar. When the natives were put to the test they were found to be Christians for life or for death.

The L. M. S. made a way for others until by the time of the French seizure it may be asserted with positive assurance that the Malagasies were as Christian as their conquerors and are by many thought to have been more Christian. The French conquest found not only a great work that had been done by the L. M. S., in which they had been supported and encouraged by their government, but there were also the missionaries of the established Church of England, the Roman Catholic, the Norwegian-American organization and some others.

The L. M. S. had enrolled more than half a million Christians under their own standards. And there were many thousands enumerated as followers of the other churches.

One of the greatest works of the American-Norwegian missionaries has been among the lepers. There is more leprosy in Madagascar than among any other people of the world in proportion to the population. Among these unfortunates the Norsemen have lived and served and died deaths of horror. There is no district free from the awful plague and no tribe that is immune. It breaks out there as in the Philippines and elsewhere over the earth in the most unexpected places. In the wilds of Africa, where I saw much of its horror and devastation, it is least frequent among the naked tribes because they are sexually cleaner and for the further reason that it is not hidden by covering and as soon as it manifests itself the victim is fed to the hyenas.

Although the French government had established as many as thirty leproseries they had not tried any cure that made headway. Now that good results have been obtained in treatment with chaulmoogra oil and some other remedies there may be more hope for the poor Malagasies, who have been cursed beyond all others.

When the French took possession of the island they were not any too friendly to the missionaries and they were especially hostile for a while to the British, charging them with sympathizing with and aiding the natives in opposition to the French seizure of the territory.

| RADAMA II | RANAVALONA I | RANAVALONA II | RANAVALONA III |

In their hearts all the missionaries were opposed to the French and felt sorry for the Malagasy, but they were discreet enough not to show it. In addition the French record at home toward churches did not tend to gain their good wishes.

No missionary work in the world furnishes more thrilling and encouraging pages of history than the labors of those who have buried themselves for a century in Madagascar.

CHAPTER XVI
THE FRENCH CAMPAIGN OF CONQUEST

THE French campaign against Madagascar in 1896 so nearly synchronizes with the American campaign in the Philippines that in a good many respects they might be considered together. Their similarity extends no further than the matter of date nor is there anything favorable to France in the conduct of that country after the conquest in comparison with the unselfish attitude of the United States. In fairness I must repeat here that next to the United States the French are the kindest and most considerate and reasonable in their treatment of subject peoples, if those adjectives can be used in describing the exploitation of a people at all.

Somehow when the colonial realm of France slipped away as the result of unfortunate wars and made a part of the map of the British Empire, the right to Madagascar was preserved, as such things went. This may have been because that right was so diaphanous as not to be seen or recognized or because the British failed to realize the value of the great island. France had lost Mauritius and ever since that event had looked with covetous eyes upon the Great African Island, as their writers were wont to call it. No others since the days of the Arabs perhaps had as thorough an idea of the value of the territory.

Larger than France itself by a considerable margin, with both developed and undeveloped resources and a capable and tractable people, it was the most worth while part of the world that was to be had. So the French went after it and not in the half-baked way of their campaign of the 'eighties, even though the attack on Madagascar was not brilliant as a military achievement. Instead of attacking from the Tamatave side on the east as before, they landed on the west coast near Majunga, and although the distance to the capital Antananarivo was much greater the real effort required was much less. By this strategy they escaped in some degree the strongest ally of the Malagasy—tazo and hazo—fever and forest, which had laid low thousands in the campaign of the 'eighties.

But the thing that really told most against the Malagasy was jealousies and intrigue at court. In their earlier victorious repulse of the French they had been ably led by Englishmen of military training and capable of developing and directing the best the islanders had. It appeared to some of the Malagasy courtiers who were close to Queen Ranavalona III to have been so easily done that they had no great trouble in driving the British out of places of authority and leadership by the argument that their own people could win the war without the aid of the foreigner. This, they persuaded the queen, would be of immense advantage in establishing the military prowess of her people. It had been said, they reminded her, that they could not have won without alien leaders. Now was the chance to disprove this and win on their own account.

So out went the able men who had led to victory before and the Malagasy made a sad mess of it. At the royal Kabary, which is their word for indaba or shauri or a mass meeting of especial purpose and significance, the party that had unsuccessfully opposed the dismissal of the English commanders was deposed and the new régime of theoretical chauvinism was set up. There was not one single serious battle or even an encounter that could be called a battle at all. The Malagasy are brave enough when well led, but in the hands of the inexperienced native generals they would not stand their ground at all and, in fact, the Malagasy leaders themselves were greater cowards than their followers. Worst of all were the false reports of victories made to the queen and the public so that when the end suddenly came it was a shocking surprise to court and people, who thought the war had just begun. It upsets some nice philosophies to have things turn out in that way.

The truth may easily be that it is the duty of forward peoples to take in hand backward peoples whether they will or no and that the great wrong in the past which must be corrected in the future if the world is to be peaceful and happy is the mistreatment that has always characterized the dominion of the strong over the weak since the beginning of time. It is as though one were in duty bound to treat his dog kindly, and possibly also human beings, whose destiny is as much in the hand of the strong as that of the dog is in the keeping of his master.

General Duchesne was in command of 20,000 French regulars in the 227-mile march, almost unopposed, to Antananarivo, the capital. There were also irregular troops made up of some Madagascar natives other than the ruling class, the Hovas, and these were principally Sakalavas who had been "conquered" by the Hovas; Senegalese, and a few so-called Turcos from the northwest coast of Africa. The naval force in Madagascar waters consisted of three third-class cruisers, eleven dispatch, scout and gunboats besides transports. Against this showing of the French the Malagasy had land forces enough and munitions of war but no navy. There were the usual outrages and brutalities of warfare that reflect upon the French.

The best and almost the only accounts of the war written in English are by Bennet Burleigh, correspondent of the London *Daily Telegraph*, and E. F. Knight, correspondent of the London *Times*. Although the French government refused to allow foreign correspondents to follow their campaign and were not even disposed to welcome their own war correspondents and made it so disagreeable for them that they were driven out of camp, both Burleigh and Knight managed to land in Madagascar and supplied their papers and the world with all that is popularly known about the conquest.

As showing the policy of the French and indicating their treatment of those who might spy upon their methods not for military purposes but in a way to inform the world, Burleigh relates that five South African gold miners were on their way to prospect in Madagascar and were arrested by the French. He says they were innocent workmen, but that did not keep them from being thrown into a vile latrine, kept there for several days, cursed and spat upon by French soldiers and otherwise maltreated until they were put in irons and placed aboard an English steamer bound for Mauritius. But that was a way not peculiar to the French at all, but just the way of war.

Can you blame the Japanese for their Chosen (Korea) policy when you remember that Nippon only opened her ports to the world after 1859 and that her first real convulsion of western fever was in 1868? She has been taking lessons from the civilized—God save the word—nations since that time. Fine example we have set barbarians, as we call all who have not mastered the specialty of enslavement and robbery on a grand national scale. Talk of the World War being started by the Kaiser! Where was the Kaiser when the other world wars started? There were other kaisers, you say? Yes! And there were other ages of oppression to create the conditions that kaisers feed upon. Just to show how they did things and made their case to warrant the seizure of a people and a country—and it is only typical—the official demands made by the French upon the weak Madagascar government are here given. These demands are not ancient history; they were made in 1894 by a republic:

"(1) The government of the queen of Madagascar shall consent to have no dealings with other powers or their agents, except through the resident general of the French Republic in Madagascar.

"(2) All concessions granted by the queen's government whether directly or mediately to French subjects or other foreigners shall be registered at the Résidence Générale for approbation and failing that they shall be null and void.

"(3) The government of the French Republic shall have power to place soldiers in Madagascar as they shall consider necessary for the security of those in their jurisdiction and foreign residents.

"(4) The French government shall be allowed to carry out works of public utility, such as roads, railways, telegraphs, canals, etc., calculated to develop the country; and to receive all moneys accruing from such public works, unless the government of the queen will undertake to carry out such work.

"(5) In case of any misunderstanding arising from the construction of treaties the French text alone shall be authoritative."

Of course the Malagasy government objected and the French Republic took them by the neck and fastened their yoke upon them. It is not as galling a yoke as the Japanese and the Dutch and the British have used, but it is a yoke and if the case were reversed the French would sing the Marseillaise with a new meaning.

CHAPTER XVII
SEIZING PEOPLE BY WHOLESALE
ONE KIND OF ENSLAVEMENT

FRANCE had no right to conquer and occupy Madagascar. It may be said that she had as much right as England has in India, although that is not to be easily admitted because there was in Madagascar a better government than the Indian peoples possessed; better than in 1857, when the British crown took things over after the Sepoy rebellion and after more than a century of grinding exploitation by the East India Company. The last hundred years constitute an epoch of wholesale seizure of territory and enslavement of nearly a billion people against their will and it is not hard to see in the great war that shook Europe something of retribution; only it is tough to see those who may be the unwilling receivers and custodians of stolen property suffer so grievously for something they might not have done themselves. And the world will continue to be filled with woe and bloodshed as long as mankind in strength ruthlessly rides the neck of mankind in weakness. The mills of God grind slowly, but they grind exceeding small. It is such an old story and yet we never learn to apply it. Shall we some day learn? I think so, after enough people die.

Within the last hundred years the nations that composed the Allies in the big war have grabbed nearly three-fourths of the earth's surface and more than half the population of the world have been made unwilling subjects. England, or rather Great Britain, has been busiest, with Russia following close, and France, Belgium, and Italy taking all they could lay their hands on. In that time the United States has increased its land holdings more than two million square miles and not always by the consent of the governed. This matter of the consent of the governed and self-determination does not worry me, but I am concerned as to whether we grab a people to cure them or to rob them. In almost no instance has the grabbing been either benevolent or philanthropic. It is true that the United States has taken less out of subject peoples than the other grabbers. Most of the big brothers have worked the little brother for what he was worth or are in process of doing so, and this makes a terribly sick world. Now do not try to annoy me by saying that this is pro-German stuff; the German Empire would have been the greediest pig in the trough if stronger hogs had not been there first and shoved it away.

When France finally seized Madagascar in 1896 (it had set up a claim in 1642 and had fought the natives for two years, 1882-1884) there were twenty Christian churches in Antananarivo, the capital, or more per capita than in Paris. Christianity was introduced into the island in 1810. Out of a population of between three and four millions there were more than five hundred thousand known and registered Christians and others that were not counted. Nor were they ordinary perfunctory followers as so many have become where Christian civilization is said to be in a high stage of development. They were simple folk with the mind of a child in such matters, just believing the beautiful story as told them by self-sacrificing missionaries and willing to die for the faith that was in them, as they proved time after time when the Sublime Truth was first brought to them to replace the shadowy myths, helpless and hopeless idolatry and arts that not only kept them plunged in gloom but also the superstitious slaves of tricky jossakeeds, the mpanao fanafody of the yearning Malagasy. Years of remarkable work, the most remarkable in missionary annals, I think, had really developed a ruling Christian people and a Christian government.

At the time of the French conquest France itself was at a low moral ebb that the sufferings of the World War have not entirely retrieved. The ruling attitude of France manifested itself in Madagascar to a degree possibly more extreme than in the mother country itself. The talented men of the London Missionary Society were swept to one side as a result of the unproved charge that they had not only sympathized with the people of Madagascar but had actually espoused their cause and had given them material aid. Even the wise Gallieni, who lived to rush troops in taxies to the defense of Paris as commander of the city, was more than cool toward the British missionaries. If the invaders after their victory had invoked the assistance of the L. M. S. it would have been gladly accorded, and for the good of all concerned it was both a misfortune and an injustice that this was not done. In my earlier travels I was both ignorant and prejudiced in matters of foreign missionary concern, but I have since become an enthusiastic believer in the work and if I had yet been in need of conversion to their cause the missionaries of Madagascar would have found in me an easy subject. From the standpoint of morals the Malagasy would have been more warranted in taking over France than in being taken over.

Agriculture was at a stage of development that offered great hope for the future. The Malagasy owned more cattle per capita than any other people in the world. This accounted in some degree for the high physical development of the people and especially of the Hovas. They were great consumers of milk and its products. The people of the world who use milk can be distinguished at once and easily both physically and intellectually from those who do not. In very many ways the Malagasy were a peaceful and superior people and were on the road to become more so when they were seized by France. What happened to the grabbers makes one pause and wonder about the God of retribution; only the ones who do the evil die and go to hell and those who survive them have their hell on earth.

CHAPTER XVIII
GALLIENI AS GOVERNOR
OF MADAGASCAR

WHEN the German armies got nearest to Paris in the big war it was General Gallieni who sent out reserves in taxicabs and won a name for emergency resourcefulness. From his youth his admirers adulated him as a second Napoleon, supporting their belief in him on the fact that he is a Corsican. His ancestors were high-grade Italians and not from Corsica originally. Gallieni is a good man anywhere, or was—he is now getting old. As the first governor (Resident General) of Madagascar he did good work.

The Malagasy generally were not hard to manage. The usual procedure was adopted of dividing the island into military districts over which military vice governors ruled. The half military code used by France in all her colonies was put into effect as rapidly as possible and at the same time a provincial constabulary was organized to which the native bent willingly and fairly efficiently. Soon came the taxes, at first a charge per head and then in addition trade taxes and concession fees levied wherever any possible income could be seen, for the French are

FRENCH GOVERNMENT TRAINING SCHOOL

NATIVE POTTER'S SHOP

not in the colonization business for their health alone. It was slow work bringing the island people to pay the fiddler, but they sooner or later were all laid under tribute.

Perhaps the Sakalavas were the last to be reached as a source of revenue, although they were supposed to have been already under the dominion of the Hovas when the French took possession and trained to give up and down, a fiction the French had to weave into a fact. From time to time they would round up a prominent Sakalava chief and show him the sights of Antananarivo with especial reference to French pomp and power. It was an effective way and usually the chief, after entertainment, medals, and presents had been quite showered upon him, would return to his people and tax them additionally in the British Indian way and send the required levy to the capital. I saw a big, fine-appearing, coal-black Sakalava king–their chieftains are all kings–taking his first automobile ride, looking with astounded eyes and gaping mouth at the French barracks and fine cannon and generally having it impressed upon him that it would be quite futile to try to side-step the new powers, no matter how successful he might have been with the Hovas.

Gallieni was rather hard on the missionaries at first, but they really fared better than they had feared, being English and under suspicion of sympathizing with the poor devils whom they were honestly trying in their way to keep from going to hell or being taken by the French, one and the same thing with these

good folk who were well informed of the official godlessness of the Paris government. Their religious schools were regulated severely or closed.

Another thing that was a bitter dose to the missionaries was the removal of all restrictions upon idolatry. Through missionary influence Queen Ranavalona had issued a decree accompanied by punishment severe enough to make it effective against all idol worship and kindred superstitions such as voodoo practices. This law was set aside and the result was most noticeable.

The most ignorant among the natives reverted to the abject adoration of the old idols, which had been hidden and not burned as had been ordered. Native charlatans soon began their practice of the revolting orgies that depend upon temperamental neurosis which is common among all primitive tribes. This was never a practice of the most advanced Hovas, but was common with nearly all others. In no part of the wild world have I witnessed more abandoned acts in the guise of worship or medicine than followed in the wake of French liberalism in Madagascar. What they actually do is indescribable and would be unmentionable if it could be told. One cannot put a frenzy or a fit or a degenerate sex act into language. On a certain Sunday at one point I saw hundreds in a state of wholly irresponsible dementia; by which statement I do not mean to imply that there is such a thing as responsible insanity, although the point may be debatable according to Freud, who is no authority for me.

Gallieni began the construction of a system of roads—something needed more than anything else—and in the French way the roads were planned as a whole and the work on them well done. Within a decade a railroad had been built from the principal port of Tamatave to Antananarivo, 369 kilometres, and is being extended towards Antsirabe in the direction of Fianarantsoa, with 65 kilometres in operation in April, 1922. Auto stage service was started on the routes made possible by new roads. An elaborate botanical garden was being developed where experiments were being conducted for the purpose of increasing the productivity of Madagascar in spices and other things that the natives had not bothered with.

Very little has been done in the direction of education because the policy of the French is against anything that is apt to equip their subjects to make trouble. They claim that the failure of Britain in India and the movement in the Philippines for independence are due to that education which in certain doses is a very dangerous thing, at least in an exploited nation. Those who look at the problem in this light trace the conditions in Russia to the association of too much knowledge with too little. It is a thing to think about in this age when education has for a primary purpose the fitting of the educated to prey upon the less educated and which takes for its standard of success the effective application of learning to the arts of acquisition.

French activity was entirely put to sleep by the war and is only now beginning very slowly to awaken. It is interesting to note that the claim is made that not one Malagasy served willingly in the French army during the war while the other subjects of all the nations involved were generous in enlistment and docile when conscripted or impressed. The ruling policy of France in Madagascar, even to a greater degree than in those of her colonies which are near the center of the world's stage, is all for France, exclusively. This would of course be justifiable if the world system of riding the necks of the backward peoples were right. It is not just nor humane, although it has been going on since man first knew how to organize and extend his avarice. The French and other western nations demand the

open door in China, but do not practice what they preach where they are in control. It is such an old, old story as to have become disagreeable in selfish ears, but it is the one greatest source of woe of the world. No great religion, at least none great enough, has been devised yet to cure the disease. Christianity would cure it if it were actually practised. From the dawn of events until the present the golden philosophies of Athens, the code of Sargon and Hammurabi, the ethics of the Epicureans, the wisdom of Marcus Aurelius, the religion of Lao-tse, Confucius, Buddha, Mohammed and that perfect lesson of the gentle Nazarene have all been bent and twisted to serve man's selfishness.

Now of course this is not the fault of the religion but of man and there can be no cure until man is changed and man can only be changed by each individual recognizing this and admitting it and taking care of his own case. As it now is the average of us think we are quite all right and that it is our neighbor who is wrong. It is a delusion that has not been classified in the insane lists where it belongs. Shaw's "Back to Methuselah" and Wells' new Bible will not do it. If anything we live too long as it is, unless we live better; and as for that new Bible, we would not know any more about it than we do about the old one we have.

Ibsen and Francis Hackett—long jump I hear you say—have the right of it; man must be made anew whether it is by being born or by his own volition. There is no reason why man cannot reform himself instead of forever trying to reform some other body except that he will not do it and up to now has never tried seriously to do it.

What has all this to do with Madagascar? It has everything to do with that island and with all the world. Upon it are builded rules of life and action. In our own America we interpret it in the oddest way. We try to make a goody-goody showing before the world in our little colonialisms and at home practice industrial slavery that sporadically knocks the spots off anything described in "Uncle Tom's Cabin." Harriet Beecher Stowe dared to indict negro slavery, but when the Inter-Church movement had the courage to tell the truth about industrial despotism in general it was put out of business in no time at all. And yet no one nation alone has the disease that kills. We are all sick. It may show on the exposed surface or it may be under the shirt, but we have it. To admit and quit and cure is the thing.

And as for myself I think each one of us must get the help of the huge Power that plowed the earth with the glaciers and furrowed it with the torrents and mixed it in the bowels of Vulcan and ground it with sun and wind and ice. But the average chance is that we are too selfish or vain or cowardly even to admit this simple fact. There were thousands who cried three cheers for the Kaiser when he was kaisering, but I have never heard a crowd give three cheers for God.

CHAPTER XIX
FROM THE FRENCH
OFFICIAL STANDPOINT

THERE are all kinds of people in every nation and as Philip Gibbs says in "More That Must Be Told," one is not justified in blaming all for the acts of some, although there does come to exist an average national character, tendency and temperament. Burke was not entirely right in his declaration that you cannot indict a whole people; individually considered one perhaps may not, but nationally considered one may. Nations are justly quick to take credit as a whole, but are slower in accepting blame. There is a French way of doing things just as there is an American way and a British way and none of them is so bad as some charge nor so good as those interested would have the world believe. The French way is better rather than worse.

No more adequate presentation of the ideals of the French in Madagascar has been made than is given in the official report to his government in 1898 by Lieutenant-Colonel-Breveté Prud'homme de l'Infanterie de Marine, Chef d'Etat-Major du Corps d'Occupation de Madagascar. This report not only comprehends a survey of the situation as the French saw it, but it includes an illuminating study of the Sakalava and of problems that confronted the new government. Much of this information has bearing on the affairs of to-day in view of the adoption in the Treaty of Versailles of the principle of mandates under the League of Nations. Many of the wild peoples of the world are in even a lower state than the Sakalava as portrayed by Colonel Prud'homme. This report was made for two purposes; for the government and for popular consumption, as showing the beneficent trend of French policy. It is not to be concluded that its recommendations were carried out to the letter. The French since Napoleonic times have understood better than any other people the wisdom of inducing their own citizens and the world to entertain a good opinion of their public work.

The ancient world leaves us but distant and very faint echoes of its maritime achievements. These, judged by their results, must have been considerable; first the dissemination of the human race throughout the world, and later, the establishment of communications and commerce, uniting peoples and countries. Primitive man was possessed of an audacity and intrepidity incomprehensible to us. His rashness is explained by his ignorance, which like a veil hid from him the folly of his imprudent ventures on the deep.

It is about thirty centuries since the fleets of King Solomon, manned by those famous navigators the Phœnician sailors of Tyre, sailed to the land of Ophir in search of gold, ivory, and precious woods. This is authentic history as given in the First Book of Kings, Chapters 9 and 10, as follows: "And King Solomon made a navy of ships in Eziongeber, which is beside Eloth, on the shore of the Red Sea in the land of Edom. And Hiram sent in the navy his servants, shipmen that had knowledge of the sea, with the servants of Solomon. And they came to Ophir and fetched from thence gold, 420 talents, and brought it to King Solomon. For the King had at sea a navy of Tarshish bringing gold and silver, ivory and apes, and peacocks."

And the Hebrews extended this traffic over a long period. Where was this land of Ophir so rich in gold dust? It has come to be a generally accepted conclusion that it was almost opposite the upper end of Madagascar about where Sofala is now situated, across the Mozambique channel. I followed the old Phœnician road from the African coast of the Indian Ocean to Great Zimbabwe where the Phœnicians got the gold for Solomon.

In these voyages of Solomon's fleets the vessels through stress of weather or other circumstances must have touched at different points on the shores of Madagascar. There can be no doubt that Madagascar has been known for at least three thousand years. Although there seems to be small record of the fact, the Phœnicians and Arabs were in hot competition and both races and the Jews probably knew of Madagascar and they must have left their blood and some of their people on the great island. Even to this day many acute observers think they can detect traces of the type produced by the commingling of these three races.

It is certainly true that the Malagasy are a mixed people. As soon as the Romans learned the secrets of the periodic monsoons they wrested the Indian Ocean trade from the Arabs at various times; then it would be won back, until there was a surging back and forth for centuries. The Roman conquest of Arabia and Egypt made them the masters until their empire fell, whereupon the Arabs came back again and assumed sway anew. With the coming of Islam there was a stimulation greater than avarice and the Arabs and their kind made conquests and sailed farther upon the waters than ever before. Cities were built and converts made to the beard of Mahomet. They mixed with the natives more than ever had them as wives and concubines, reared prodigious families, taught their language as well as their religion and left marks that will never be effaced.

When the Portuguese came to compete there were large towns at Sofala, Mozambique, Quilamane, Zanzibar, Mombasa, Melinda, and elsewhere. At that time there appears to have been no military instinct among the Arabs—a fact supporting the economic philosophy of Norman Angell. They had no forts or soldiery and were not prepared to fight and did not expect to fight. Their policy was to treat the natives as of themselves, to teach them their religion and generally to use just and kind and pacific means to win their friendship and their trade. This made them easy victims in a way to the Portuguese except where the natives resented the coming of the men of Bartholomew Diaz and Vasco da Gama, which

was often enough to be noteworthy. The Portuguese swarmed up the East Coast of Africa after rounding the Cabo Tormentosa and spread terror everywhere. It was the Cross against the Crescent and the Cross won temporarily. Lusitania's mighty men burned out their fire and again the infidel came back, and the Sultan of Muscat was the power in these waters.

In spite of the number of upheavals that have taken place the moral vestiges of the Sultan of Muscat are still apparent in Madagascar and exercise an undoubted and considerable influence; blood relationship with the followers of Mahomet, habits of Arab trade, customs, manners, superstitions, traits, tendencies. I take it that we can, have no adequate understanding of the people of Madagascar and perhaps least of all of the Sakalava without taking into full consideration the Arab relationship.

The region comprising Menabe, whose inhabitants were among the slowest to accept French rule, has been for three centuries a land of promise for the Sakalava. There they have preserved best their original peculiarities, even to their physical appearance. It is difficult to trace their origin. They are like tall trees that tower above those about them. There are no accurate data to illuminate the Sakalava of even the almost immediate past. So we shall have to study them as we find them now.

From tradition it may reasonably be concluded that they are of very ancient origin. Out of a pre-tribal state they emerged a strong people, almost a nation from the very first. Once at the apex of their power they occupied all of the western portion of Madagascar and exerted suzerainty over the entire island; over even the Hova. It was not unlike the case of Timur Leng perhaps. The rulers whose genius built up their power had no successors and they lapsed almost as quickly as they had magically arisen.

The origin of the Sakalava may be traditionally traced to the region south of the river Onilahy, a section now occupied by the Mahafaly people. The tribal story of the Sakalava may be taken as a type tale or proto-history of aboriginal Malagasy. Menaced in the sixteenth century by a foreign invasion, probably Arabic, a strong man in the person of Andriamandizoala came to the fore and was made a big chieftain over all. Under his leadership the invaders were repelled and the Volamena dynasty (Family of Gold) was founded. The chiefs of the Sakalava to this day trace their origin to this source. But the ruling stock ran out long ago with the result that the tribe occupies a secondary place and some of them were paying tribute to the Hova when the French conquered the island in 1896 to 1900. That is to say they were paying in spots widely separated, for the Hova conquest was largely on paper.

In the ascendency of the Sakalava there was much action. Their first great chieftain or king, Andriamándizoála or Zoala, had several children, amongst them Andriamandresy and Andriamisara, who founded a settlement on the river Mangoky and called it Sakalava. This finally gave the entire tribe the name it has borne ever since. Andriamisara left a son who became as distinguished in Sakalava annals as any leader they ever had, and with just cause, for he ruled wisely.

He made war against tribes north of the Mangoky and defeated them so signally that they begged to come under his rule. Afterwards his sons continued the wars and subdued all the tribes to the boundary of the river Tsiribihina. They called the territory between the two rivers Menabe from a stratagem employed by the Sakalava that gave them an easy and important victory. Arriving near the enemy just at nightfall they dug a huge pit before morning. They put a big red bull into the pit, leaving a hollow log for air. Then they restored with great care the natural condition of the surface. In the morning the enemy heard a fearful subterranean bellowing and fled precipitately. The ruse was so successful that they called the region Menabe, meaning "Great Red."

This great Andri died about 1680, leaving his people in marked ascendency. The son Andriamanetiarivo was a worthy successor and made the tribe still stronger. His brother was likely to make trouble unless given an outlet for his ambition and ability, so he was sent still further north and aided in driving out the hostile population and establishing an auxiliary stronghold called the Kingdom of Iboina. About this time they learned the use of firearms. They also began to trade more widely with foreigners through their port of Morondava, exchanging slaves

and products of the country for ammunition and arms. Andri II saw the great advantage of this and sought to prevent the interior from trading except through his representatives. He was so successful that even the Hova became vassals in order to get guns and powder and the merchandise that the people were fast learning to seek. Andri II died about 1718, when his subjects virtually ruled the entire island.

Before the creation of the Volamena dynasty wars had resulted in wholesale massacre and the practical extinction of the defeated tribe. The Volamenas changed this policy and endeavored to save and incorporate their enemies into their tribe, with the result of strengthening themselves greatly. It was the first taste of mercy in Madagascar, and although its basis was self-interest it had a good effect. Sometimes as in other lands the assimilation was not all one-sided, as the victors were affected by taking on many of the manners of the vanquished and almost always an improvement all around resulted. At the time of the founding of the Kingdom of Menabe about 1670, the Sakalava swept all before them. The Hova were completely obscured for the time being.

When the brother of Andri II, who was named Andriamandisoarivo, went to the north with the help of that ruler he had ample military assistance. His first encounter was with the Vazimba (Little Folk) who fought, then fled and then joined his forces in large numbers. It was the method of Alexander and Cæsar that won the enemy after conquest. The victorious march continued to the extreme north of the island and then Andriamandisoarivo turned West and south, crossing the Betsiboka, the largest river in Madagascar. It was a fair land and he decided to build a capital on the bay of Iboina, near the mouth of the Betsiboka which he called Tonga. On the shores of Iboina at that time were a number of Arab settlements of some importance. When the Arabs learned of the warlike nature of the Sakalava they withdrew to an island in the bay of Iboina. Here they were attacked and forced to submit to the conquerors, which they did with good grace, and taught them the Arab methods of trade.

Revolts broke out among the tribes that had been mastered as soon as their overlords were far enough away, but these too were ironed out by force until even the Hova, the Antankara and the Sihanaka, the most powerful tribes on the island, were submissive to the Sakalava. Then dynastic troubles arose. Sakalava kings and princes took foreign wives and concubines and there was a large issue of children of varying strength and ambitions. These made the trouble, as is often the case, that outside enemies had not been able to develop. Enemies inside and out fanned the flames until the solidarity of the kingdom was affected and there was a near return to the segregated tribal state. Finally they could not agree on a male ruler and the throne fell to a succession of women who really restored for a period the prestige of their people.

The first queen was Andriamaninarivo, daughter of Andriamahatindiarivo. The greatest of the female rulers was Ravahiny with the passing of whose beneficent reign went the glory of the Sakalava as a consolidated and conquering people. Among the big things that Ravahiny did was to increase foreign trade. She built new towns and went to war to aid Andrianampoinimerina, her favorite chieftain, in his successful design to subdue Vonizongo and Imamo with the entire central plateau. She died about 1810 and at once the Hova asserted themselves and became the stronger power. They maintained this position until the coming of French rule.

Mikala of Menabe and Rahiny were the last of the independent Sakalava rulers. While the Hova never reduced the Sakalava to vassalage they did compel them to admit the Hova suzerainty, and in fact conquered the entire island, although the Sakalava seldom paid the head taxes levied upon them and for that matter the French are having the same trouble, as their rule over the Sakalava is still only nominal. The big chiefs swagger like Othellos and seem to realize that the French are nearly if not quite afraid of them. In any event their attitude is far from that of fawning vassals.

The Sakalava are a shifty people. When the Hova drove them into a cul-de-sac they pretended to yield, only to gain time to send to the Sultan of Muscat, who came to their relief, but saw the impracticability of resistance and withdrew. This led to a renewal of a Punic fealty to the Hova which lasted only

until the accidental arrival of the French Captain Passot in 1839, who had been sent by the Governor of Bourbon, to whom the Sakalava had got word.

At various times for three centuries the French had endeavored to obtain a permanent foothold in Madagascar, but had made no headway of any account and did not now. But their intervention enabled the Sakalava to stand off the Hova and to come to an agreement that they would yield if the Hova did not ask too much of them. In fact the Sakalava played the French against the Hova and the Hova against the French from that time on for more than a quarter of a century. It was their instigation and encouragement that led to the war between the Hova and the French in 1883 in which the French were worsted owing to skillful assistance in leadership supplied by the British.

In this war the French were the aggressors. Captain Pennequin landed troops at the town of Ambodimadiro on the bay of Pasandava. The Sakalava flocked to him for a while and he trained them as recruits and riflemen. But in the back of the heads of the Sakalava was no loyalty to anybody except themselves. They aided the French in a small battle or two in which the Hova were whipped and then when they saw the French and the Hova were in for it they ran away, hoping that the French and the Hova would eat each other up and leave Madagascar to them as the rightful rulers. But the Hovas under British leadership were too much for the French and they had to make a peace that was not altogether one-sided, but it left the Sakalavas rather out in the cold. So when pressed the Sakalava would withdraw to impenetrable forests and swamps, whose poisons and jungles they knew how to withstand better than their enemies.

These are the people that the French are having their liveliest contentions with at the present. They cannot be compared to the fanatical Moros, who were and are the cause of friction in the Philippines, but they offer almost as difficult a problem in colonial government. All efforts of a constructive nature practically stopped with the breaking out of the World War and will not be seriously renewed in Madagascar until France is reconstructed at home.

CHAPTER XX
FRENCH GOVERNMENT IN MADAGASCAR

IT is asserted by the French that after the war of final conquest they really tried to rule the island through the old Hova organization, but soon found themselves thwarted and even the object of open insurrection. This led to a change of policy and the organization of French units. General Gallieni, the hero of Paris, where he commanded during the World War, won his spurs in Madagascar. He was the first governor, or, as he was entitled, Resident-General. With the same initiative that led him to rush recruits to the front in taxicabs when Paris was in imminent danger of falling to the Germans, General Gallieni attacked the numerous problems that arose in the work of taking over four million civilized people who had been surrendered by a handful of traitorous officials at Antananarivo.

His first work, as he saw it, was to convince the people that they would be better off under French rule than they had been before. If anyone could do this Gallieni could. Brave, courteous, and a combination of tenderness and strength, he soon began to make real headway until the new subjects could feel that outside of that nebulous thing called freedom and liberty they actually might be better off. His grace and tact were infinite and had it not been for inefficient successors who kowtowed politically to Paris he might have done a work of permanent value to both France and Madagascar.

Captain Torquenne was commissioned in 1897 to establish order in the provinces of Analalava and Nossi-Bé. Here were the Sakalava, who were the traditional friends of the French. But they were not so friendly at close range and broke out in armed rebellion in 1898. After some fighting and fatalities on both sides the revolution came to an end and the French again pursued lenient policies after the example of Gallieni. And this time they made better headway until now there is peace and good prospects of its continuing until some attempt is made to put pressure upon the inhabitants to collect taxes, when it may be expected confidently that the relations will be strained, to say no more.

Oddly enough the Sakalava, who were supposed by the Hova to be a conquered people and who really aided the French against the Hova, have made more trouble for the French than the Hova or any others. When the French sought to open the Tsitibihina river to navigation their expedition was attacked and they had to kill Toera—or thought they had to kill him—the first chief of Menabe and a descendant of the Volamena dynasty. This act caused a general uprising and the French were defeated in some skirmishes and several military posts were captured by the natives. Then the French created the Territory (Territoire) Sakalava and tried to set it apart. This too was a failure and the district was cut up and included in the second and fourth military Territories.

This did not work out as had been expected and the Territoire Sakalave was reëstablished. There followed active military operations under General Pennequin, who had been promoted and charged with the task of subduing the Sakalava. Finally the Sakalava chieftains consented to a conference with Colonel Prud'homme, chief of staff for General Pennequin, and the war was ended by granting big concessions to the Sakalava, but not until there had been devastation and loss of life on both sides.

There were the usual horrors of war between the combatants, although it was a merciful proceeding if compared with the practices of the World War or even with our occasional policy of extermination of the Moros or our heartless segregation and deportation of Indians, notably the Creeks and Seminoles. Perhaps not much worse than our shipping off of alleged undesirables and unloading them on the defenseless peasantry of Russia! Villages were destroyed and there was living off the country, but so there was in Sherman's march to the sea. Wholesale slavery means just these things and will continue to mean them as long as the methods of the immediate past are continued. There is no such thing as benevolent exploitation; either the native must be cared for in his own interest or let alone. A curse follows his abuse.

CHAPTER XXI
MADAGASCAR
AT THE FRENCH EXPOSITION

AT the Paris exposition in 1900 there was an especial attempt made to introduce Madagascar to the French people and thus to justify the seizure of that island, for there is a subcurrent of opposition among the French to anything that smacks of injustice and trespass as they understand such things. The basis of this is the Gallic temperament in which always on the average the humanities are richly proportioned. So the government made a brave and interesting exhibit of Malagasy things as soon as they had a chance after the conquest. They took full advantage of the Paris exposition. The Madagascar section at the exposition was in the center of the square of the Trocadéro on a raised platform. It was housed in a pavilion that was supposed to suggest the island architecture but with too much of the Byzantine, perhaps.

Arabic influence predominates in Malagasy architecture. Remote tribes have no set style of building that can be dignified by the term architecture. The Parisian pavilion façade had three ornate entrances over which, with outspread wings, was the voromahery (peregrine falcon), the royal emblem, and oddly translated by the French to mean vulture, an error not to the taste of the Malagasy.

My descriptions are taken from the official guide book for the Madagascar exhibit entitled "Exposition Universelle de 1900—Colonies et Pays de Protectorat, Madagascar." On the ground floor was presented a varying panorama of island landscape with methods of agriculture, wild and tame animals, and native life in hut and field. There was a clever reproduction of the big island in miniature in the basin of the Trocadéro, which was large enough to give an idea of the forest and jungles, in which were lemurs, birds and serpents. Huge crocodiles hid in the thick foliage of the banks and the whole made it easy to visualize Madagascar. In one place the rice fields were well displayed in their four stages of cultivation and development. Preparation for setting out in the rice fields by digging them with the wooden angady or native spade; the working of the soil when flooded with water by driving cattle backward and forward through it; the work of transplanting in which the women assist, working to their knees and deeper in mud and water; and finally the harvesting, were all shown vividly. Rice is the Malagasy staple, but there are several products that compete with it in importance.

Near the rice fields the rubber industry in all its parts was portrayed. Almost genius was applied in the many little gardens that were exactly as they are in real life in the island. There was a coffee plantation. The coffee berry is coming into prominence as a fine product, much better than any grown in Brazil. Also was shown the fertilization of vanilla, and the cacao bean and basic chocolate industries were displayed. The rofia fibre was prepared under the view of the visitor and that fine product was a revelation to the French, competing as it does with silk and even possessing some advantages over the worm which also was at work in the Exposition on amberivatry and tapia shrubs, which are perfect food for the silk worm. As the shrubs grow wild and are very plentiful in the island it may be understood that Madagascar will be heard from more and more in sericulture.

A close competitor with the silk worm, in Madagascar, is the silk spider, which yields a delicate material that is woven into the most diaphanous of fabrics. Tea and tobacco were gathered and the entire agricultural resources of Madagascar were displayed and impressed the visitor indelibly. Natives from all the leading tribes lived and worked in their huts as they do at home. They wove rabanas of rofia, and lambas of wool and hair, shaped pottery, made fine baskets and hats which rival those of Panama and the Philippines, turned out lace and wrought skilfully in wood and metal. The native gold mines, both placer and quartz, were shown and there was a suggestion of the graphite industry, most of which has developed since the time of the Exposition.

In one place there was a farm with a corral containing domestic animals, including the valuable and serviceable zebu or humped ox which used for everything, including riding. Not only were assembled a lot of native workmen, but there was also a good showing of the insular constabulary and

ROFIA PLANTATION

NATIVE SPINNING ROFIA FIBRE

some of the native regulars who were being beaten into a colonial army. In fact I think there were more of these at the exposition than in Madagascar. There much opposition in the French Republic to foreign service and the government sought to show that not only would the new territory pay in income but it would provide itself with soldiers.

The Exposition greenhouses contained a fine collection of orchids from the island. There was a topographical map, colored as to districts and elevations; another map outlined the railways that are to be built, some of which are running now and doing a good business. Care was taken to have the visitor understand that the island is so large that even as much as was given did not nearly reflect what there is or afford an adequate idea of the riches of Madagascar. The harbor and bay of Diego-Suarez were shown, as that is the naval station and rendezvous of the French fleet in Indian waters. Wax figures portraying a party on a journey gave the best idea of the filanjana that can be had without actually being carried in one. Just about all the contents of the royal museum at Antananarivo were moved to the Exposition and they were numerous and in many instances impossible of replacement. Consequently I was told with pride at the museum later that not a thing was lost and the curator rubbed his hands in satisfaction as he said so.

There was a collection of fine native woods, some finished and others natural, with furniture made from them, and a piano entirely of Madagascar

ebony and mahogany. The æpyornis egg they had was a good specimen, but not so large as the one in the university museum at Ann Arbor, Michigan, that I was so fortunate as to secure.

At the various American expositions since then we have shown natives and their methods of living. This idea was copied from the gathering of Malagasies at the Paris show. There were twenty-four soldiers, fifteen militiamen, thirty-five musicians, twenty Hova, including eight women, two pairs of Betsileo men, four Sihanaka, a man, a woman, and two children, two couples of Tankarana, four Sakalava men and one woman, one man and two women of the Tullear Mahafali, a Tanosy man and woman, two men and one woman of the Taimoros, two couples of Betsimisarakas, one Tambahoakaa—a total of one hundred and twenty-four, which gave a comprehensive ethnic idea of the tribes and peoples.

There were was panoramas of the French campaign in Madagascar. Also valuable and interesting exhibits were shown by the various missionaries. In all the Exposition was almost as good as a trip to the island and quite justified the conquest in the eyes of the French people.

CHAPTER XXII
MALAGASY NATIVE HISTORY

As the most important portion of Madagascar the history of Imerina and the history of the Hovas taken together give as good an idea of the island

PLAYING FANARONA

as one can well have. As that history is recited by natives it is more oriental than Wellsesque; a phrase sculpture in style. To be detected in the composition and style of the Malagasy are many inherited Arabic traits of imagination. There is the same spiced and florid flow of language, as plentiful as the sun of the desert and as warm. A mixture of the ancient Arabic with the north of Scotland style ought to produce both warmth and solidity.

My attention was called to a voluminous mass of papers left by one Raombana, who was born in a late year of the reign of Andrianampoinimerina and lived until the beginning of the rule of Radama II, which would make his life cover a period between fifty and one hundred years ago. Mr. Raombana was a minister to Great Britain under Radama I and spent three years in England. From his writings I have taken liberally in translation.

In remote times the forefathers of the Hova race dwelt in an unknown island far across the sea. They were, however, not to remain there, for God in His inscrutable wisdom, Raombana says, ordained that they go to the fair land of Madagascar and take up their abode. In order that they might have a way to cross the broad waters, the Almighty made a bridge for them by causing great water lilies to grow in the sea and spread their expansive leaves over the face of the waters. Moved by a divine impulse they set out in steadfast faith to travel westward on foot. They crossed the miracle bridge in safety and settled on the coast of Madagascar near the mouth of the river Matitanana.

There they lived until malaria drove them elsewhere and they went inland and found a more salubrious spot. Under the leadership of their chief, Andrianamponga, they forced a passage through the grim and silent forests and at length reached Ifanangoavana. The remains of a town are to be found there to this day. It is about thirty miles east of Antananarivo and a likely spot for a town. About all that is to be seen now are some stone pavements. In the center of the ruins is a great rock on which Andrianamponga and his chief men used to sit basking in the sun, playing the native game fanorona. The ruins are now held so sacred that no person of any rank dare break any of the trees or shrubs and use them for wood. If they do so they will drop dead, as the spot is protected by the gods and is "tany masina." Andrianamponga died about five hundred years ago.

The favorite folk tale is that the Hovas are descended from one man and one woman. God placed the man on the summit of the mountain Andringitra and the woman on the top of the Ankaratra; the man thirty miles south of Antananarivo and the woman forty miles north. They knew nothing of each other and wore no clothing. But the Creator had made them for each other and He gave them a mighty hunger which led them to each other. But before the happy design was fulfilled there was a trial of strength and fortitude. They were made to wander for months through the lonely valleys and over the trackless mountains. Their longing grew only the more fervent. Each night they were given blissful dreams and the promise that at the proper time when their love had been tested enough they would find each other and be happy. One day the man made a fire to cook his simple meal of manioc. This fire spread into the dry forest and made a huge mass of smoke that could be seen for a long distance. On the same day the woman made a fire to cook sweet potatoes and it also ignited the woods. Each saw the smoke made by the fires. They took heart anew and felt that they were soon to find each other. The man started towards the smoke on Ankaratra, building fires on every crest as he proceeded. The woman went in the direction of the smoke she saw and lighted fires to guide the man for whom her heart yearned. Six days after they saw the smoke the first time they came face to face. There they stood speechless, enraptured with the beauty and love and radiance that each saw in the other's face. In just a little time their voices were heard in words of love and endearment and they perfectly understood why they had been sent to each other. No snake, no apple, no punishment; just perfumed bliss such as the world had not known up to that time.

So from these first lovers from across the fragrant Indian seas came the great Hovas and the founding of Imerina. They had all they could eat of good things.

It was Ralambo, an early king, who discovered that roast beef and brown potatoes were fine food. Up to that time vast herds of wild cattle had roamed everywhere. They were not afraid and were not molested because a forerunner of Dr. Kellogg had told them that the flesh of the wild oxen was poisonous. One day Ralambo was taking a walk over the plains with two slave attendants. A fire caught in the high grass and as the wind was blowing it soon became a roaring, rushing conflagration. Even the swift wild cattle were cut off and roasted alive. There was a savoury odor in the air. It made the slaves hungry and they said so. Then Ralambo, for a joke, asked them why they did not eat of the roast oxen that smelled so inviting. They recoiled in horror at the idea of being poisoned. But Ralambo, not liking to have his authority flouted, choked some of the grass-grilled flesh down their throats and, to his astonishment and theirs, they liked it and it did not kill them. Whereupon the king also tried it and pronounced it good. It was a little rich for his blood, so the king looked about him for something to go with it, Protruding from the ground he saw a tuber nicely baked by the prairie fire and he tasted it after trying it out on his slaves. It was fine and went mighty well with roast beef. The tuber was a kind of potato; not a true potato, which is autochthonous in America, but a vegetable almost as good. From that time on roast beef and browned tubers were the very thing for the king and his people and the fashion crept over the world. Ralambo was an early-day Morgan. Before he told his people how good

HINDU MAGICIAN IN MADAGASCAR

beef was he had corrals built and thousands of cattle driven into captivity and tamed. Then he made a feast and summoned his subjects. They were served with beef roasted, barbecued, grilled, broiled, fried, braized, in ragouts, and were made to eat. Then he told them to go and capture wild cattle. But there were not enough to go around after the meat habit was formed, for they all wanted T-bone steaks. There is where the king cashed in; the people had to come to him and buy. Armour, Swift, Cudahy, and the other packers heard this legend a long time ago.

The founding of Antananarivo, the capital of Madagascar, is credited to Andrianjaka, son of Ralambo, king of Ambohidrabiby. One day he thought he would build a new city to be his own and such as would suit him, like Peter the Great. So he climbed to the top of the mountain Andringitra to view the land. On the farthest horizon he saw an eminence that invited examination as a possible site. He sent fourteen wise men to look it over and report. Making their way through the tangled forests—and the forests are like a maze in Madagascar—they reached the summit of the eminence and to their surprise found a clearing and a cluster of huts. They concluded that these must belong to the primitive inhabitants who had been encountered at Alasora and driven out by the chief Andriamanelo. Not a soul was at home, as all of the men had gone fishing.

Report was duly made to the king, and he made plans to seize the hill and build at once. When his men returned in force for this purpose they found

FAT OXEN AT THE FAIR

that the Vazimba had fled. Seeing signs of the visit of the strangers and remembering the treatment accorded not only their ancestors but their relatives that lived at Alasora, the little people fled to the Sakalava country, where they sought asylum and were treated so kindly that many of them joined that tribe and served the Sakalava faithfully and taught them many of their arts, such as making poisoned arrows and trapping and trailing, and the use of blow guns for hunting.

Andrianjaka had a huge stockade built and inside of it houses for himself and his numerous wives. His people built their huts outside of the stockade in a circle. Thus was started the great capital of Madagascar.

The most celebrated of the sovereigns of Imerina before the time of Adrianampoinimerina was Andriamasinavalona. Some time after he had begun to reign at Antananarivo as successor to his brother, who had been driven from his throne by a revolution, the land was beset by a sore famine. It was India and China and Russia all over with no American Red Cross or Santa Claus Hoover to help out. That was before Santa learned how to get and spend others' money and make a name for himself as the apotheosis of human kindness, no matter what the cost of the overhead.

The hunger time was caused by a fierce storm of rain and wind that lasted for twenty-one days—and it can blow and rain in Madagascar as nowhere else in the world. Then it hailed for three days and nights

in order to shred anything that might have been left undestroyed. There was complete destruction of the rice in the fields and manioc and sweet potatoes in the plantations so that the real wolf of despair, gaunt and gleaming toothed, was at every lintel. One day the king sent men with twelve pieces of overweight silver to the village of Ambohipiainana, where lived a man named Andrianinoana, who had a lot of rice stored away just like a lot of people did sugar during the war; real Christian persons you wouldn't think it of. So it may be seen that selfishness was not born to-day. When the messengers of the king asked Andria to sell them rice, adding that the king and his wives and children were starving, the brute replied that he and his had not eaten since their last meal, nearly three hours before, which was one way of saying that he thought the king a liar. "Tell the king he is no more than a two-spot now and that I have no rice for him or any of his." This message was carried back to headquarters and there would have been a lot of blood shed, only there was not much blood left, as men fought on their stomachs then as now.

But some revenge must be had, so the king drew himself up as the Kaiser was wont to do and said he would curse Andria not with ordinary bad-road profanity but with an old-time Biblical curse. Then the king roared as loudly as his condition would permit; did this fellow refer to the king's family as if to say that he and his were as good as the king and his? The king went on to say that if the fellow had only refused the rice without comment and had sent a few sweet potatoes there would have been no hard feelings, but as it was he was bound to lay a curse on him. In that time a real king's curse told. The rice hog and his family perished and have remained extinct to this day. Some say it was acute indigestion and not the king's curse that carried them off, but that only goes to show that doubting and envious persons have existed in all times and places.

The passing of Andrianinoana did not satisfy the appetite of the king, so he sent to Antsahatavoka, where dwelt a man named Andrianomemboninahitra, who had never been called upon to eat his name or take it to the chiropodists. This man also had rice hidden away, but he was as clever as Will Hays and sent word to the starving king in the kind of language used to appease a person who believes that civil service reform is not an ignis fatuus. "Tell the king that I would send oodles of rice if I had any and ask him to remember that the fields are his and that the people who till them belong to him also and that whatsoever they have is his as well and that all he would have to do would be to say the word if only there were any rice any where." These honeyed words pleased the king, but made no impression upon his waist. As a last resort the king sent his men to Andriasisa to make solicitation of a man named Andriandrivotra, not forgetting to send along the twelve pieces of overweight silver. The messengers were nearly paralyzed by the attitude of the man.

"Certainly," he said, "we have rice and shall my king starve?" Forthwith he ordered the rice to be pounded and cooked and a sheep that had been fattening for three months to be killed. When they were ready the provisions were placed in big baskets; the boiled mutton filling three and the rice four, and to these he added seven baskets of paddy. When the twelve pieces of overweight silver were offered in payment the man refused to take them and was nearly insulted.

"To the dogs with your silver," he said, "for is it not the same as that the king did me the honor to call on me when he sent you, his men? And for the king to call is just the same as a call from God, so instead of taking the money here are twelve pieces of silver that weigh more than those of the king. Take them to him with this 'skoff' and 'pasha' as a present from his humble and well-fed servant."

You should have seen that hungry king eat. As soon as he had filled up he gave a lot of food to his wives and children, parcelling it out in accordance with their favor with him and nibbling as he came to a special titbit. Then when he had time he said to the good subject who had sent the feast, I Thank You, after the style of K. C. B. Andriandrivotra felt amply rewarded.

Several years before his death, to beat the inheritance tax, King Andriamasinavalona, to the grief of his counsellors, divided his dominions between his nine favorite sons, leaving a lot of other

Manioc and patates market

sons and a grist of daughters to grin and bear it. They were allowed to live at their capitals, while the old king really did all the reigning there was to do, leaving the young fellows to live a sort of Prince William of Wied life. They were perfectly willing to be vassals of a good old scout of a father for the time being, and play polo golf and have a good time with the girls who rolled their stockings in that time too.

One of the sons had to spoil the show. His name was Andriantomponimerina. He married his cousin Ravololondralambo and then treated her so harshly that she ran away and complained to the old king, who had his son beaten in public and also dissolved the marriage, giving the hand of the princess to another son who had a longer name than her first husband. Furious at his disgrace, the injured husband, who had done nothing but beat the princess, resolved to be revenged. He got together a snappy army and hired several thousand Sakalava fighting men and went after the brother, who was still enjoying a honeymoon with the princess, who was coyer and sweeter than a widow. The love feasting brother was no sybarite, so when he was attacked he left the side of his bride and told her to watch him go to her first husband. There was a fight and about as the second husband was on the verge of being beaten the princess put her head out of the window and shrieked a curse on the first husband. The Sakalava chieftain saw her and heard her and thought she was putting the Indian sign on him, so

NATIVE WORKING CATTLE

he got scared and ordered his men to run and they ran as if they enjoyed the change. This turned the tide of battle, which goes to show that if Cleopatra had been as quick-witted as the Malagasy princess and had not kept a pet asp things might have been different with Mark Antony and a lot of the rest of us.

This defeat did not cast down the tough son. Quite on the contrary, for he began to plan to get even with his father in any way possible. His first act was to pretend to be sorry and to ask his father to forgive him. Then his next step was to kidnap the old king and force him to agree that he should succeed to the throne. There was to be a public declaration and then in a little time he would have his father murdered and take over the Kingdom of Imerina.

In carrying out these designs the son invited his father to come to his palace on a visit. The old king was received with a great outward show of filial respect and affection, but as soon as he had entered the palace courtyard the heavy doors were closed and his attendants kept out. The amazed bodyguard was told that "sikidy," a sort of fortune telling by divination, had said that the father was to remain for some months with the son, who was to take tender care of the old king and see that he was given a rest and made happy in his old age. The bodyguard believed this, as all had faith in "sikidy." No sooner had they gone than a strong guard of the son's men, armed with spears, was put around the palace.

Up to this time the old king had not been

suspicious. He ate and enjoyed the repast that had been prepared for him. But no sooner had he finished than he was informed that he was a prisoner and would remain one until he made a public acknowledgment of the wily son's right to succeed to the throne of Imerina. At first the savage old man nearly had apoplexy and he refused even to consider the demand. Consequently he was kept in close quarters, but was allowed as much freedom as his health needed and as much as could be given without offering him a chance to get word to his people outside.

After several days had passed the old king's bodyguard called to ask for orders. They were given no satisfaction and this aroused their suspicions to such an extent that they informed the other sons. In consternation and anger the sons held a meeting and decided to make an attack at once and restore the freedom of their father. Just as they were setting out they consulted an elder statesman who had a Secretary Hughes reputation of being the wisest man in the nation. He told them their course would almost certainly result in the death of their father, that as soon as there was any chance of their success the bad son would have him murdered. This they concluded might be the result of an open attack. The wise counsellor told them to pretend that they had no suspicion and thus make the bad son think that they believed that all was well. At the same time they sent reinforcements secretly to the bodyguard and gave them rigid instructions to keep a close watch and if a chance presented to rescue the king but not to make a mess of it. The wise man said God was on their side and would rescue the king in His own time. Despite the sharpest lookout the son was not caught napping and the old king was a prisoner for months.

His release was finally accomplished in a melodramatic way by his thirteen-year-old grandson, the son of Adriantomponimerina, who was as natural and loving as his cruel father was unnatural. The old king and this lad Ratrimobemihisatra were permitted each other's companionship. The boy's father thought he could be trusted at his age as harmless and he wanted secretly to have him know his strong old father, in whom he had pride in spite of his lack of true filial love. A strong affection grew up between the grandson and grandfather. Day after day the two would sit on a mat on the east side of the palace. The old man told the boy brave tales and gave him much wise counsel. So the time passed sweetly between the two, only broken discordantly by the raucous laughter and jeers of the bad father, who sat all day with the headmen drinking toaka and playing the game fanorona, gorging themselves with rice and fat meat, and twisting their manes about their necks.

For a long time the boy did not know that his grandfather was a prisoner. But from seeing him weep frequently he wondered and finally asked why he cried so often.

"Ah, my child," he replied, "has your father not told you that I am his prisoner and that he will not release me until I turn over to him the throne of Imerina? I will not do as he bids because he is not fit and if he were it would be an injustice to my other sons, his brothers. I long to escape and do not know why I have not been rescued by the others."

As the boy heard this sad story his eyes blazed with anger and fury. He broke into bitter words against his father and called him a beast and a dog and a socialist and said he would beard him before all his headmen and thrust a spear through him. With gentle words the older man soothed the child's fury and told him that to do as he threatened would only insure the destruction of them both. The boy became calm and began to brood, and made a resolve to assist his grandfather to escape at no matter what cost to himself.

A few days later, pretending to make a screen against the hot sun, he placed it as near to an old and unused gateway as he could and bided his time. One morning while the recreant and unfilial son was at his revels the boy led his grandfather to this hidden gate and bade him pass through, which he did and found waiting his trusty bodyguard, which had been informed by the boy.

In order that there might be no suspicion the boy reclined under the screen and placed a stick of wood with his grandfather's cloak over it and his hat of fine woven reeds just showing as if the old man slept. From time to time the boy's father, as if

VILLAGE SMITHY

dimly aware that something was going on, called to his son and asked how the king fared. Always the boy bravely and unfalteringly replied that he was asleep and not to bother but go on with the feast and games.

No sooner was the king through the hidden gate than one of his exulting attendants placed him a-back and off they went in a dog trot even where the trail was steep and hard to follow, on towards Andrianty, across the bottom lands of the river and through brambles, first one man and then another taking the old man on his back.

At the river canoes were in waiting and they swiftly paddled away, threading the winding channels of the shallow lake that lay in their course to Andohatapenaka, whence the king was taken overland to his palace at Antananarivo.

When his people heard about the great wrong that his son had done they were more savage in their desire for vengeance than they had ever been before.

Meanwhile what of the brave boy whose affection and courage had righted the wrongs of his wicked father? It came near being another case of Ivan the Terrible and would have been but for the intervention of Providence. When he was certain that his grandfather had enough of a start to make it impossible for them to overtake him the youth stalked in where his father was, erect and with his head thrown back defiantly, and told the story of what he had done.

A homicidal impulse seized the cruel father and he

BETSIMISARAKAS DANCING

grasped a big spear, the one that was best balanced and sharpest, and hurled it at his son's breast. His passion was so great that the spear missed its mark, although it tore through the lamba of the courageous son, who screamed defiance as if to challenge the murderous father to throw again and do his worst. More enraged than ever, the insane man grasped another spear, but his arm was seized by one of his headmen who had recovered his senses. His anger somewhat spent, the bad man realized that he must try to overtake the escaping party, as it would mean immediate war if his father got away, and he was not yet prepared for war. They went in pursuit as rapidly as they could and continued to the river only to find they were too late.

Instead of making war, which would cause death and suffering to so many who were innocent, the old king decided to put the William Randolph Hearst king's curse publicly on his worst son. This he did at a solemn "kabary" called for the purpose; and as the son died in fearful agony soon after, the efficacy of the curse was proven.

The old king, always popular, now was increased in regard and still more so when he appointed his brave grandson to succeed to the rulership which had been held by his wicked father. In the fullness of his days the old king died and was gathered unto his fathers. He was 150 years old when he passed to the Malagasy heaven, and had never used tobacco nor drunk moonshine.

In the early part of the eighteenth century or about 1720, Andrianjafinandriamanitra succeeded his father as king of Ambohimanga, the capital of the populous and prosperous subkingdom of Avaradrano. The old king Andriabelomasina was a kind of feudal lord under the king of Imerina, but they called them all kings if they paid their "hasina" promptly. The young king turned out to be a good-for-nothing. He was weak, profligate, self-indulgent, cared little for his people and left the affairs of government to his favorites, who were worse than he and in addition clever and daring and thievish.

While the king was submerged in sensualities, these headmen and the king's greedy relatives planned wholesale robberies and executed them. They oppressed the people grievously, seized their cattle and slaves and the land groaned under their evil doings. One of the schemes worked by this vicious crew of parasites was to abuse the practice of the "tangena," trial by ordeal. The belief in the efficacy of poison in the detection and punishment of crime was deepseated in the minds of the superstitious and ignorant people. Their credulity was their undoing. At this time the people of Avaradrano were rich in cattle and slaves. They had a foreign trade with whaling ships and slavers, and Spanish dollars, received in exchange for slaves and cattle, were plentiful. The king permitted to be issued in his name a call for a great assembly or "kabary" at which it was announced that the ruler had been pained to learn that sorcery was rife in his territory. People were being bewitched by black art and many were suffering and not a few had died. The people had not heard of it, as they were not subscribers to the *New Republic*, but if the king said so it must be true. The proposed cure was a general resort to "tangena," so that the guilty might be detected and the realm cleansed from the iniquity. Within a short time the poison was administered to thousands and very few escaped death. Most of those to whom poison was given died from the effects and those who did not die were killed as having shown signs of guilt by being made sick by the ordeal. The entire property of the victims was confiscated, and as the richest and most powerful had been selected, not only was the loot tremendous, but those most apt to lead a revolution were dead.

The people realized that their deadly custom had been abused and that they had been violated, but in a little time, with no leader, they seemed to forget, until they heard from Indiana, Pennsylvania, Iowa and North Dakota.

In addition to the great crime there were petty annoyances which they appeared to care more about and resent more tangibly. Some of these consisted of the monthly pilgrimages to the towns of the wives and relatives of the king. The citizens were expected to do them honor and entertain them lavishly. If they did not whole towns were fined and some of the best subjects were imprisoned. The people stood this as long as they could and then they arose in rebellion. The man of the hour to lead them was found in Ramboasalamandrazaka. He was of royal lineage and brave and able.

His first act was to call a secret meeting of twelve good men upon whom he could rely. This meeting was held in his house. He recited the abuses briefly because all felt as he did and were at the limit of endurance. But the thing they had to contend with was the disinclination of the people to rise in open revolt against their established rulers, who were generally thought to come from the throne of God, a primitive idea of the divine right of kings. Not only would they be doing a wonderful thing for their countrymen, he told them, but he would give them as well a big share in government and all of its proper emoluments and would ennoble them and their children for all time.

The big twelve then and there swore fealty to the death. They did not have long to wait to start their plan. Ten days after the secret meeting the king and his staff started for Ilafy in the early morning. The king and his outfit had barely passed the gates when Ramboasalamandrazaka, on the pretext that the king wished to issue orders that had been forgotten, sent a crier among the people widely and they assembled quickly in large numbers. To their open-mouthed surprise they found Ramboasalamandrazaka and his twelve rebels on the ground armed to the teeth. Every man was a fighter and was known to be and the leader had a reputation for eating people alive when hungry. A profound silence fell upon all as one of

AT THE FAIR AT SOBIKY, BETSILEO

the conspirators stepped forth to recite the argument of the drama. The speaker told the assembly that a leader long wished for was ready, that the king had tried to kill him with all others who might rescue them, but in this case had providentially failed. He asked them to rally to the standard of independence and said that certain victory awaited.

To make matters more tense a prominent man of courage who had been treated better than most by the king and who had not been invited to join the original twelve arose and denounced the scheme in fiery terms.

"Close your ears to these rebels," he said. "Do not let them lead you astray. It will mean failure and death to all who join Ramboasalamandrazaka." No sooner were the words out of the speaker's mouth than one of the revolutionists rushed upon him and drove a spear through his heart. The effect of organization upon those who were not organized was most apparent. The act of death was so sudden that the people made up their minds that the new movement was likely to succeed. At the psychological moment Ramboasalamandrazaka came forward out of his circle of magi. He was clad in a scarlet lamba, the insignia of royalty, and looked more a king than the real king ever had looked. Standing erect with an extended spear in his left hand and a big gun in his right, he was a stunning figure. It was not his idea to act the brute as the king had done, but to pretend to be kind as well as strong. Things were happening quickly. Thus artfully he spoke:

"My friends, I am deeply grieved at the death of the man who has just been slain before your eyes. It was not my desire to have him killed, but my followers in their ardor have done it. There was no time for consultation and they have gone beyond what would have been my will. I seek no man's death and if there are those among you who do not want me to be your ruler I will not force you to join us. You may go your way even to following the king who is here in his weakness and has been frozen to the spot by cowardice. It is fair, however, to tell you that if you do not join us you will have to leave Ambohimanga. My sole desire is to bring you deliverance from this coward and tyrant, and make you more comfortable and happy. I solemnly promise that if you join me I will win and make you free and that I will be a loving and clement ruler, whose first purpose always will be to promote your well being."

The effect of these words upon the agitated and dumbfounded assembly was as magic. They rushed to where Ramboasalamandrazaka stood, knelt at his feet and with many fervent voices proclaimed him their king forever and forever and that they would live for him and die for him.

Ramboasalamandrazaka took them at their word, although he suspected that a good many of them were emotionally affected in a manner that might be temporary and that others were scared into the game.

Now the king was not such a coward as Ramboasalamandrazaka had charged in his speech for was he present at the assembly. As soon as he caught the early drift he saw that he could not arrest the rebels with the force he had with him so he stole away, and sped for reinforcements in anger and chagrin. He thought all that was necessary was to appear at the head of a force and the people would be restored to normalcy (origin of the word unknown).

In a very short time the absence of the king was noted by Ramboasalamandrazaka, who set out at once with his armed men, leading the rabble toward the citadel. The guards, suspecting nothing, allowed them to enter and when the king returned in strength and sought to enter the royal eastern gate they were ready for him, even the palace guards having joined the revolutionists. There were a charge and firing and a number of the king's crowd fell and some were killed. The war was on and the king retreated to Ilafy.

Ramboasalamandrazaka knew it was not over with and that he had to keep busy if he wished to hold the advantage he had gained. If defeated it meant death to him and his followers. So they fortified Ambohimanga in all the outer places that had been neglected and prepared for war to the death. Next he turned his attention to other important towns in Avaradrano. His trusted agents visited them in great haste and made lavish promise of favor to the citizens of Ambohidrabiby and Amboatany and to the people throughout the country. They were told of the advantages to be secured by supporting Ramboasalamandrazaka and that the alternative would be the death of the men and the enslavement of the women and children—a precedent for the march through Belgium.

The powerful clans of Mandiavato and Tsimahafotsy, whose territory made two thirds of Avardrano, rallied to Ramboasalamandrazaka, but the clan of Tsimiamboholahy, which occupied the remaining third, could not be won and were attached still to Andrianjafy. Ramboasalamandrazaka changed his name as kings do and assumed the cognomen of Andrianampoinimerina, of whom we have heard before in an earlier recital of brave deeds. He had more warriors than his opponent, but that did not cause the occupant of the throne to lie down. The men of Tsimiamboholahy were also brave, and on the defensive he hoped to more than hold his kingdom.

Chiefest of his loyal followers were a great noble named Andriambao and his three brothers, grandsons of Andriantsimitoviaminandriana, the predecessors of Andrimbelomasina as sovereign of Ambohimanga. These four nobles lived in the town of Anosimiarinimerina. This was a veritable stronghold, located in relation to an impenetrable swamp so as completely to command all communications between Ilafy and Ambohimanga. , Ramboasalamandrazaka quite understood the strategic importance of this place and tried in every way to win the chiefs to his standard, but they were not to be moved from their attachment to the ruling king. Try as he would he could make no headway with pacific measures, so he tried threats. The strong men laughed in the faces of Ramboasalamandrazaka's ambassadors and sent insulting messages to their chief. They wished to make him so angry that he would attack them in their entrenched position. It worked as they had hoped.

Ramboasalamandrazaka determined to take the place by assault. Amidst a tumult of battle cries, clashing of spears and reports of musketry the fight went on with valor on both sides. The loyalists were not only protected by palisades but also had a wide moat without a break around the town. Time and again Ramboasalamandrazaka's men waded this fosse and seemed to be bridging it with dead bodies. Finally Ramboasalamandrazaka called a retreat and the sore remains of the attacking force withdrew. Undismayed, Ramboasalamandrazaka tried to take the place by storm several times, but failed in each instance. Encouraged by the defeats, the king thought he would try to recapture the capital. In his assault, which was as determined as the struggle for the stronghold, he was no more successful than the enemy had been, so difficult was it in that time to take a fortification by storm, and the temperament of the people did not lend itself to sustained sieges.

As is the way with civil strife, within a couple of years the country was in chaos, the fields were idle, food was scarce and there was bitter suffering even more among the noncombatants than among the warriors, to feed whom every strain was made as is also the usual way. Necessary food was commandeered no matter whose it was or whether it was needed to keep starvation from babes, old folks, delicate women or the sick. Such is war in all ages and among all peoples. There may be a veneer of civilization, but with the coming of war that is found to be the thinnest of surfaces, and the human being relapses to a stage of murderous savagery. Rice fields and manioc plantations were not worked and there was not even a sweet potato, usually the most plenteous of foods, to be had in Madagascar.

Thus the strife went on for seven years.

Ramboasalamandrazaka saw that he could not win in a fair fight so he decided he would Newberry his enemy. Remembering that the king had kept around and nearest to him a lot of crooked politicians who had brought on all the trouble by robbing and killing, he sent secret agents to some of them and not only offered them large sums of money but showed them the color of it. The trick worked as the wily rebel thought it would. It was for the traitors to decide how they would do the deed which was to deliver their victim to him who had bought them. They went to the king and told him that they had good news for him; that they had been going into the capital as spies at night and that they had disaffected a major faction who only awaited his leadership to rise and overpower the usurper.

The king was so frantic with joy that he almost had a heart stroke. He went over in his mind what he would do to Ramboasalamandraz and his followers and finally asked for the plans of carrying out the coup. His treacherous chiefs said that all he had to do was to follow them some dark night and the sooner the better and that all would be settled; but they did not say how. He agreed to the plot, but as they were about to start he suddenly became suspicious as if by instinct. So he asked them if they were leading him into a trap. There was deeply simulated grief at even the thought of such a thing. They asked the king if they had not followed him through thick and thin for seven bloody years during which they had risked their lives many times until their fortunes were lost and their families even scattered? This appeared to satisfy him, so they proceeded toward Ambohimanga.

The night was dark and just fit for evil deeds and treachery. Oomagh! Oomagh! At a gloomy spot those who were leading him fell upon the wretched monarch and bore him heavily to the ground. Then they bound him and some of them started at full speed for the capital to tell Ramboasalamandrazaka and his men. They were admitted through the gateway and told their exciting tale. Ramboasalamandrazaka sent a body of his men, enough in number to insure that he was not being tricked.

After consulting the trusty twelve who had followed him from the first he gave orders to throw the king into an empty rice pit, there slowly to starve to death, as they did not wish to put spear or knife or bullet to the throat or body of royalty, whose blood never must be shed. Royalty must die some other way and always more horribly. These instructions were carried out to the letter.

They stripped the king to the buff and threw him into a rice pit which appeared to be bottomless and filled with murky water. In fact, they said that they heard a splash when the body descended and they were certain the fall had so stunned him that he drowned. However, they took the precaution to cover the pit with earth and stone and went their way to report to Ramboasalamandrazaka that he could now be assured that there would be no trouble; that his rule would not be disputed longer and that there would be peace and safety in the land under which his people would come to love him as they had never loved a king before.

Magic of magic; the end was not yet. The horrible rice pit was on high ground and was drained by a subterranean passage that did not show on the surface. It is supposed that robbers had made the tunnel long before and had not told anybody about it. Anyhow, the naked king found the passage and followed it, not knowing whither he was going but that he was on his way, as far from where they had dumped him as he could go.

Presently to his amazement he saw a spectral light which turned out to be the faintness of the dawn, as the night was now spent. Peering about cautiously and making certain that there was no one near, he emerged into the sweet morning air and felt as if he had been born again. There was inspiration in the miracle, for he traced it all to the goodness of God and wondered how it could be when he had been so cruel as a king. Pondering as to what to do, be concluded that he would go southward and try to reach his son-in-law, who was Andriamboatsimarofy, king of Antananarivo. He had gone only a little way when he was seen by a slave who was on his early way to the capital. But the king did not see the man, who had almost fallen from fright, as he thought he was seeing a ghost that had risen from a secret sepulchre, and in fact the king looked like nothing else than a naked apparition.

Gathering all the courage and strength he could muster, the poor slave fled for his life. But he overdid himself and fell in a sort of faint. Half recovered, he looked and saw it again, as the king had accidentally taken the same course as the slave. And he was as scared as the minion because he was sure he would now be captured and there would be no mistake a second time; they would torture him to death. Nor had he any common sense left, so crazed was he from what he had gone through. But suddenly a gleam came to him and he ordered the slave to kneel and disrobe. Donning the garments of this man, he started with renewed courage. But he made a terrible mistake, for instead of going to where he knew there were faithful friends, only a little distance over the main road where no one who would molest a man in slave's garments would have seen him, he plunged into the jungle, and as he did not know the way in the forest without a guide he was soon hopelessly lost.

Meantime the slave had proceeded, naked as he was, and went so swiftly that he caught up with the executioners on their way back to report on the regicide. Although naked he was dripping with perspiration from nervous strain. The men of Ramboasalamandrazaka saw that there was something unusual in his demeanor and appearance. They demanded why he was in such a sweat on a cold morning and with no covering for his body. The poor devil tried his best to be true to his king and the harder he tried the more confused he became. Finally, under threat of immediate and severe punishment, he told the story of the naked king, how he had seen him and had been stripped of his clothes and then had been ordered on his way without turning his head.

There was something about the tale that fastened itself upon the hearers in spite of its wildness and improbability, for had they not just killed the king; then how could he have appeared to the slave? They questioned and cross-questioned, but the slave stuck to his story and they knew that he was familiar with the king's face. Finally they were convinced that the slave was telling the truth and they realized that immediate action was necessary. A swift messenger was despatched to Ramboasalamandrazaka, and the others divided into two squads and began an eager search.

As soon as Ramboasalamandrazaka heard the bad news he was all action because he thought that if the king got away and told his story there might easily be a change in affairs. So he sent a hundred of his swiftest warriors in pursuit and stimulated them by offering large rewards. Tangled in the jungle, the king lost his mind in a deep-woods frenzy and began to call for help. It came all too quickly in the form of men from the party of Ramboasalamandrazaka. This time there was to be no doubt of the disposition of the king, so they strangled him before they threw him into another rice pit. When the partisans of the king heard of the attempt against the king from flying rumors they hastily mobilized their fighting men and marched towards the capital to demand his release, and if he had been foully dealt with to mete out revenge.

The astute Ramboasalamandrazaka had foreseen this action and to meet it he sent a strong party headed by his most eloquent chiefs to intercept and harangue the royalists. When they came upon each other there was a great confusion and some fighting, but as soon as there was a lull the stoutest throated of the chieftains Ramboasalamandrazaka had sent began to talk. Other chiefs started to harangue, and if there is one thing a Malagasy enjoys it is talking, either as performer or listener. They are congenital Chautauquans. Soon all was quiet enough and then the one with the big message from Ramboasalamandrazaka held forth and was heard.

"Know, O ye people," he began, "that the Almighty in his wise and irresistible way has ordained that Ramboasalamandrazaka is to be king of Avaradrano, and more than that, the divine decision is that he is also to be ruler over all of Imerina. The late cruel king's death is to be ascribed only to a Higher Power than ours, for how could we alone have taken him from your strong arms? No, the decree had gone forth that his hour had come. Our noble and generous master, the new king, has empowered us to offer to you his friendship, his forgiveness and his good will. He solemnly swears that if you will lay down your arms and acknowledge him as your king he will elevate you in his perfect esteem and will ever hold you in dearest affection. Place yourselves under him and he will forget your past ill will and will make your lives brighter than ever before by his bounteous favors."

These honeyed words, together with the fact of the new king's strength, made a vast impression upon the opposition. Then also the legitimate heir to the dead king's throne, as even they admitted, was a youth of decided weakness. So they went into a consultation and decided that their interest was with the new régime.

A courier sped to the capital, where Ramboasalamandrazaka was engaged in spirited preparations for the coming attack. He experienced an ecstasy that he did not show on the surface.

At once he ordered three hundred of his fattest cattle driven to the new followers and invited the headmen to come to him immediately for a conference. The warriors divided the cattle among themselves and the chiefs repaired to the capital, where they were ostentatiously received. Shouts of "Long live the King!" filled the air as they had done before when success crowned ambition on one side and the grave claimed its own on the other. Ramboasalamandrazaka addressed his guests as follows:

"My friends, I take you to my heart in truest love. Let us put away from heart and mind the strife and animosities that have kept us apart for so long. The prowess and fidelity with which you served the late king, so far from hardening my heart towards you, have won my highest admiration. It proves your courage, your fidelity and your high general character. Under my reign you shall have due' rewards and honors and meanwhile I beg of you to take these bags of money as a token of my good will and earnestness. To your chief noble I promise now and here to give the lordly manor of Iharanandriana as a proof of my respect for his great worth and valor."

This finished hooking them to Ramboasalamandrazaka and the hoops were steel.

Now that there was peace and opportunity to heal the bleeding land Ramboasalamandrazaka inaugurated measures for relief and reconstruction.

By his kind treatment of the late king's son he more than pleased the royalist clans and confirmed his popularity among them.

His encouragement of agriculture, stimulation of trade and industry and renewal of intercourse with European and other alien traders soon had a marked and permanent effect, so that the people attached themselves to him in real affection.

One reform that was most popular was the exemption from military service of all who had tonsilitis or toothache and those whom the diviners said would fall in battle. However, Ramboasalamandrazaka selected his diviners with assiduous care.

In order to make the sovereignty of Imerina more than a mere claim Ramboasalamandrazaka had to defeat the king of Antananarivo and the king of Ambohidratrimo. To this end he sought an excuse for hostilities. Nor was this long in abeyance nor hard to make.

The ruler of Antananarivo had promised to give his beautiful young daughter Ravao to Ramboasalamandrazaka as wife. In order to perform his part of the contract Ramboasalamandrazaka sent a large treasure in silver and added as extras not agreed upon a number of jewels and coral ornaments. The father of the prospective queen bride took the treasure and the jewelry and did not send the girl, offering as an excuse that she was too young, a matter he had not thought of before he got the valuables. His concern as to age was caused by a larger offer for the sale of his daughter made by Rabehety, also a petty king to whom the ravishing Ravao was duly delivered.

This was just the thing that Ramboasalamandrazaka had been looking for. What was a wife or two to a monarch who had dozens and many of them as youthful and beautiful as Ravao? But he pretended to be grossly insulted and acted at once by declaring war on Antananarivo. Then the grasping ruler who had twice sold his daughter and could only deliver her once got scared and offered to return to Ramboasalamandrazaka all his treasure and presents. The big king told him to throw it into the Ikopa, a convenient river that would hold a lot of such stuff, and added that he demanded either Ravao as a virgin or Antananarivo. Neither of these demands could be complied with, as the girl had already occupied the nuptial bed of another. The king in a poke tried to buy Ramboasalamandrazaka with offers of several times the value of what he had sent, but this had no effect. War was the alternative and so he began to strengthen the defenses of his capital.

Ramboasalamandrazaka acted with furious activity. He marched at the head of his army and delivered a tremendous assault upon Antananarivo. The defenders knew that it meant death for the men and slavery for the women and children if they were taken, so they fought with grim determination and to their own surprise drove off the assailants. Then followed a desultory warfare for several months with partial besiegement. Finally Ramboasalamandrazaka was successful and there was terrible slaughter.

The king of Antananarivo escaped and fled to his next strongest city of Fenoarivo. Here he recruited another army and renewed the war. For two years he tried repeatedly to retake his lost capital and finally he was successful. Taking advantage of the absence of Ramboasalamandrazaka and the engrossment of the soldiers in the celebration of the New Year, he planned an attack and his forces actually reached the big hill overlooking the city before they were observed and were able to rush right in among the people. Great confusion arose and there were many killed. Hundreds of women and children were taken and sold to European slave traders. Many fugitives were drowned in the canal near the village of Ivandry.

Ramboasalamandrazaka was not cast down, for he knew that his enemy had become dissolute and was much given to the drinking of toaka and also that he had become more and more unpopular from his crooked way in dealing with even those nearest to him, frequently boasting that crooked politics were more successful than honest methods, that any fool could be honest but that it took a clever man to intrigue and get away with it, illustrating this by the saying that it was hard to get a piece of meat out of the pot with a straight skewer as compared with the ease of hooking it out with a crooked hook. Ramboasalamandrazaka recaptured the city shortly without great difficulty and compelled the king to flee again to Fenoarivo, where he soon died in a debauch.

Things were coming Ramboasalamandrazaka's way from other directions. Rabehety, who had got the pretty bride away from Ramboasalamandrazaka, was ambitious to try titles to Imerina with him. In order to prepare the minds of the people for such an undertaking he planned the assassination of Andriambelomasina, the king of Marovatana. This king, a kindly ruler, was sitting with his family at a meal one day when Rabehety with a band of cutthroats of his own stamp burst into the room and killed him. Rabehety at once proclaimed himself king and made the people swallow him. But they hated him for the way he had gotten the throne.

Ramboasalamandrazaka kept his spies on the ground and when the time was propitious got up a convenient boundary dispute and made war on the regicide who now was king. The fellow, though a brute, was a fighter and the war lasted for seven years and would have gone on indefinitely if Ramboasalamandrazaka had not resorted to his old game of buying off the strong supporters of his enemy. Rabehety was captured and hanged.

The only remaining strong king, seeing the growth of Ramboasalamandrazaka's power and how he made war, and influenced by the advice of his chief nobles, who had been corrupted by the secret agents of Ramboasalamandrazaka, decided to capitulate and become a vassal of the conqueror. Ramboasalamandrazaka received him with many words of affection and told him he would treat him as his own beloved son, which he really did until a revolution was hatched and it was proposed to restore him to his independence. Then Ramboasalamandrazaka had him killed. This did not end the trouble. It had come to be deep-seated in the hearts of the Manisotra. These were the high-class slaves of the nobility. There were really able men among them, as many of the affairs of importance and all the real work had been done by them until on the average they were more efficient than their masters. They easily enlisted the low slaves and civil war was in the land and a bitter war it was. The first act of the slaves was to seize the town of Ambohijoky

and fortify it anew. Ramboasalamandrazaka sent his best men against it only to be defeated time and again to his discomfiture and chagrin.

The Manisotra handled their battle axes and spears with more deadly effect than the royal army. No sooner did they learn this than a great confidence came to them and they took the offensive. Sallying from swamp and plain, they defeated the royal army all the way up to the foot of Antananarivo. Just what the attachment was no one clearly knows, but the Manisotra said that they proposed to capture Ravao, who had been taken to wife by Ramboasalamandrazaka after he had killed Rabehety, and place her on a throne as their queen. This was the situation when royal troops led by Ramboasalamandrazaka were pressed to their utmost to defend their capital against the lowly terrors.

A little time before this Ramboasalamandrazaka had traded fifty beautiful slave girls to European slave traders for a small cast iron cannon and some of his men had been instructed in its use. Time and again the Manisotra forced their way into breaches only to be swept by the fire of the cannon, which not only caused fearful havoc but frightened them, as they did not know what to make of the thunderous enemy. It was a repetition of the revolution of the .Roman slaves. Their Spartacus was as brave. Even with the cannon it took a week to drive off the Manisotra. Very often they were on the point of victory. Their greatest blow came when Ramboasalamandrazaka had Ravao and her two children by him killed so that they could not be a nucleus for the hopes of the slaves. Ramboasalamandrazaka had the fact distributed among them and their change. in morale showed how hard they were hit. There seemed no longer anything tangible to fight for and, their spirit dropping, they were easily defeated. During the battles Ramboasalamandrazaka was in the thickest everywhere leading his men. Nothing else won; it was a contest between the thoroughbreds and the mongrels, he said, and the side won that had the best breeding.

In order to make up for the vast outlay of the war with the slaves Ramboasalamandrazaka raided the Betsileo and took booty and slaves of huge value. He

MAKING HATS FROM AHIBANO GRASS

readily disposed of these to European merchants, as the native chronicler terms them.

Again there was peace and the ruler was able to devote himself to internal matters that had fallen awry. It was his practice to hold court in person and when he could not he delegated the trustiest nobles, who in turn did not decide but reported to Ramboasalamandrazaka, who rendered the decision. In complex cases where it was difficult to reach a verdict in the usual way sometimes two dogs were taken to represent the sides in dispute. They were subjected to the tangena poison test. The dog that died was concluded clearly and finally to have proved the guilt of the side it represented.

Ramboasalamandrazaka was a strong man, but he adjusted himself to the superstitions and customs of his people. Their system was the product of centuries. Occasionally Ramboasalamandrazaka would order that entire towns be given the poison test to discover witchcraft. Children were exempt. This was a convenient way to kill enemies and to obtain wealth, for all the property of the guilty was confiscated and became the king's. At times there were thousands of victims. As he grew old Ramoasalamandrazaka became hard-hearted. He was cruel especially to his numerous wives. If ne of them came under the slightest shadow of suspicion she was killed at once either by spearing or drowning.

In this way he disposed of more than thirty. Their suspected gallants were also killed ignominiously and their bodies left to be eaten by the crows and dogs. His great care was insuring the succession of his favorite son Radana. To accomplish this he killed his eldest son and sent his mother and her three other children into the fever district, where they soon perished from the pestilence as he desired. A full hundred friends of his eldest son were slain and their wealth seized by the crown. Another hundred were subjected to the tangena and more than half of them died from the poison.

Trade grew as never before. Europeans, Arabs, and East Indians came in numbers. They bought slaves, the Europeans for the plantations at Mauritius and the others for shipment to America. These traders introduced lying, venereal diseases, firearms, gun-powder, and other vicious things. The native historian declares that before this the Malagasy were strangers to lying but that the more they had to do with these foreigners the more viciously they lied.

Ramboasalamandrazaka was eighty years of age when his fatal illness came and he attributed it to magic and witchcraft. This moved him to invoke the tangena so that his life went out on a wave of death that surged over hundreds. Diviners were called and no matter what they prescribed it was done, which had the merit of hastening the death that was hovering near.

And so died Ramboasalamandrazaka, who was Andrianampoinimerina, with his feet bare. The tale of his reign is given as a typical period of the golden age of Madagascar. Other kings and chieftains did as nearly what Ramboasalamandrazaka did as they could. By the time the French came there was only a feeble queen and she was controlled by a circle of incompetent and dishonest and vicious courtiers who were no match for the invaders. There are thousands of Malagasy who are firm in the belief that Ramboasalamandrazaka will come back some day and rescue them. In the event that he does not they hope eventually to reform and improve the French.

CHAPTER XXIII
MORALS, MARRIAGE AND VIRTUE

MORALS and marriage and virtue are so much a matter of convention and habit and custom and man-made law that what is all right in one place and among some people is all wrong elsewhere. From the open and above-board Christian standpoint most of the women of Madagascar are unvirtuous and immoral. From their own standpoint they are as good as women are anywhere in the world and for this claim they have better foundation than they realize themselves, and the same can be said for the men. Their customs differ with almost every tribe. However, whatever system they pretend to follow and whatever custom prevails, they openly and honestly and honorably adhere to them. This is not true in America and Europe. We pretend to be monogamists and are a lot of sneaks and cowards, for we really practice polygamy and concubinage and all sorts of looseness under cover. In this way of double dealing and double crossing we are the most adept of the world and the so-called Christian peoples are alone in the way they behave in this regard. It makes here for illegitimacy and disgrace and woes without end.

The contrary is true in Madagascar. If a man wants a woman he gets her one way or another, but always openly. He may go marauding and steal her or he may buy her or he may try her first with her consent and never without, or he may win her in the way of sweet, pure and lofty passion. If he has one and wishes another he gets her in the going style. But mark you, it is all done openly and there is never disgrace of bastardy and shame among the offspring. Nor is there woe or want, because everybody in a tribe helps everybody else. The same is true of the woman. She may be divorced by mere decree of her man or she may go off with another man and if she gets tired of No. 1 and No. 2 she takes on No. 3 and not infrequently goes back to No. 1 and is welcomed just as though her first experiment had been found best after all. Now, I do not advocate this in America, but I do say that it is better than the loose way in which we practice monogamy. There is a lot of Christianity in Madagascar, but it

SILKWORM COCOON ROOM

has not yet made of the people a horde of domestic crooks. It seems to me that the way they do things in the big island is very attractive to the French.

As the men practice polygamy so do the women in some tribes resort to polyandry and have several husbands. Plural wives and husbands live amicably and really are out and out partisans of their ménage. In several tribes the custom of couvade is in vogue. In case of the birth of a baby the man instead of the woman takes to bed and rests up, receives congratulations or commiserations as the case may be. That could never be introduced into America until modern athletics do as much for women as the athleticism of savagery does for the primitives and did for our own mothers not so long ago. If a woman gets up, as the saying is, before nine days she takes her life in her hand in this great land, but in Madagascar the mother drops her babe naturally as a foal and goes on pulling. I have witnessed this also among the Bedouins and the Tartars and also in Poland and Russia and Finland and in hinter-China.

Civilization has its penalties that are visited unsparingly on both women and men. I don't know what the automobile is going to do to us, but it can be depended upon to do it; perhaps at last our legs will become rudimentary and we shall grow wheels.

There is no prostitution in Madagascar as we define it and until the arrival of outsiders there were no venereal diseases. A French captain of fleet tells that he had a hard time keeping the comely women of one of the coastal tribes off his ship, although he was anchored quite a distance from land. Several of the women swam out and were not repelled by the sailors and some of them were even willing to accompany the ship and their new mates, although they had no idea where. There was no blushing nor confusion; all was a matter of natural mating, he says, quite like the birds. He drove them ashore, but in doing so had a near mutiny on board as the sailors liked the bronze girls very well. The captain reports that at one time there were more than half a thousand women on the beach, all young and pretty, clamoring to come aboard; which beats any tale told by Fred O'Brien of old worn-out Tahiti.

I have been in both places and I know that the girls of Madagascar are prettier and cleaner and in every way superior to those of Tahiti. The seas are as languorous, the spices as sweet and stimulating and sensuous life as compelling, if that is all we are on earth for. Most of the men and women of Madagascar are clean bodily and wear clean clothing and practice the bath more than the Germans were wont to do at home. All in all it impresses me as being a clean land and a fine people.

Woman has been everything in Madagascar. Often she was the ruler and the last queen was a strong woman as Malagasy women go. When she was queen no minister or courtier tried to ingratiate himself in any other way than that taken by Disraeli with Queen Victoria. Very often the Malagasy woman is strikingly handsome. There is a lustre in her eye, love in her lips and passion in every gesture; but it is the lustre and love and passion of life and not of death. It charms heart and mind to see her in her robe of coarse palm or finer rofia. Her garments are as flowing as those of any of Athenæ's daughters when the Greek maid was a type of love and beauty for Phidias and Praxiteles. Done right now in Parian marble by one of them, she would march down the pathway of the gathering mornings as her Hellenic sister tripped the evenings of yesterday.

CHAPTER XXIV
TRIAL BY ORDEAL:
COMMON USE OF DEADLY POISONS

THE method used in Madagascar to detect and punish the guilty and to prove innocence is as primitive as any custom the people of the island have. It is trial by ordeal and is common among many of the wilder peoples of the world. In Madagascar it is practiced by all the tribes from one end of the island to the other and is called tangena. For the most part poison is administered, but there are other ordeals that are not even as intelligent or as fair as trial by poison. If a man is charged with a crime or if designing officials wish riddance of him, he is forthwith summoned or dragged to the court of ordeals. Here, depending on the grade of the crime, he is given poison to drink. If he dies or is made ill he is guilty. If he does not die and is not much affected he is adjudged innocent. As a general thing they know only a few deadly poisons. They are mostly vegetable and more than any other of the nux vomica. In preparing the poisons some are made as strong as they can concentrate and there are degrees less poisonous until some are practically innocuous. The court can get any result it wishes. If there is a person the king desires to put out of the way the deadliest of the mixtures is administered and that is all there is to it except the burial. Some of the tribes do not know how to prepare the poison so that it will be of the strength they desire and guess at it, which is unpleasant for the victim or would be if he knew about it. This ignorance, which goes very well with the poison custom, results often in weaker toxins and indeed they are more likely to be weaker than stronger. Once in a while a person is found who is immune to any strength. This is so seldom as to be most notable and the person is either killed in some other way or is a marked and free and worshipped man.

Not infrequently two persons will present themselves for the adjudication of a bitter difference and ask to be given the ordeal. More than likely both are made very sick and both die. Then the property in dispute goes to the king. It is quite safe to assume that the court of ordeals knows its business and gives the poison that fits the crime.

Up to the time of the French occupation trial by ordeal was common and it is still widely in vogue. There are other ordeals that unfortunates are subjected to. The commonest of these is the crocodile test. Inasmuch as this is the way with the wilder tribes it is still followed more than the poison practice and it will be a long time before the French reach in a corrective way those who employ it. The crocodiles of Madagascar are huge man-eaters and infest rivers and some lakes in unbelievable numbers. I have seen them so numerous in the head waters of the Betsiboka that it looked as if one could cross the stream on their backs, which of course is an exaggeration, but not of appearances. When the crocodile ordeal is ordered, the victim, as he almost always is, is made to try to cross an infested river by wading and swimming. If the saurians do not eat him he is innocent and if they do he is guilty. The chances are overpowering that he is guilty because he next to never gets across except in the belly of a crocodile, and it is not so hospitable as a whale.

In the old days, when the property of some man was desired by the king or when certain persons were odious, court killings by tangena under the guise of law and regularity were by the thousands. Perhaps this is worse than the law's delay in this country, but the difference does not seem so great when a rich litigant can keep a poor one in court forever and just wear him out; or worse yet if all the law is for property and not much of any law for the human being or if the big power of wealth selects or controls the court. The conditions are improving in this respect in both Madagascar and America.

CHAPTER XXV
MALAGASY BURIAL CUSTOMS

WHERE there are hundreds of tribes there is a considerable variation in customs. But they are sufficiently general for one to suggest the other. The custom of burial that I shall take as a type is the one practiced by the Betsileo. In fact I am endeavoring to go to one tribe for one thing and to another for a different thing so that perhaps a composite may be obtained that will supply an

idea of what may be encountered in Madagascar.

When a Betsileo falls seriously ill all of his relatives assemble and get as near to him as possible. This is likely to insure a fashionable funeral. If he doesn't die and they think he should they get on top of him until he is red hot and faint. Then they proceed to nurse him in their laps, taking turns until all have had a whack at him. The medicine is changed as rapidly as possible and the witch doctors are called and often the sorcerers and diviners. The witch doctors outdo the other frauds and say, as evidence of their interest and confidence, that if the patient dies they will bury him in their foreheads. The treatment tends to give the man no chance, but if he still clings to life they close his eyes and will not permit him to open them again. Then death steals in and the corpse is bathed, a thing that is rare in life. A strong piece of cloth is tied tightly under the chin and around the head; the knee;s are fastened together and also the great toes. There is much weeping among the women and children, but it is not allowed to be heard outside the household for fear they will be charged with feigning grief.

At once a message is sent to all who are at a distance and they are certain to come. A special bed, placed along the east wall, is prepared for the body. The corpse is placed here on its back. The family and near relatives hold a council to decide the style of the funeral and the cost, both depending upon the wealth and social position of the deceased.

In case of a rich man a great deal is spent on toaka rum, lambas, and ox feasts. The winding sheet is procured and the ceremony of presenting it is as if the corpse could hear and appreciate. The presentation speech is as eloquent as the head of the clan can make it. Then the death tax, called the "tandrahova," is paid to the head of the village in oxen or their equivalent. Until this is done the funeral is in abeyance. This calls for a lot of sharp bargaining.

A great day is chosen for the funeral feast when the oxen are killed, although perhaps the mourners could not wait and have already killed two or three and gorged themselves. The barbecue of death is called "miahy ormanao fiahiana." As many as an hundred oxen have been killed on occasion without anything being left over for the very poor. If the people bereaved are poor they bury the dead man in four or five days. In some cases the feasting and games and dancing and drinking of rum go on for months until it has sometimes happened that the ones responsible for the expenses have had to sell themselves into slavery to pay the bill.

The actual burial summons all the mourners. If a woman, the corpse is carried out and then back into the house, for she might have forgotten something, as women are ever doing, the Malagasy say. The cortège does not move straight to the grave, but loiters on the way, singing and dancing and even playing games. When they arrive at the grave the head of the family makes a speech, reciting what the deceased died from, the cost of the funeral, and closes by thanking the people there for coming.

A guest replies and thanks the family for making the funeral such a success. It is an occasion for speech-making all around and the utterances are invariably tactful and have the purpose of influencing the hearers rather than of giving any useless praise of the dead. When the talking concludes the body is buried without the coffin, which, however, is destroyed.

The body is wrapped in a mat which is removed and taken home to be washed and dried and kept, for they say they cannot love their relatives if they destroy it. This mat is often a source of contagion, as it is never washed clean and is filled with bacteria and smells to heaven.

It will be noted that the east is the ruling orientation. When the body is lowered into the grave care is taken to see that the head is toward the east. It is the direction whence their ancestors came and they are to return there. Hence there is advantage and consideration in placing the corpse so that the spirit will not be confused and may easily get a good start.

Their campi santi are good places in which to study the growth of architecture in Madagascar, and it really deserves to be thus denominated. The graves of the poor are not apt to be marked at all, but all others are in an orderly scale of pretentiousness, depending upon wealth and power. Sometimes strong families have totem poles significantly and

intricately carved and the work astonishingly well done. The tombs of the kings of old were marked by huge monoliths in the rough. They were' often rolled great distances from the mountains and still are stately and effective. The modern royal tombs have temples that would not discredit the Greeks. It is their own work, for the Malagasy is a clever fashioner. Some tribes bury treasure with the corpse, but not much of it and it is not a general custom as it was among the Incas and pre-Incan peoples of South America, who sent enough with the dead person to set him up at housekeeping in heaven, a trick that would be an advantage if it could be attached to those who are born unto the earth.

Next day the family kills more oxen and the ceremony occurs of rolling the mats that have been used in the obsequies. Then there are prayers to the ancestors and the dead is given over to them for keeping. After this they drive out the ghost of the dead, saying that the deceased has no wife nor husband nor father nor mother, as the case may be, and is expected as a decent dead person to clear out and keep away.

They believe that there is a spirit of the dead that goes to lratra, a holy mountain, where in the bowels of the earth it pounds rice, fires guns, beats drums, plays music and keeps at something consequential all the time. There are myriad spirits at this holy mountain and they welcome the newcomer.

Despite the fact that they drive out one spirit from the house there is another that abides there and knows what goes on and has power to bless, protect, make rich or cause bad luck. Because of this conviction they pray to all the dead and engage and believe in ancestor worship.

When they pray to their ancestors they assemble in a room and all must be present. They turn to the east; then take into the palms of the hand a big silver ring that is worn in the hair. Thus disposed they pray to a long list, always mentioning Andriananahary (God) first, for the Malagasy are monotheists or at least believers in a chief God.

One reason the custom is frequently resorted to is that it is a time of eating and drinking; a fowl for each worshipper is prepared and there is copious resort to the toaka jar. In the feasting they do not, however, forget the spirits, for they place food and rum to the east and bid them help themselves.

There are those who sacrilegiously say that if good things to swallow were served at the weekly prayer meetings in the Christian churches they would be better attended. The Malagasy believe devoutly in all the prayer ceremony, even to the presence of the spirit, although they eat the food that is left after they have given the spirit a fair chance at it.

It is a common thing for them 'to lay at the door of the household spirit certain illnesses, claiming that the sick person is possessed by a "lolo." To drive out the "lolo" they have the ceremony of "salamanga" in which they compel the sick one to dance until he drops exhausted. This produces a violent perspiration and often is followed by relief. Much like the folk belief among the Canadian half-breeds of the "loup garou" they think the "lolo" carries its victims off into the fields and sometimes to the water and may forget to return them unless it receives some sharp reminder.

Some tribes believe that a good many become "kinoly" when they die, which means that they rise from the grave and assume their original form except that they have no stomach and speak through their noses. The "kinoly" live in the west and eat only burnt fat. I did not see one. If Malagasies have good fortune they say that the dead are blessing them and if ill luck comes they say that the dead are angry.

CHAPTER XXVI
MALAGASY MARRIAGE CEREMONY

As with funerals, there is a variety in marriage ceremonies. There is no written service in the island and often there is no semblance of a wedding; just a consorting that does not take on even the small dignity of our common law marriage. The French law of registration will cause more regular procedure, although the French are not such great sticklers for a wedding ceremony as they are for statistics. The Fombandrazana of the late Rainandrimampandry has the best account of the native wedding. From it translations have been made that I was fortunate enough to have access to. The bride having as a rule

been selected by purchase and all the preliminaries of payment and amount arranged, the day is set. The "mpaka," who are friends of the bridegroom, and whose appellation means those who go to fetch the bride, put on deep red silk shawls called "lamba mena" and go to the home of the bride's father. One of the "mpaka" makes a speech to the family:

"This then is what we have to say to you, sirs, for there is a small private matter to be considered under your roof. We are met here as a family, including the father and the mother and the elders who are as fathers, and the younger members who are strong to have and to hold. And now we have to open the business, so pray pardon us. After all proper apologies have been offered we wish long life to the queen. May she not suffer from disease but live as long as her people. And now that the thanks and salutations have reached our royal lady they will also apply to all of noble birth to whom they should be addressed; and may we as a family be rendered safe from all evil and witchcraft. The matter before us is such a simple thing that we may now proceed. We are the messengers of the bridegroom. He comes in speed and haste; he knocks at the door; he asks for heirs and successors. If money were given by you or many oxen or a grand house all could come to an end, but heirs and successors to continue forever are what is sought. The bridegroom knows he is not climbing up an unknown tree, but is like the tall man who was lying by the fireside and exclaimed: 'Why, this is the rim of the pot; this is not another person, but is the same as myself; like the rim of the pot that is the same all the way around.' And so he comes to you as one to his own family to talk details and enter into friendly consultation. So please open the door unto him."

To this some member of the bride's family replies in the same elastic way:

"Yes, that is true, sirs, and a truth demanding an answer, so allow us to reply while you listen. This is a family meeting and at such we do not thrust one another away and so I have been asked to represent her in talking for the bride. All blame has been removed and your good wishes are speeding to our sovereign in her royal abode. May we who are assembled here be blessed by God and our ancestors, and have many heirs and successors. May our family spread and increase on every hand. You have come in haste to open the door and we welcome you and it is pleasant and acceptable to grant your request. For even if one not like your friend had asked we should have given, then how much more happily do we give to you, for him, our relative. Going out he is dear to us and coming in he is dear to us. But although we grant your request our ancestral customs must not be slighted; households are not all alike and a cloth with ragged edges must be trimmed. Marriage is not tied in a fast knot but in a slip knot, for it is a matter of mutual agreement. Unless you agree to abide by those customs that are observed by sovereign and people such as three bundles of fire wood; two to be taken by the man and one by the woman, we cannot give our consent. Also when the end comes our daughter is not given to be retained by the brother-in-law, but like the feather of a fowl which does not die except at the corner of the hearth, so our daughter is not given to be the wife of many men, but it is only to whom you represent that we send her forth. Also if any debts are incurred our daughter shall not bear any responsibility, and the children in sufficient numbers anyhow from two upwards are to be ours. This is our answer and do you make it known to your bridegroom."

The messengers reply:

"That is all quite correct. You are not following wood and stone but you are dealing with a human being; not following all mazes of stars in the heavens but only the three stars that bind (Orion's belt); so be assured as to all the proper observances, for, as our saying of the wise goes, the widow of a brother-in-law is not a wife but is already a sister."

The bride's spokesman answers:

"The child is still young and does not know much of housekeeping, so you are to promise to tell her so that she may learn without too much scolding; also you are not to expect her to work without materials to do with and in this is wealth and happiness. They are but man and woman and there may be quarrels such as arise very often among married people; for anger is like scalding water, crushes the eyes, knocks out the teeth, and breaks legs and arms. If such be done to our child she will leave her husband and compensation will be demanded."

This is answered thus by the representatives of the bridegroom:

"This is all quite true; it is not those children who marry but we grown-up people and if there should arise faults in their conduct as man and wife and the husband should use cross language and harsher and the wife' should become a hen that crows then all the members of the family will be angry with them and not you only."

For the bride there is then an acceptance of all the agreements and they say jointly that the blessing shall be pronounced at once. The senior member of the bride's family then prays:

"Thou art appealed to, O God, the Creator, also our ancestors and the sacred things. May the destinies of these children never be contrary to each other; may they have many heirs. May they enjoy property by reason of the blessing now pronounced."

All of the household say: "So may it be." Money as a bridal present is now given and. the bridegroom's proxies say, as they give it, that it is not sufficient for such a bride, who deserves also a ram with a large fat tail and an ox with spreading horns, but as it is only the custom to do as is now done this will have to be satisfactory. For the bride the reply is that it is all right because there might have been a custom that called for nothing, and the present is very liberal.

Then follows the wedding feast. The father of the bride asks the messengers to overlook the fact that he could get nothing that would do justice to the occasion; to which the messengers reply that it is most substantial and that every- thing will be just right if they all enjoy it together in proper spirit. All the time the guests are urged to eat and they retort to the host that he is not eating at all and that the meal is like a piece of one-sided masonry. "Yes, but we are happy to have you eat first and if there is anything left we will eat at our leisure afterwards."

After this first feast is given a banana leaf is placed in front of each guest. On the leaf a piece of fresh beef is laid, which is called "tolotra," meaning a present. During this ceremony the bride's grandmother, if she is living, must be present but must sit without moving at the base of the principal pillar of the house until the party has gone. At the home of the bridegroom the same doings as at the bride's house are carried out in minutiæ. There are speeches and feasting and the giving of meat and the wedding duly proceeds.

The bride is conducted to the abode of the man and together they are marched around the house accompanied by a sacrifice to prevent evil. This varies in different tribes. In some there are sacrifices of human beings by proxy, some small wild animal being selected to represent a baby that is supposed once to have actually been a victim. Among the nobility the groom remains at home, but in the common ranks the bride is taken to her home by the groom, where she remains until old enough for the bridal bed, for these marriages are made at all ages, even at infancy among some of the tribes.

The furthest departure from this ceremony is that of tribes which are phallicists. Some of these conduct their marriages in a nude state with decoration of the phallus and the linga. They have ceremonial cleansing and unless the contractants are healthy and free from disease they cannot be married. These were the strong tribes and the claim is made that their phallicism is both a sane and a hygienic religion. It makes for cleanliness and prevents prostitution.

Other tribal wedding rites are confined to tying the garments of the man and woman together and compelling them to eat out of the same plate. Divorce is easy and as referred to elsewhere there is both polygamy and polyandry, with couvade, although some tribes are strict monogamists. As a general rule sex consciousness and conscientiousness are not in bold relief.

CHAPTER XXVII
AVERAGE MALAGASY
CONDITIONS OF LIVING

HOUSES of the common people are from eight to ten feet in length, seven feet wide and six feet high. The better ones have wooden frames enclosed in woven bamboo. The door is three feet off the ground and is only a hole, sometimes round or square or oval, and not bigger than is necessary to crawl through. I had a lot of clumsy trouble getting used to them, but the native scuttles through in fine fashion and never bumps his head.

The door is always in the west and the holes for windows are in the north and south. The latter are not much larger than a good chicken coop would call for and there are chickens of several kinds in the native houses. A fireplace beside the door has no chimney, the door acting in that capacity as well and it is nearly as good or as bad as a chimney as it is as a door. Behind the fireplace is a large earthen jar in which water is kept. Over the fire is a sort of mantel for wood or fagots or whatever is used for fuel; in some cases dried dung. Where the roof touches the walls a shelf runs clear around the room. On this are straw baskets in which are stored the rice and manioc and whatever else they have to eat. The roof is grass indifferently thatched. There is more than likely to be no bed, although now and then I saw a sort of little bed in the northwest corner of the room. Mostly the sleeping is done on floor mats and that was satisfactory to me because I have spent three-quarters of the nights of my life on the ground and rock and like it.

One thing I did not approve was the soot that hung in ropes from the low ceiling of grass. It had a way of getting into the mouth if one opened it while asleep, and to awaken to eject a throat full of stringy, black, choky stuff is not so pleasant as swallowing a chocolate parfait, even of the same color. I could not get used to it.

In striking contrast is the finely carved center pole of the house. The little frames of the doors and the windows were also artistically carved in many houses. Man has ever been an artist with a sharp implement, whether of bone or stone or steel.

There is no furniture and sitting and eating as well as sleeping are done on the floor. This is not true of the best houses in or near towns, but it is true of the country dwelling. In the towns are quite elaborate houses of stone and brick and wood. Both sexes are together and recognize no inconvenience or impropriety. One thing invariably present is the bamboo guitar on which music is made that is sweet and has arrangement. I have not seen a people in the world of any degree of development who did not love melody and have some kind of musical instrument.

Rice is the staple of the population and they raise more than enough for their use, and the island could be a great exporter of this most nourishing of all cereals. They eat it unpolished and hence are free from beri-beri. Of other foods there is an endless variety, including succulent herbs, manioc next to rice, with sweet potatoes nearly on a par, fish, wild and tame birds, beef, mutton, edible caterpillars and spiders, and wild animals. In some tribes lemurs, the most plentiful of all the forest things, are eaten, while with other natives they are "fady" or forbidden.

There are earth nuts like the peanut and there are many luscious fruits, including the mango, peach, loquat, pear, banana, pineapple, and many more. Only the near rich eat fowl when they wish, but there is beef to be had by all. Cooking of all kinds is done in earthen pots except in towns, where iron utensils are coming in. Native soap is being displaced by what they call sweet soap, that is, any kind from the outside.

Coffee and tea of fine quality can be raised, but they are not native beverages. The Malagasy drinks warm water that is poured into the rice pot to soak the burned rice which adheres and in this way the pot is cleaned and their rice water tea is made.

Rum made of sugar cane, a kind of coarse "aguardiente," was widely consumed, but the French have interdicted its use so that there may be a market created for French wines and liquors and baleful liqueurs.

Britain has grown rich at times selling poor people opium and France has done the same thing with alcohol products. Fine business! And still they wonder at wars and their curses. Oddly the Malagasy resents the taboo of his moonshine and the result is less drinking just now and better social conditions.

Cane raising is successful and all the sugar needed can be raised, but none is refined in the island. There is a considerable importation of refined sugar.

The usual dress is loin cloth and a "sarimbo" lamba woven at home by the women. Women also wear a low lamba often so disposed on the torso as to leave the mammalaries bare and they are beautifully developed and rounded. The breasts even in old women do not hang sagging and wrinkled as among so many of the wild naked people.

In olden times all the lambas were made by the natives from the fibre of the dombeya tree, which they call "hafotra," for the common ones and of the rofia palm for the finer ones. Now, however, they are made of imported cottons and have been for a long time.

This cotton was first obtained from America, but our trade disappeared with the war and the discovery that we have a better market at home. In towns one now sees a sprinkling of European dress and it is ugly in comparison with the elegant native garb. Even at the huge public markets there may be seen some persons attired as they would be on the back streets of New York or London.

Also the Malagasy is learning to have faith in the modern medicine man. This represents a real progress, for in the old time nature did not have a chance and now, in spite of what Shaw says in his "Doctor's Dilemma," the sick person is not so often doctored to death as formerly. If an abuse exists in this direction it lies in America and in other countries where the profession has its highest development, but where people of ignorance and wealth think that they have all the better chance the more doctors they call. Not long ago I was told of the son of wealthy and loving parents in a large American city who was stricken with quite an ordinary malady. He was an only child, robust and fine in physique and vitality. The parents got scared and also wished to be able to say that they had done a lot so they called a half dozen doctors from outside towns and in the competition of treatment among these the young man was murdered. It is safe to say that they have not reached this point in Madagascar as yet.

It is claimed that the Malagasy women are healthier who wear a woven coarse mat about the body from the waist to the knees. This is a fashion of the tribes least developed. At night this mat is rolled and used as a pillow and even as a bed.

The Malagasy is a natural linguist, which is a characteristic of insular people. It is surprising how soon many of them acquired a working knowledge of French just as English began at once to replace Spanish in the Philippines with the change of government to the United States.

Until recently towns were builded on heights and points that could be defended and were difficult of approach. Houses were surrounded by deep ditches where water and slime made approach difficult. Now the people are feeling a greater sense of security and are coming down from the hills. When lawlessness was at its height there was a truce at the great markets which are more important in Madagascar than in any other land, even the Orient, where the bazaar has its highest development.

One of the first fine roads, built by the French from Masindrano to Fianarantsoa, was most astounding to the natives. They had not seen a road of any kind and it had been the policy to discountenance roads or even trails because they facilitated the movement of an enemy and permitted an intercourse that was held to be undesirable. But they are now enthusiastic about roads and vehicles and while the filanzano (native palanquin) is to be seen commonly even in the capital, its days are numbered.

There is a big change in the matter of money. From none at all to cut money, which was simply the chippings of native silver, they have come into French coins and like them. They are still in a state of amazement over the mails and telegraph and are beside themselves over the wireless and the flying machine. But the Malagasy are quick-witted and it will not be long before they will be operating all of them.

Already there is a native flying corps and several adept wireless operators. It may be said that there is freedom but not encouragement of religion by the French. The few French government schools are open to all, but their attendance is not compulsory. There is a free social relationship between the French and the Malagasies and frequent intermarriage. Mr. Gascon has never drawn the color line here nor in Martinique, nor in Africa, nor any place. Often I saw at the levees in Antananarivo a handsome French bride and a coal-black husband or the reverse. This makes no doubt for a kind of assimilation that is at least commercially desirable. It is even claimed that the black and white marriages are more constant than the French average at home. Anyhow they are getting on.

CHAPTER XXVIII
MALAGASY NEW YEAR FESTIVAL

THERE are a great many festivals in Madagascar. I have taken that of the New Year as prominent, important and typical in order to give an idea of the people in matters of this kind. Native customs will not survive in their purity and all that will be known of them must have been recorded before they are lost.

The festival of the New Year is called "Fandroana," or the Sacred Occasion of the Bath. Ceremonial bathing is a chief point in the program. The Malagasy word for bath is "mandro" and it is often given as the title of the observation of the new year. As the Malagasy year is eleven days shorter than ours and as it is good luck there to celebrate only on Sunday or Thursday the chance that their celebration and the first of January will synchronize is very remote. The celebration of which I am giving a native description occurred in 1864 in March. The affair took place each year eleven days earlier and thus made the circuit of the seasons. Every thirty-four years they gained a year and many of them thought for that reason that they were longer lived than Europeans and found thus a blessing in their faulty chronology.

Theirs was the lunar month and they called moon and month by the same name, "volana." Their New Year's day is the first or new moon of the month called Alahamady (of Arabic origin) from Aries of the Zodiac. Ranavalona III, who became queen in 1883, instituted many reforms and among them was the arbitrary royal decree that New Year's was November 22, which was a way she had of signalizing her birthday, and she made it stick. All they did after that on the old Alahamady New Year was to fire a salute of cannon at sunrise to propitiate the conservative spirits that still clung to that date.

The celebration starts on November 22 and continues for five days. The chief day is either a Sunday or a Thursday. It was and still is a big day. Diviners work the "sikidy" or consult the oracles to get the signs right and no work is done for a week before by anybody. If a person dies within three months of New Year it is good luck and the main funeral is made a part of the celebration of that day. But it is a bad sign to die during the week that New Year's is being celebrated because it is hard to alter the program to adapt it to a burial. Therefore the people, abetted by the diviners, refuse to die at the hoodoo time, and, astonishing as it may seem, comparatively few shuffle off then. If some one was unlucky enough to become a corpse at New Year's the body was hidden and buried a long time after, which may be one reason for the claim that few die then.

Tradition has it that the uniform program on New Year's originated with Ralambo more than three hundred years ago and it must have been of long custom, for all the tribes celebrate in the same way and have done so ever since records have been kept. Not only do all knock off work, but it was a sin to kill any living creature within five days of the feast. In more recent times it is by law and the consent of the chief spirit permissible to kill geese, ducks and chickens because it is so hard to have a feast without them. Such food is called "fo-tsi-aritra," meaning "heart not enduring," as a balm for not having other fine animal food for the time. In earlier times it was expected that those within reach of Antananarivo would go there and pay their respects and take a present to the ruler. Of course only the nobility saw the ruler, but all were required to take a present. Sometimes whole tribes would make the pilgrimage to the capital at New Year's and they turned the occasion to account, as they made their "hasina" or royal head tax do for a present.

With Ranavalona began the custom of showing herself to the people at that time in some such way as the sultan does, or did in selamlik days at Yildiz Kiosk, an ancient Arabian custom.

The queen, dressed in a striped lamba called "arindrano," would take a position on the first balcony of the largest palace Manjakamiadana under a red umbrella. She would be surrounded by her women of the bed chamber, clad in a slouchy open way in lambas of the same kind but not so fine. Often they were naked to the waist.

The roads to the city would be thronged and the town crowded with people and there would be everywhere piles of rice, fine mats, sugar cane, manioc, honey; and those who brought their tax

had cut money or silver cut from a bar and there would be a quantity of it in evidence and no guards.

It was the belief that if anyone stole anything he would be detected either by the sorcerers or through the tangena. They also carried firewood. It was a time of general and even required present-giving. All slaves had to carry presents to their masters and in addition a bundle of firewood. One day was occupied with a huge fair. The one at the capital was held on Zoma or Friday, the day it is still held on. Fine exhibits too were there; much poultry because it could be eaten; and also herds of wonderful humped cattle that had been fattening for the New Year and would be killed and barbecued as soon after the regular ceremony as was permitted.

Always on the evenings of the market days occurred the "hasendrina" or the firing of grass. Bundles of dry and very inflammable grass were tied around long light poles and carried mostly by children. These were lighted by thousands and waved to and fro, making a bewilderingly beautiful spectacle. During the spectacle a vast and not unmusical chorus arose from myriad throats shouting "hasendrina, hasendrina." As far as one could see these serpents of fire crawled through the air gracefully. From an elevated position the sight was memorable. In Wales and Scotland and in the North of Ireland they do something of the kind as a relic of ancient fire worship. They drive cattle over grass fires and wreathe them in flames amidst much bellowing, and have given the custom the name of "beltain."

In Madagascar it was usual to have two fire nights; the first for the king and the second for the people. On both nights there was noise making of all kinds and in the later period much cannon firing.

The big act was the bathing of the queen as proxy for all the people, and they were content for the most part to have her act for them. This royal bath took place in the big palace on Sunday or Thursday evening. The courtyard would be dimly lighted and the palace guard would be on duty. Only those who had been received at court were invited to the affair and these were of the nobility. The bath was given in the large central room of the palace on the ground floor. Into it were crowded the guests and those who were at all late and could not enter were seated on the ground of the courtyard with open windows in view. Inside were those of special favor and the highest rank, wearing striking red lambas of silk. In the northeast corner, the sacred part of every house and the same in the huge palace room called the "zorofirara zana," the ceremonies were gone through. Here "rary" or prayers and chants and all worship are performed. It is the place also of the family idols and charms.

On the night of the royal vicarious New Year's bath the queen took her seat on a low platform erected for the time, dressed in a flaming lamba of red, a glittering crown upon her head and sheltered, although under roof, by a big red silken umbrella. Near to her were the prime minister and in proper relationship the other officials of the government. To the west of the queen a huge temporary fireplace of earth kept in by boards had been made. Many fires were kindled upon it of a smokeless wood. Rice and other eatables were cooked for the inevitable feast. Early in the program a procession of royal cooks and serving maids marched in, bearing earthen pots to be buried in the coals. These contained all the things that they know are good to eat, including honey and other sweets that are heated and poured over everything. The Malagasy has a sweet tooth. The royal cooks are called "madiotanana," meaning clean-handed, and were supervised by a gorgeously caparisoned royal steward who bore and continually waved as a wand a horn-like "zinga" bound with silver bands; all most impressive. The queen was the only one who ate from this "zinga." It is held sacred. The cooks seated themselves on the floor around the fire and saw that it was kept burning and that the cooking food was done just right. Not only were they under the closest observation by the queen and all the court, but the utensils were sacred and must have especial care as they have been used at New Year's for centuries and may be seen to this day in the royal museum at Antanananvo.

While this was going on the maids of the bath were preparing the annual bath in the same room, and for years no screen was put up, but with the coming of the Europeans a sense of sex consciousness came and up to the banishment of the queen they had a sort of hide for her tub. It was not much of a shelter, for there must be a certainty of the bath or else some one else would have to bathe and the bath of the queen was supposed to go further in cleansing the nation and everybody in it than any other. In fact, they always managed to satisfy the public that the bath had been administered to her majesty.

The queen's tub was of finest silver. It was in the corner and the only screen was made by the lambas of the maids of the bath, who held them as high as they could. Then the queen was assisted to the corner by the prime minister; he withdrew a step; there was a sound of splashing waters for a moment only and her majesty appeared .to all with wet hair and face and with water actually upon her body, which was shown in glimpses between the upheld lambas. Before any towels were used her majesty exclaimed: "Samba, samba, Andriamanitra, Andriananahary, ho arivo, tratryny taona anie tsy hisaramianakavy," in a pitched and chanty voice. It translates: "Blessed, blessed be God the Creator; may we reach a thousand years an unseparated family."

To this as an antiphone all present replied: "Trarantitra," meaning "reach old age," referring to the queen and all hands.

Holding in her hand the "zinga" horn filled with sacred water from secret springs, the queen passed among the guests. She sprinkled them and now and again took a sup, which was another vicarious act. Nor were the soldiery left out, as they were held to be aided in valor by this, and to the general in command a sloshing baptism was given, usually causing him to cough and strangle, which was taken to indicate that he would confuse his enemies. One of the chief things to be assured by this sprinkling was a bounteous rainfall at the season when needed by the rice fields.

Even those rulers who were converted to Christianity believed in the "fandroana" ceremonies and the immersion part was preceded by a hymn and prayer by one of the royal chaplains. Immediately after the baptism the rice must be ready and was ladled out upon banana leaves for plates and hot honey poured over it. Of course the queen was served first. At the side a piece of meat called "jaka" was placed. This meat had been kept edible for an

FESTAL DAYS: DANCING ON A FÊTE DAY

entire year and got its name "jaka" from the canned stuff aboard the whalers that came into ports and especially at Antongil Bay. In fact everything that came from the foreign ships was called "jaka," from jacktar. It was "jaka has come" and "we can get 'jaka' this and 'jaka' that from 'jaka.'" It is likely that the term "jack" for money used by Ring Lardner and George Ade and other masters of slang had its origin in this way. Anyhow the natives called the money they get from the jacktars "jaka" and that is near enough to "jack."

The food at the queen's New Year's feast was eaten with a spoon made from a banana leaf twisted and rolled so as to make it quite handy. This spoon was tied with a pliant vine that is used for string and is tough and suitable for tying. All the rice is not eaten; enough must be kept to spread on the head, after which the words of the queen's bath benediction were repeated, and that was the end.

After the bath and feast the nobles and chieftains present passed in review and made addresses to the ruler and gave their "hasina" and other presents. Then the prime minister made an address and paid the best tribute to the sovereign that he could compose, accrediting to her all the power that he comprehended. In this speech the prime minister discussed politics, domestic and foreign, and it was supposed to be an important pronouncement. It was followed by a royal salute by the guard and after they got cannon there was much firing of cannon all night. When it comes to liking noise the Malagasy

is a savage and a torchlight politician combined. Singing of the national anthem concluded the bathing of the queen.

Next morning when time had been given for the operation of the queen to take effect all the heads of households went so far in imitation as to have warm water poured on their heads as they repeated the queen's prayer. And at this time special mention was made of those for whom any were in mourning, with regrets expressed that they could not be present and asking the kindly watchfulness over them by their spirit.

As soon as it was proper to kill the fatted beeves the entire land was a shambles. Very early in the morning the killing began by the slaughter of an ox of a certain color called "omby volavita" and "omby malaza," in the royal courtyard. As soon as the throat of the beast had been cut a knife wet with the blood was carried reeking to the sovereign and it was licked and a blessing asked and an admission made that the ruler had already tasted of the harvest of the new year. Then the bloody knife was pressed against the elbow, the knee and the great toe in order that the claim might be successfully set up that the majesty had bathed in blood for all the kingdom. The fat hump was carefully saved and conveyed to the royal tombs, where there was a sacrifice of burning fat to the ancestral spirits of the reigning dynasty. Always the doors to the little grave houses were opened and the spirits were implored to take notice.

There was much interchange of meat as presents, but the slaves were expected to give more than they received and it was seen to that they did not forget. In the households there was near imitation of the practice of blood bathing by the king. Each member of the family would take a stem of the "zozoro" rush and, dipping it in blood, would then hang it over the doorway, something suggestive of the habit of the ancient Jews of smearing their lintels with the blood of the paschal lamb. The great granite monoliths that mark the tombs of the powerful were blooded and so were the sacred cairns that all over the island designate a significant place, a battle or a spot where there was a birth or death of importance or where the king made a journey or a victorious army marched. Fat humps were also left at these places so that any hungry spirits that might be around or might pass that way could help themselves. Nobody is forgotten on New Year's at the feast of "fandroana."

The feasting continues for weeks as it falls at a time between work and harvest. The entire island relaxes and goes merry-making. There is much gorging when they begin to kill the fat cattle. Perhaps the favorite dish of meats is the one called "tonombilany" and it tastes as it is spelled. Portions of the entrails such as tripe, intestines and liver are finely hashed and mixed with blood and fat and then braized brown in an earthen pot in the coals. It is not forgotten to save some meat out to make "jaka."

The children are not left out. It is a memorable time for them and they are allowed to eat to the stretching point and then picnic and play until completely wearied. At their picnics they cook and eat as do the grown-ups. Each does something in the way of entertainment and they have little individual cooking pots. Their games are of swinging and dancing and the singing of simple songs of childhood that are really sweet. In their dancing there is more gesturing and posturing than foot action and they are a graceful people. The royal youngsters are permitted to play with the others and without too much consciousness as to who they are. Finally New Year's is over.

CHAPTER XXIX
TRADITIONS AND FOLK LORE
AND LIFE AMONG THE NATIVES

THE legendary and folk tales of the Malagasy are richer than anywhere else in the world of partial civilization. They all betoken centuries of development. John H. Haile and other missionaries have done a creditable work in studying the myths and ancient customs and in preserving as many of them as possible before it is too late. Even now it is necessary to see the very oldest of the natives if one is to learn much of the remote yesterdays, for the stream of modernism is a forceful and seductive current, sweeping all before it.

It is possible also to learn a good deal from the

FESTAL DAYS: OPEN AIR THEATRE

ruins of ancient, towns and by tracing the Source of fixed habits that have been in vogue so long that the people think they always existed. As in the feudal times in Europe everywhere, the towns, and even what might be called castles, were built on the tops of mountains or high hills and always with the idea of defense uppermost. They were surrounded by wide fosses and dense hedges of prickly pear about as impenetrable as any wire entanglement ever devised in the most modern warfare. Massive stone entrances were guarded day and night and the cattle and sheep were driven home at night and put in a place of as great security as could be provided, just as did the people of San Marino, who still dwell upon the Three Towers of the Apennines, although their independence has been an aggravating contrast to those who have surrounded them for more than a thousand years.

Anarchy prevailed and there was constant feudal and tribal war. That was the only intercourse they had for centuries. Those who were captured were either killed or made slaves. Home wrought spears and big knives were the weapons that succeeded clubs and stones. Gradually the stronger tribes conquered the weaker ones and absorbed them and there came to be a caste of warriors and another caste of timid, servile subordinates.

There developed a class of women that were the most peaceable of any on earth. It is common to see several of them living under the same roof as wives and never a jar of jealousy. Instances are given of a divorced wife; simply kicked out, taking up with a servant of the former husband and no friction at all resulting, although all live in the same compound. They learn to take what is given and make the most of it, partly from callousness, and with a perfect measure of stoicism, if there is feeling that requires control.

A husband will go away with another woman and stay for a period and then, tiring of her, will return to No. I and say not a word in explanation and offer no endearments to wife or children. Nothing is thought of this, nothing is said and all goes on serenely as before. There is no bickering and quite a degree of happiness subsists.

If you ask the average native how his health is or where he is going, or what he is doing he will assume a beautiful air of mystery and reply in a whisper close up to your ear that he is "tsara madina," all right, and going nowhere and is doing nothing and all with peering about apparently to see if anybody is listening or spying. It is just as funny as can be and quite reminds one of Whispering Smith. They do not propose to say a word that will illuminate the task of the head tax man and so they have acquired the habit of saying nothing—in many respects not a bad idea to follow. Talking too much begets more trouble than any other one thing that people do, say the Malagasy "hooray" (wise men).

Ancestor worship is brought down to practical cases by paying great deference to the parents and especially the father, who is the big chief and autocrat of his house and clan, if he has one. Children are taught that they must not eat until their parents have at least made a start and often not until they have finished. If urged they positively refuse and are not to be budged. Men with beards are deferred to almost abjectly, probably because very few can raise whiskers; the longer and more scraggly they are the more attention they attract and the more power they wield. It would be an ideal place for Jimhamlewis, by which I mean no disrespect, for Jimham is quite a boy. At this moment a man with umbrageous pink whiskers could go to Madagascar and organize a monarchy and expel the French, one, two, three, even if this is an epoch of low ebb for kings.

Most of the medicine men have long beards; in fact all have who amount to anything. If a man with whiskers appears he is taken to be a medicine man until evidence to the contrary is forthcoming. I was told of a longbeard traveling with a man clean-faced. On the trail everybody salaamed to the bearded person, but finally they saw both of the travelers eating and noted that the one with the beard took second place. There was such indignation because a man who had such a gift did not practice with it that they caught him and scraped it off with a sharp piece of flint as thoroughly as they could and finished by pulling the hair out by the roots, as do many of the American Indians who cannot have a good beard and so take care to see that the stragglers are done away with.

Among the pacific tribes there is next to no acquisitiveness. They are not traders and any huckster of a Hova can beat them just as the Hovas in turn have no chance with the Arabs and East Indians. They work in the rice fields and elsewhere industriously and are humble and shy.

When a girl is to be sold into wifehood her parents say she is "adala," meaning she is practically a fool and cannot do things and that much must not be expected of her until she is taught, although the fact is she knows how to cook and spin with the best. It is a sort of anchor to windward and is something like the philosophy of a Yankee I know who has taught his sons and daughters to be at their worst on first appearance in order that every discovery as to their character and habits shall be better rather than worse.

Lazy women are an abomination and are not often to be met. Such a woman is scorned and is given only greens to eat and a scant mat to cover her nakedness. Usually it is not long before her indolence is cured. To the working Malagasy the ox is as sacred as the reindeer is to the Laplander. It is everything and must not be referred to as a mere animal. Cattle yield manure and labor for the rice field, milk for food, bones for implements, skins for dress and harness, hair for paddings, and the money to be had from the sale of oxen supplies a fine lamba to be buried in and an imposing tomb.

In many tribes all refuse to touch anything in

CHILDREN PLAYING FAMPITAHA
OR COMPETITION DANCE

THE GAME OF KINDRIANDRIANA,
OR "PLAYING HOUSE"

another's house. If an object is to be removed it must be handed out through the window; no chance is given to charge theft or loss.

There are stories without end, all of which point a moral. An old fellow, who was in the neutral zone of life, was collecting cow dung to dry for fuel one day when a young woman passed. He accosted her and asked her name and destination. She knew that he did not need to be so penurious and that he was rich but so stingy that nobody would have anything to do with him. With this in mind, and being a fast young thing who had been tried out and rejected by several husbands she started in to vamp the old man. With rolling eyes and insinuating pose and honeyed tongue she replied that her name was Razaranao, meaning "Miss Yourportion." The old man answered: "Ah, ha, mine is Rasoatsihiova," or, translated, "Mr. Allrightifyoudonotchangeyourmind." That was sufficient and they hooked up then and there without further ceremony. The Malagasy vamp had had enough of philandering, so she made a good wife and finally got a chance to poison the old man and get all his money and she did so. The moral, not according to George Ade, is that there is a time to quit. Young brides in Madagascar are as coy and devious as elsewhere.

They are supposed to show all sorts of odd traits. It is bad form to have an appetite and they are compelled to refuse almost everything until they are on the verge of starvation. The great test is honey,

of which they are as fond as a bear. One coy young thing was offered honey and of course said that she never touched it. Her newly made husband thought he had the best helpmate in the world and went out to catch a catfish, which is the first food the bride can take with form and fortune. When he returned he was horrified to find his wife dead with her head fast in the honey keg. She had tried to eat some without having to say to the spirits that she had touched it with her hands and so she stuck her head in, got fast got excited and perished. The groom mourned almost all afternoon and then went and procured another bride, offered her honey and caught a catfish for her within thirty-six hours, which is said to be the record for such things in the island. The moral they attach is, "Look out for honey in a keg."

Another newly married woman had a quarrel with her husband and left him in a honeymoon huff. She took a lonely road through a forest, but when night came she got frightened and went back home. When she arrived she went in dramatically and told her man that the forest spirit had appeared to her and had told her to go home quickly or something dreadful would happen to him. It was a pretty good story, and the husband accepted it, but the neighbors were not so easily taken in. To show their view of the matter they renamed the forest Analmananatra, meaning, "The woods that give seasonable advice."

Another popular tale is of a woman who had

a paramour. The husband was too fat and as a consequence was the dunce of the community. He invited his wife's lover to the house to an ox feast, which is a big event. But before the feast came off he got suspicious and cancelled the invitation. The lady was not to be deprived of the joy of her gallant's presence, so she had him concealed in a bundle of fuel. To dispose of him she hid him under the bed, a common place of retreat for lovers and a spot that is never investigated in Madagascar. They never look for what they do not wish to find. Choice morsels were carried to the hider and he choked on one of them. In his anxiety to keep from being discovered he tried to swallow his spasms of coughing, which brought on a heart attack and he died.

When the delinquent wife discovered that her lover was dead she made an outcry before she thought and in came the husband. Then she made a clean breast of the whole thing, confessed that she had loved the dead man and had brought him to the house and bade her husband kill her. But he was a fair man and replied that he had a half dozen mistresses and that he would forgive his wife, who was really sweeter than all the others combined. The problem was to keep the neighbors from learning about the affair. Not far away was a very jealous man who kept his wife imprisoned part of the time and watched her night and day. The dead man was dragged over to the jealous man's house and propped against the door. Then the fat man whistled a signal as if calling for the wife. Out rushed the husband with murder in his eye and heart. Falling upon the corpse, he dealt it several stunning blows, knocked it down and kicked it in the head until he was weary. As soon as he got over his insane anger he examined the body of his supposed rival, and found it to be that of a man he had suspected, as he was suspicious of everybody. He had killed him, he concluded, and next to the satisfaction of being a hero, he was proud of his fighting ability.

There was no doubt at all in his mind that he had done the work. When he cooled he began to consider the consequences. The dead man belonged to a powerful fighting clan and the murderer would have to answer to them with his life. It was at this juncture that he told his wife and asked her advice.

She was diplomatic and invented a story to the effect that she had been pursued by the dead man and that her husband was justified in killing him and that she was glad he was dead. But that did not relieve the situation so far as the dead man's relatives were concerned. So the husband and wife put their heads together and decided that the best plan was to carry the cadaver to a cattle pen and place it beside a vicious cow. They got a pail and a rope with which the cow's legs might be tied and disposed them near the dead man. Next morning they ran to the neighbors and with great show of excitement told them that they had discovered the man in the cattle pen, where he had evidently gone to steal milk, and that there was no doubt that it was the wild cow that had killed him, for his face and head were marked with the hoof kicks of a cow. Thus the poor devil was killed three times.

This story is one of the most entertaining of all they have and is most often asked for. It is listened to with tears, laughter, suppressed breath and a demonstration suitable to the part that is being told. There are many professional story tellers and they are quite histrionic if there is a chance in the story for acting.

The natives are of all shades of color. Some of them are as black as Nubians and these have thick curly hair, sometimes kinky. Men carry a wooden comb either around their necks or at their belt. In the hot country bathing by both sexes and often together is common. When they are hot and tired they will plunge into the water and then sit in the boiling sun and comb their hair for hours or until they are compelled to go at some other task. The women are more fond of open air dressing of the coiffure than anything else and they dote on combing each other's hair. They will add false hair to lengthen the tresses and then will plaster all of it over with fat after the ancient American style of using bear's grease, until the head is a malodorous, glossy, pudgy mass. Next they work different parts into many designs. It often takes an entire day to comb the hair of a woman of quality. Mutual hair dressing is one way of managing it, but the rich usually have their slaves do it.

It was once the style to wear colored beads around

BLOOD BROTHERHOOD, COMMON AMONG SAKALAVA AND BETSIMISARAKAS:
AN INCISION IN THE BREAST IS BEING MADE IN THE FIRST PICTURE, AND THEN THE MIXED BLOOD WITH
WATER IS DRUNK FROM A BANANA LEAF

the arm above two silver bracelets and the same around the lower leg or ankle. In some parts the girls wear a heavy silver ring around the back hair. In eating not many of the natives are fastidious according to our standards. When a beef is killed they stand around with mouth watering until it is opened in dressing and then proceed to taste everything, raw, bloody, and uncleansed as it is. Like the old Georgia Cracker they adore chitterlings, only they eat them raw and without cleaning. A guest at a meal is served with rice and meat, as often as not in his hand, and it is frequently red hot. If the burned person blows on his fingers or whistles or purses up his mouth or snaps his fingers or in the slightest manner indicates that the portion is hot he not only commits a major faux pas but is guilty of insult and may even be charged with an act of witchcraft. Manners are important in Madagascar.

There are sports everywhere. One of them is cock fighting and a chief one is bull fighting. Sunday is their day for all things and bull fights are arranged whenever it is possible. The Madagascar sport is more humane than the miserable man-bull fights of Spain. Crowds gather in the open and are not deterred by wind or sun or rain. Bulls from anywhere and everywhere are brought to fight each other. Some of them are stock of a well-known fighting strain and are kept for the purpose. An interesting feature of most bull fights is that the herds of the respective bulls are assembled to cheer their chiefs

on, as it were. And bulls really seem to be braver when the cows are looking on, at least the Malagasy think so. There is a rush and a roar and the great humped beasts meet in a crashing impact and snort and bellow and gore. The cows set up a fearful din and the onlookers cheer and yell wildly. This keeps up until the vanquished bull turns tail. As a rule nothing is hurt seriously. In the interlude there is singing and music on the crudest instruments and much drinking of any kind of liquor they can get, principally toaka of home brews. Always there is a poor old blind musician, whose blindness is often simulated and who has always a crowd to whom he tells stories and sings songs and plays on his fiddle or blows on his pipes.

Tales of long ago compete with those of salacious quality and the story teller takes up a good collection of knick-knacks.

When a person dies the relatives, friends and neighbors proceed to the house; women marching in single file with straw mats around their loins and torso bare; hair tangled and pulled and twisted, features contorted and woebegone, but they do not weep aloud or wail on' the way. The men go together and are as stoical as possible. The corpse is covered with a silk lamba even if it is necessary to borrow one. The room where the dead is laid out is crowded and the mourners sit on the floor. One woman begins to rock to and fro on her loins and sing in a quavering voice what may be translated as "O me, O my," and all present repeat it as an exclamation. This, with rhythmic clapping of the hands and beating of the breasts, make a death scene that is not easily forgotten. Through it all they drink quantities of toaka, their native moonshine.

A week after childbirth the mother is ready for the birth ceremonies. Relatives and friends and those who wish to get acquainted carry presents of rice, honey, meat, poultry and ornaments and garments for both mother and babe. An ox is killed and there is a feast and a procession of eaters, celebrants, musicians and even children. A record is made of the gifts and of those who gave them as they are to be returned as soon as a birth occurs in the giver's family. It can be safely asserted that there is no race suicide. Hundreds join the festivities and the conclusion is a dance, the feature of which is the competitive dancing of the father and an uncle of the babe. The father is told that if the uncle beats him in the trial, baby and mother will be taken from him and given to the winner. This is never done, for the father enters into the game with all his might and his relative lies down, so to speak. The birth festival is one of the best of the native doings, as they see it, and one of the common inquiries is, When are you going to have a baby so we can come and have a good time and repay you for what you did when we had one? Some of the brides are very young and their husbands are old. This makes the dance for possession a funny spectacle; so humorous that it is not uncommon for a young husband to disguise as an old man, and that is the best acting of all.

A rival of the childbirth feast is the "tsikonina;" which may be translated accurately as the Harvest Home celebration. The natives assemble from miles around and there is no need for acquaintance, for even tramps come and it is said that there are those who nearly live off the dispensers of hospitality at the harvest home barbecues and banquets. They eat hugely of rice, sweet potatoes, manioc, pork, beef, greens and everything that is considered good in Madagascar. The eating is followed by a religious ceremony in the nature of a thanksgiving. There is a song of pagan praise and then the father asks the continued blessing of the deities which have increased his herds, filled his granaries, and given

him all the bounties he has received. There is not likely to be so much thankfulness as there is asking. During this part of the festivities petition is made to all ancestors to continue their love and watchful care. To propitiate them their deeds of bravery, which have grown in imagination to, prodigious feats, are recited and the admission is made that no Malagasy such as they were is alive to-day. An outdoor dance is held and there is wrestling and boxing, drinking and fighting. The missionaries charge that the harvest feast is a time of gross immorality, judging by our theoretical standards.

Native ingenuity is elastic and productive. Some of their devices could be adopted with profit anywhere and not a few have been. Their threshing floors are all arranged with reference to the prevailing wind, so as to take advantage more often than they could otherwise of using that agency to blow away the chaff. This is burned and no ashes are wasted. They are carried to the field and scattered as needed for sweetening the soil.

Ox pits are walled and are near the houses for safety. They are often so located with reference to the rice fields that when they are filled as full of manure as is desirable, a stream of water is turned in and liquid fertilizer in the most approved modern way is carried over the fields and distributed evenly and effectively. Sluices carry the flowing nourishment to the soil, which has been terraced, a labor involving a lot of fine practical engineering. The general irrigation of the terraces from the highest to the lowest demonstrates as much skillful work as is done anywhere.

Their cleverness often astonished me and won my admiration completely. Nowhere do I remember seeing exactly such fishing. Instead of the usual seine of fibre or twine they weave of withes and make an excellent net. As they draw it or drag it they leave both hands free by balancing a flat basket on their heads. With great skill they throw the fish into it as they are caught, never so much as once touching the head basket to balance it, although they are in all kinds of postures.

A Malagasy may select his own primitive religion from many varieties that are prevalent in different tribes. Perhaps a majority of them are monotheists.

Their God is One, while people go in pairs, they say. This one God made the earth and covered it with grass and made the sky and stuck in all the stars for ornament. He lives far, far away beyond everything but sees all and knows all and has as his servants the ancestors from the very beginning of things to guide, guard and punish those on earth. These ancestors are poised between heaven and earth, beyond the sky and in the bottom of the sea; in fact they are everywhere and they are so alert that it is impossible to cheat God. It thus becomes a Malagasy proverb that a man is foolish who cheats himself, but more foolish who tries to cheat God.

Ancestors when tried and proven in service advance until they even become minor deities with some super power of their own. Thus they could get even with those who might have done them a wrong in life on earth and this belief is so strong in some tribes that there is a high degree of justice.

Gods and mortals in some tribes have intercourse much as in Greek mythology. Others think it is a sure sign of disaster if the gods come to earth. When it is assumed by the native sorcerers that some god, as they say, is monkeying around on earth, he has no good intention, and as he is off his reservation he can be circumvented or appeased. One way to send him back where he belongs is to take a piece of sacred stick, which the tribe wizard will supply for a reward, and some holy silver and some rice that has been blessed and cache it all at a place where paths cross. Here the god will find it and it will act as a bribe to him and he will go back whence he came. Of course the medicine man steals the bait away and the simple native is satisfied in his belief. As a coincidence the imaginary curse will often disappear.

Some of the wiser ones are not so easy to fool. They say they can do their own bribing and praying. A favorite prayer is to ask a god to come down to them on the wire of gold that connects earth and heaven and bring to them a gift of cattle and silver and at the same time poisonous spiders and centipedes for their enemies.

Others are absolute fatalists and from the Arabs have learned kismet and Allah il Allah and let Allah do it. No use to buck against the will of the Almighty, which they take to be any bent they have. They pray to the moon, the stars, the sky, the sea; to many things. I have seen them at night pulling tufts of grass and throwing them at the moon as they say "You die ten times and I live ten times. You get fat and get lean but I am as I am always for I am a child of the sun." In this way they propitiate the sun. Ten is a lucky number.

In their idea of creation they do not go farther back than to the time when the earth was covered with a dense forest. There were gods somewhere and they started a fire which burned all the trees but two and these agreed that two trees alone were not worth anything so they changed into a man and a woman, by what process is not stated any more satisfactorily than in most cosmogonies. They began to walk and talk and learned from a talking crocodile that they could create their own kind.

According to other Malagasy there were several gods engaged in making man and woman; they were made of clay but the thing called the spirit was supplied by a finer workman than the potters. To account for death they say that the first man and woman were given their choice as to whether they would die as the moon passes or as the banana; the former with no power to procreate and the latter with many stalks and bunches springing from their dying roots. They chose to be as bananas and act like them to this day. Thus they have an idea of both mortality and immortality. There are not so many religions as tribes, but there are a great many of both.

No people on earth like and prize the dog more highly; not even the Igorrotes in the Philippines, who eat them. How they came to be fond of the faithful canine is told to all the children so that the attachment may be assured in perpetuity. There were two brothers. One was a bright, kindly and clever fellow and the other was stupid, stubborn and base. Both got as far as the golden gate of heaven and were met by Rakonativokoka, the ancient gate-keeper, and told how to act if they got inside. His instructions were that if they entered they must watch their step and at every turn act as if they were not surprised and then, as if they were, and not to accept refreshments served in gold vessels nor accept anything from those of radiant hue, who

MALAGASY PREVENTIVE MEDICINE

would probably tempt them. The elder brother got along all right, but the younger one was taken in by everything and everybody that baited or tripped him. He drank the gods' nectar, reclined on celestial shining and downy couches and naturally took all of the things that he had been looking forward to and expecting in the heaven he had been told about. For his disobedience and foolishness and sybaritic and sensual tendencies he was turned into a dog. Hair, tail and ears grew at once and he became the attendant and shadow of his brother. The tale ends abruptly with no sequel or moral. The story tellers point any lesson they wish and these differ in accordance with the inventiveness of the raconteur.

In fact the heaven believed in by many Malagasies would not be much of a place anyhow and there is more reason for living and making the most of life than for dying. There are in Madagascar many primitive Christian Scientists who never heard of Mary Baker Eddy, or of America for that matter. Their lamba is disposed and draped so as to be different and thus they are recognized. As they pray the eyes take on a dreamy stare and are not closed. When they pass they salute none and act like a yogi. Medicine and doctors are an abomination and an insult to God. Faith cures disease that is scattered among people by devils as seed is sown. Great numbers are baptized with a paint brush, and if they are not cured the sick are told their faith has been insufficient. Their founder was visited by an angel clad only in a bright golden light, who

ordered him to go forth and heal the sick. Also they have the gift of prophecy. This is only exercised by those who follow as disciples and have reached a state of exaltation.

According to these prophets the next year is always to bring a famine to those who do not believe and pray as they are told, so within the territory they work belief is general and a good income is shucked out. If the famine story does not work on some of the hard-heads they have an earthquake and world-ending tale that puts them on the sawdust trail with shaky legs and downcast spirits and the proper humility that leads to surrender and subscription. Aside from scaring a living from the people they are not to be criticized and really are a wholesome influence as they teach honesty, justice and all the finer virtues. The followers are among the best and most trustworthy of all the natives.

It is unlucky for a Malagasy to touch a blacksmith's forge with a stick and if it is done the unfortunate person squares himself by sacrificing a fowl where the smith can get it. If a bird called the "takatra" (or a crow) meets one as he starts on a journey it is bad luck. If the person thus hoodooed does not return home and make a new start he is done for. It is superfluous to say that they all start over more rigidly than we duck a ladder or a black cat. Cattle are not dehorned. If they are born without horns or have them knocked off they are driven into the jungle in the hope that they will acquire horns in some way and when they happen easily to capture wild cattle or they stray in with the tame ones, as they sometimes do, it is the return of the hornless ones they had before. If an ox is presented to a child the animal must eat some of the youngster's hair, or it is pretended that he has done so, in which case no one can take the ox away from the new owner and good luck follows. If the ox takes naturally to hair eating it is a sign that he will be easily kept, will eat little and will not be particular as to what his forage consists of. They have a sacred wood called "hazomanga" that is used exclusively by the medicine men, the magicians and the sorcerers, between which classes there is not much distinction. Any wood and water that the tricksters use become forthwith sacred. It is a common thing to call in one of these diviners, when two people or more have a difference or even a serious quarrel. There is arbitration and the trouble is settled. This is made binding forever by dipping sacred wood in sacred water and then scratching the arm or leg of all the parties to the dispute until the blood comes freely. Blood thus drawn is mixed with the holy water and all drink the potion.

They never go back on a compact made in this way. It is the blood brotherhood as known to nearly all the African tribes. There is substance to the belief that it is a relic of the time, centuries ago, when Madagascar was a part of the continent of Africa. So sacred is this oath of blood brotherhood that there is no record of its violation even when administered to foreigners, as has been the case so frequently in Africa. No great traveler has failed to realize its helpfulness; nor has any felt safe among savages until they had been made his blood brothers.

No extended journey is undertaken without consulting a medicine man or magician, who engages to keep the witches and bad luck away if the traveler does all he is required to do. If there is a failure and ill luck attends it is charged, of course, that there has been disobedience of the quack's instructions. Before starting the traveler is bathed and anointed. If he is going through the high country he is rubbed with sweet unguents; if through the low jungles he is given an abominable odor. Of course he carries his own food and at each place he stops he throws away some rice, thus to get rid of the evil spirits that have alighted upon him and taken up their abode in the rice as the most desirable spot for an evil one to dine. The quantity of rice thrown measures the standing of the person and if he is wise and can afford to do so he dispenses with a good deal and does not throw it farther than into some vessel where his host may make use of it. In this manner he is certain to have good luck and gets along famously. Nor must he forget his guardian angel, who also eats rice, and it must not be placed where other travelers who may chance to be out of food will get it.

The "ombiasy," as the diviners are called, are more popular than are our fortune tellers and clairvoyants and they are sought openly. Many childless women

PRACTICING DIVINATION

go to them for aid. One of the verdicts in case of barrenness is that the man and wife are not suited to each other. Consequently the woman is taken to the high mountains. In a lonely place where none other may see her she is anointed in the presence of her husband after a bath in a brook that flows from a sacred rock and has healing qualities. Then the husband is stripped and both are left in the woods as the first pair were in the garden of Eden. It is astonishing how many times a baby is the outcome, they claim.

Before the pair are left in the hands of the love sprites of the wildwood a fat fowl that has been plucked and made to bleed is drawn seven times down the face of the woman and then is tied to the girdle of the man. As soon as they think there is to be issue they eat this chicken. Some fertility doctors do not kill the chicken but make the couple carry it alive and preserve it until a child is born. As there are few really barren women this chicken eventually supplies broth for a baby. When all works right the "ombiasy" hangs his "sikidy" (divination board) on a willow bush by singing waters and no one must go near for ten days; not even the "ombiasy."

In no land are there more charms. There are charms for every kind of work. The charm for adultery keeps the lovers from being caught. It is supposed to make the wife or husband who is being deceived blind and deaf to the doings that would otherwise fasten guilt upon the lovers. To combat and counteract this "gree-gree" there is a charm that will make one supernaturally keen of sight and hearing, and so on, There is a lot of use made of both and much harm and suspicion, but the evil and good average up.

A girl may get a charm that will capture any man and especially one who is in love so deeply with some other woman that the baiting maid can do nothing without what American Indians call the right medicine.

One of the most potent magics is one that permits the owner to commit murder and not be apprehended. It takes the sorcerers more than a year to prepare this charm and invest it so that there can be no doubt that it will work, for if it does not work after the big price that has been paid for it the relatives kill the diviner. It is the only act that puts the voodoo worker in danger.

Next to the murder medicine the most sought after and most expensive is the charm that makes cattle thieves safe. Once in a while there are those who own all these charms. They may not use them often or at all, but the charms are an asset. The general belief is that no one can acquire wealth without possessing a cattle-lifter's charm, a belief tantamount to the one current in our own land that no one gets very rich honestly. Before the cattle-thief charm can be used safely the owner must get the talons of a certain hawk and draw them seven times down his face until the blood flows freely. Of course he must then wait until his face gets well or he would be under suspicion. Cattle lifting and wife stealing are legitimate sports among some of the Malagasy.

Locusts and a kind of spider are regarded as fine food, but the cicadas are so numerous and so destructive that there is a charm against them, one of the very expensive ones. Most of the locusts are of the creeping kind and sensible natives destroy them by burning them in trenches as they do in Argentina and elsewhere. The lazy man with the charm and a big cargo of superstition goes to a hilltop in the road of the locusts and there performs his incantations amidst smoke and fire. Now and again the fire and smoke turns the column of insects to the fields of a neighbor. If the charm does not work either a neighbor with a stronger one from

some rival doctor is blamed or it is recognized that God is too busy on the other side of the island to give personal attention to. the matter and the insects are too many for His assistants. Always there is an excuse and a "reason." If this were not true there would be a quick ending of wizardry. It is passing rapidly anyhow as the natives come under the instruction of foreigners, although often it is only an exchange of their superstitions for a set of new ones, as the French are as much given to superstition as any people in the world.

The crocodile charm includes great politeness and if it is impotent the owner has not been as polite as he should have been. It is an astounding fact that about every bit of water big enough to hold a crocodile has one, and when the stream or pond or lake is large it is literally infested with them. From these streams and ponds the natives get all their water for household and farm use. They are always wading streams and ponds and it is a big game to keep from being devoured by the man-eaters. It is believed, as in South America, that once a crocodile has tasted human blood and meat it will eat no other food. There is not as great mortality from them as from snakes in India, but they are held in the same dread. When the water users or waders—and they often wade out—are about to fill their jars they salute the water with a doublebent bow and say: "Dear, Dear Honorable Crocodile," or "My Esteemed Grandfather Crocodile." If they are not eaten the charm and politeness have appeased the terrible saurian, but if otherwise there is nothing more to be said or done, as they are worse off than was Jonah. Nor do they fight them, as is bravely done in South America.

Almost next to the crocodile as a deadly pest is the bedbug, and more deadly, to the foreigners, is the mite that is called the chigoe or jigger, or by the Malagasy, Senegals, because they were brought from Africa by the Senegalese soldiers in the service of France.

The bedbug is exceptionally poisonous in Madagascar. So the natives try their best to keep them out of their houses. There is a charm for them, as there is for everything, but they do a lot of work to help the fetich along. Nor is it cleanliness that provokes the attack on the bedbug, but the pain and actual danger and disease that result from the bite. There are all kinds of performances as the charm is applied. One thing they do is to entice them out with bait. They wrap rice in a scented leaf and tie it at some distance from the infested house and then say: "On yonder stick or bush or tree (as the case may be) is your food; you have been here quite long enough, so clear out and remain away." This is partly a command and also a lure. As those who are fighting the pests do not go into the house for some time afterwards the bugs are starved out and the charm has worked.

In the matter of the jigger it is not so easy for Europeans to solve the problem as it is for the natives. All the natives have to do if a house is infested is to get a crowd of children and let them sit a while on the floor, walk around and then leave the place. It will be found that nearly, if not quite every jigger will have fastened itself to the feet of the youngsters. These are carefully removed before they imbed and there is next to never a fatality. But in Madagascar, as in many portions of Africa, every foreign resident and traveller will, if he is wise, have his feet examined without fail by a sharp-eyed native girl each morning. It has come to be that there is a class of girls who are famous for their eyesight who make a business of taking out jiggers.

The deadly pests get under the toe nails and in the callouses of the bottom of the foot and occasionally into the finger nails. They are not much larger than the point of a needle, or at least do not present more surface by the time they have dug in. Given just a brief opportunity they will disappear into the flesh, and often it is too late to overtake them and death is the result. The jigger is not a trichina, but it acts like the trichina and is, if anything, more deadly. Nor is it a joy to have the girls dig them out from under the toe nails. If they are not removed at once they bury themselves and then grow rapidly and encyst and incubate.

When they reach the size of a grain of wheat the yellow cyst breaks and there is no cure. Countless numbers journey through the body in every direction and eat as they go, destroying tissue and causing death. I dug out a nest from the foot of a person who had been heedless and barely caught it in time. It was imbedded about a quarter of an inch and was just about ripe. Within a few hours the victim would have been done for. There was no more pooh-poohing of the jigger. Astounding tales of the numbers they kill in Africa were told to me by persons of high accuracy and intelligence.

When it comes to preventing and detecting theft the Malagasy think their witch doctor charm is a system that beats Scotland Yard, Bertillon and the finger-print sleuth. In making this charm there is a lot of acting that impresses the purchaser. The magician blindfolds himself and gropes about until he finds a chicken that has been previously placed where he can appear to stumble upon it or be directed to it by the powers that control him. This will give potency to the medicine. Immediately he seizes the fowl he digs out its eyes and thereupon exclaims in the voice of the ghost of Rienzi that so shall it be with any and all who shall dare to tamper with anything in that household. Not only will he be blinded, but he will be caught. It is more of a disgrace to be caught than it is to steal. After the declaration, made in tragic tones, the charm is placed at the gate or is buried at the foot of a tree near by. At worst, if there is theft, the stolen goods will be returned with apologies. Inasmuch as the workers of magic see to it that those who do not patronize them are robbed and that those to whom they sell charms are protected, there is a lot to the game. Whenever a new witch doctor sets up in business the dickens is to pay until they get together and form a combination, after which all goes pretty well. If a person owes and cannot pay or is a chronic dead beat or is in hard luck generally he must get a "mohara" charm, which does not cost so much if he will help the sorcerer make it. The "mohara" may be a hollow doll or a cow's horn. It is dressed in fantastic garb and inside is a pair of scissors stuck in sacred wood. This cuts all responsibility. If the owner can fill the thing with oil and honey he is square with the world. Also his luck is permanently changed for the better.

No lightning rod peddler, the country confidence man of years ago in America, who had about as much character as the old time life insurance agent—both of whom have experienced a renaissance—need go to Madagascar hopefully, although it is a land of deadly lightning and the people are scared to death by it. George Bernard Shaw would be disgusted with the Malagasy because they believe in vaccination and utilize it to protect themselves from lightning. He would say it is as efficacious in that regard as in smallpox. Anyhow they vaccinate for it on the forehead and between the toes and fingers. Just what they use as a virus I do not know, but it costs and that is to the purpose. It is business. After the protected has bought safety thus he must do his part. If thunder and lightning come on he must sit out on the doorstep and take the rain or hide in a dark and suffocating place where the old man of the bolts cannot see him. Nor must he eat from a cracked pot, nor rice that has been in such a pot, nor bananas that have fallen from a tree. If he does the things that are "fady" (taboo) it is all off.

If it is dry and they need rain they say that some big medicine man has tied up the spirit that gives rain. But if it rains too much their dead relatives are having a sorrowful time and are weeping.

The charm for children with rickets is to rub a potsherd on sacred wood that has been spat upon and if the spitter happened to be a big man, so much the better. This is laid upon the cranial sutures that have been too slow in closing and if it is done right and the incantation is what it should be the child will improve and grow up to be strong. Of course if there has been any omission or failure to do everything as it ought to be done then there is failure and the child dies or becomes a cretin.

It is found necessary to grade charms according to price. A good one costs a certain amount, a better one more, and a poor one less, and they all are potent accordingly. And the reasons for failure are real exercises in the powers of invention.

Youths with a charm against goring bulls must not linger at crossroads, for crossroads resemble the horns of a bull and the charm is double-crossed. It sounds like politics, doesn't it?

Snakes are worshipped as being the totem of their ancestors and the bigger the serpent the more important is its spiritual content. When Malagasies see one they close their eyes, mutter a prayer to their grandfather and pass on. If you or I should kill one it would mean certain trouble. I heard of a German, who killed a snake and had his house burned immediately by the natives and they have kept right on setting his property on fire on the anniversaries of what they call the murder he committed. For a long time they did not distinguish between snakes and eels, but they do now and eat eels with gusto.

The sacred day of the week is Thursday. Nothing must be touched that is in the house on that day. If fire or food or garbage are handled it is certain that there will be loss of wealth; it will take wings and fly away.

A house was on fire and the flames could not be extinguished. The fire would seem to be entirely subdued, but then it would break out anew in a spot where there had been no sign of fire before. The witch doctor came and after looking wise and mysterious said the fire was caused by ghosts who were angry because pigs were kept in the house against the taboo or "fady" of the tribe. To appease the angered spirits it would be necessary to kill an ox and give a big dinner to the gods at which the witch doctor would preside and eat for the ethereal guests and invite some of his friends to aid him. Also he would personally require a fat sheep and a fee of chipped silver. Soon afterwards the magician, or "ombiasy," died from too rich living and since then there have not been so many mysterious spirit fires. A few of the brighter natives put two and two together and understand.

There are so many manifestations of belief in witchcraft that one can never tell where it will break out. Once upon a time, it is told, a bad man was apprehended luring little girls and was condemned to death by beating and spearing. Generally the executioner is selected by lot and it is counted an honor and a service. The practice is to blindfold the man who is to be killed, but in this instance they omitted the precaution. In the midst of the assault with spear and club and when the guilty person was half dead he turned his eyes upon the executioner and hoodooed him. For years the victim had bad luck. His wife and children and his parents died; a venereal disease attacked him and made him miserable and odious and nothing could have been worse than his plight. At least that is the story they tell. All the best witch doctors tried to remove the Indian eye and the double cross, but to no avail; the victim died in horrible spasms. Most of these stories have an application that is supposed to be restraining and to exert a wholesome influence upon the people. And the folk beliefs and practices are the result of queer habits running over centuries of tribal life.

When a funeral is to take place one of the masculine members of the family bereaved goes to the vault to prepare for the burial. As has been stated, the Malagasy are elaborate in their burial practices and have stately tombs and monuments and temporary and permanent vaults that are creditable and distinctive. This visit to the vault has a special purpose in conciliating the gods. The man who makes it calls nervously to the spirits of the dead who have gone before and have been transformed to gods: "O ye dead, divine ones are many and we mortals in comparison are few. You have the power to abduct us into the land of everlasting shadow. Please do not lay your hands on us suddenly without warning. We shall try to have no objection to going with you when our time comes but we wish to remain as long as you will permit us to stay and we hope so to conduct ourselves that you will be lenient and grant us many more years."

Like many tribes of American Indians, they believe that the souls of the dead are quite substantial and remain for a long time in the vicinity of the body they occupied in life. Corpses are placed in temporary vaults or in vaults for a limited period. When they are removed to the place of permanent burial great care is exercised also to remove the spirit. It is told that once this was neglected and the ghost made all manner of trouble. So the relatives went to the first resting place and, putting the ghost in a pitcher, they carried it to the final place of interment. There was much fear that the ghost would break out of the pitcher, and after a week, to appease it for the neglect and introduce it to the kindred spirits in the realm to which it was journeying, they made a fire and cooked a feast of rice and meat and made a speech. There was food sufficient for many ghosts,

on the chance that some others might come. And also sufficient speech.

"O invisible ones, please to be hospitable and take this fresh man to your arms and make him comfortable and teach him the manners of the big house in which you reside. Do not let him wander back to us unless he comes in kindness to aid us. We forgot him for a week, but we did not intend to slight him and as soon as we remembered our stupidity we sought to make amends. We have fed him and some of you, we hope, and we know that he will forgive us if you will demand it as a price to pay for what you are to do for him at our prayerful request. He has done with this earth and we wish that you will teach him to mind his own business where he has gone and not to meddle with our concerns unless we send for him."

Not infrequently funerals are the occasion for the greatest license and the debaucheries are a shock to our conventional senses. The marital relation is completely suspended and acts of free love and common sex indulgence are openly practiced. There is apt to be much drunkenness and murderous fighting. If there is a widow she leads in the depraved orgy because she is taught to believe that unless she does she will not get another man and Malagasy widows are strong for getting new husbands as quickly as possible. So in many tribes a funeral is a tough event in our eyes.

I am giving these bits of folk lore and fact as I think of them and as they were told to me without further arrangement.

There are two classes of tricksters: One formed of the magic workers who learned the trade from their ancestors, who first got their tricks from the Arabs; the other is made up of native sorcerers and soothsayers. Both are charlatans and the latter are particularly crooked. Credit to the former must be given for a skill that can be traced even beyond the Arabs to the old Indian jugglers. I have seen samples of their prestidigitation. They set an empty pitcher before the crowd and let them all see that it is really empty. Then the magic words, "go fetch water," are spoken and the pitcher is at once found to be filled with water. They did the trick too quickly for my eye. Or they place on the fire a sauce pan filled with water. At the command of the magician it is found to be full of hot meat thoroughly cooked. These are the best tricks the purely entertaining class perform and there is nothing done by the witch doctors which equals the art exhibited in these tricks. But the tribesmen do not expect the magicians to cure them any more than they expect the "ombiasy" to compete with the magicians in sleight of hand.

Unless there is urgent cause a person on the way to a well with a pitcher must not be called back. If he really must be called the only safe way is to curse him as he comes with such condemnations as "May your neck grow stiff; may your tongue be split; may your belly and genitals collapse; may you be struck by lightning; may you die suddenly and at once."

This is for the purpose of befuddling the gods, who are very jealous of man's praise. For the same reason pretty and healthy children are given horrid names. The same idea obtains among the fellahin of the valley of the Nile and that may be the ancient source of the superstition. The fellahin will not wash the eyes of their babes for fear that demons will get them if they are pretty and attractive. This results in a frightful percentage of blindness among them. The way of the Malagasy is much better. They give the children vulgar and opprobrious names so that the baby snatchers from the world of mystery will be misled and not think them desirable. Such Christian appellations as Mr. Nobody (Rafoana), Mr. Dungheap, Mr. Pig, Miss Cat and no end of others will certainly be protective.

The wiser natives told me that the medicine men who were such tricksters met with retribution both before and after death. When they reach a certain age, instead of being credited with more and more wisdom and efficacy they are regarded as having no further power and are derided and disregarded and even set upon and their tricky gains taken from them. Their power goes with their virility and many of them kill themselves or move to other parts in disguise before their time of fall arrives.

The contest between the missionaries and the witch doctors was and still is interesting. The sorcerers told the natives that nothing from away from Madagascar could be as good as a thing of their own land, thus appealing to the primitive chauvinism of the natives. In this manner the sorcerers have held their own quite well against the ablest missionary organization in the world, for nowhere else is there such a record of missionary achievement. Even after the missionary physicians and surgeons had done wonderful things the "ombiasy" would be called and the first thing that he saw to was that he did not have to come into competition with the foreigners. In order to clear the decks the "ombiasy" would address his "sikidy," or divining outfit as follows:

"You that were in the silent forest where the speckled guinea fowl and the dun-colored partridge perched in the branches of the trees and won their food, will you not tell to me the kind of ghost that is possessing this person? You can see and know all things that my poor wits do not understand. You have the eyes of fowls that can peer into the tiniest nooks. I am born those who do not know unless you, who are celestial, will condescend to tell me. Do not be as a coat with two sleeves but be definite in your reply for I am stupid and it is necessary to make everything very plain to me."

After this supplication the patient is anointed with sacred water, a proceeding which amounts to a bath. Next follows a poking and punching and feeling of the body of the sick person in a search for the evil spirit that is causing the trouble. After a while the "ombiasy" pretends to find it and the spot is cut open and the spirit bleeds out. Not content with merely driving the bad spirit out of the body the witch doctor grasps a spear and phases it out of the room and even rushes into the yard, making gestures and wild passes at the imaginary thing until he has given it such a run and scare that it will not return. What with the bath and the massage and the blood-letting the sick person often recovers and great is the reputation of the wise old fraud who has performed the magic.

On one notable occasion a rich chief was taken so ill that all were certain he would die unless unusual aid could be had. So they carried him from one witch doctor to another until seven had said he could not get well and must prepare to die like a king; they saw a grave being dug and a royal shroud being woven and the chief was surely doomed. But he got well and killed all the fakirs as they do in some parts of China when a doctor does not keep them well. Worst of all, the entire group of mystic healers fell into bad repute. Nevertheless these worthies are ingenious and pull the veil of ignorance over the eyes of their people with master skill. If they cannot diagnose a case they are likely to say that the sick person's soul is suspended upside down over fires and that is what is the matter. To cure this, one must pay a big fee and give much food to the gods. If death follows it is proved that the gods are unrelenting, and if the sick person gets well the gods have been gracious.

The custom of burying a slave alive under the tomb of a chieftain is only rarely resorted to now. Not long ago it was common. It is still common to assess the entire tribe for a showy monument of carved granite and woe be to any who do not pay the tithe and also simulate great grief. There was also a custom similar to the Indian suttee of burning the widow alive. According to this custom the favorite wife was sent along with the chief by throwing her into an ox pit into which the oxen were driven until she was trampled to death, which insured that her soul would accompany her husband's spirit. This rite led to queer conduct on the part of the wives. While the chief was well every wife desired to be the favorite, but when a fatal malady was thought to have come upon him there was a scurrying to become unpopular and this not infrequently made death more welcome. Besides, on account of the danger of capital punishment if the royal husband lived the wife who had thrown away her position as favorite saw to it that he died. One common way of attending to this was to steal and administer some of the tangena poison.

Once a diviner predicted the end of the world, like the Adventists, and there was woe and fear in the land. Hundreds of the natives gave away all they had to any who would take the gifts and run the risk of being forever damned if the prediction came true. But most of the natives ate all they could of what they had and dressed themselves in burial attire. Then they hid anywhere and everywhere. When it became clear that the world had no idea of ending, they were shamefaced or thankful and tried to recover their property if they had given it away. Those who had feasted on all they had were turned into mendicants. The next prophet of the end of the world had a hard time.

As I have related from time to time in these stories of the people, all illness is caused by evil spirits that seize and hoodoo and bewitch. It matters not whether the malady is mental or physical or both, it has been caused by a bad ghost. There are all sorts of prescriptions and the "ombiasy" shows a lot of wit in bullying the natives into doing whatever he says will bring about a cure, no matter how silly it is. No illness is ever charged to bad food, careless diet, filthy habits and general uncleanliness and the other real agencies of disease.

One common cure-all recipe is to rinse the mouth seven times with water into which holy wood has been whittled and each time to eject it with as much force as possible so as to insure blowing out the evil thing that is doing the mischief. There is a careful examination by the fakir and a declaration that the spirit has been spat out if he thinks it is the right thing to say. But that is not all the treatment. Seven mouthfuls of the water are swallowed and the family is required to exclaim that the sick one is healed and they wish him a long life and happiness even if he is pretty sure to die the next day. If there is a chance for a big fee the witch doctor carries the game farther. He stands at the center pole of the house with pieces of chipped silver in his hands. These he rubs, making motions as if he were washing his hands, and tells his gods he will pay them well if they will help him to make a cure. Lastly he rolls up his sleeves and washes his arms in a bowl of water, holding on to the silver as he laves. The patient and all present swallow this water avidly, saying as they do so: "Do not waste a drop; drink all, as it will drive away the ghosts and keep us well and make us prosperous."

If the family and friends are not satisfied yet the "ombiasy" has a fat ox brought and the patient strapped to him and covered until he sweats copiously. This may be just what is needed and the patient may recover. Then the magic healer gets all his fees plus the ox, which has been made sacred to medicine by its use, although it is to be noted that the fakir has to have a new ox each time.

MAKING A LAMBA FROM NATIVE SILK

Women buy small silver rings from the "Otnbiasy" in the market. It must be agreed that they are an improvement upon the cheap leaden ones that are worn to prevent rheumatism by ignorant people in America and England. Children are protected from "lolos" and fever by wearing rings around their waists with the same object the African native resorts to "gree-grees" and fetiches. The rings of wire that women wrap in so many strands around their ankles are not only stylish but also are a prophylactic for rheumatism. They will not part with them.

If a man loses his well-spirit it is a cause of illness and it must be rounded up and induced to reenter the body. One way to do this is to roll the unfortunate in a mat and place him between two fires. When he is about dead from exhaustion and the perspiration is streaming off and he is steaming hot they push and hustle him and flash a mirror before his eyes. Insane yells accompany the performance and the man falls senseless. If he lives his lost spirit has again taken up its abode in his body. If he dies, as he very often does, the wayward spirit has been too alert to be trapped.

Rubbing the neck with a dog's foot will cure goitre. When the fakir is a good sleight of hand man he will have the patient cough violently and will show him pieces of bone, hair, rag or anything that is handy and tell him he has coughed it up and will now get well.

A barren woman is tied to a sheep. The cord is around her middle. She and the sheep are driven three times in a circle and then along the bank of a stream. At a -point where the water is swift the string is untied and fastened to a piece of light wood and to the sheep's tail. These are set afloat and as they disappear around a bend the woman's trouble has been removed and she may even bear twins, and sometimes does if she exchanges husbands as the "ombiasy" demands. She has no further "faditra."

For a certain native disorder that has a venereal origin the patient is placed with others suffering from the same malady in a cave or pen of detention where he is kept as long as there is room or until he is supposed to have been cured. While in this place the inmates must not look at human beings or cattle and are only given rice and water to eat. They must call the most ordinary objects by names invented at the moment and as readily forgotten. If a patient forgets and looks at things that are forbidden or calls articles by their right names he is at once seized and on his forehead white mud is rubbed and piled until there is a pyramid of it; all this is to confuse the bad spirits and to complicate things so that if the ghost of the disease leaves the body to get food or take the air it cannot find its way back.

If a woman has lost a babe by death and is about to be confined again she retires to a jungle hiding place and there loses the witch that killed her other babe and thus insures the life of the new one.

If there is doubt about the credentials of an "ombiasy" he takes a vessel of water and whirls it around his head, in the fashion that every American boy has practiced, without the water spilling. This proves that he is a wonder worker and can do anything. And to show his power to others of his kind an "ombiasy" who is in high repute will go upstairs, taking with him a chunk of luscious roast beef. Below he leaves the family, each with a piece of charcoal in his hands. When the "ombiasy" calls out "hano" (eat) he takes a big bite of the meat and his dupes take a bite of charcoal. Grinning as this performance goes on, the "ombiasy" tells his rivals that it will be a long time before they can have their clientele eat out of their hands like that. Sometimes, however, the clients have revolted and tortured the "ombiasy" to death. Some day this may be the fate of many of the tricksters who play upon the public credulity in more civilized lands.

If a child is of delicate health it is not unusual to have it eat with a dog. If this brings about strength or the youngster gets fat its name is changed to Mr. or Miss Dog-child. They have the alternative of giving the name of Mr. or Miss Cured-by-the-witch-doctor.

Always the witch doctor declares that he will bury the patient in his forehead if he doesn't get well, after the manner of Americans who say they will eat a thing if such and such an event does not befall. But the witch doctors take care to absent themselves for a period if things go wrong and the Malagasy is peculiarly forgetful and also forgiving. He is given to playing safe too, and knows that he may have to call in the witch doctor on another occasion and therefore cannot afford to abuse him.

The natives are taught to believe that sickness enters the body at the head and makes its way downward and finally issues through the great toe. Sometimes this toe is bruised and even amputated to hasten the departure of the disease from this last stronghold. So firmly do they believe this that they describe their symptoms as a feeling of a mouse running down inside their body and a mewing cat after it.

The "ombiasy" holds sway only because of the dense ignorance and superstition of the people. He understands this and feeds them with tales to fatten it. He has many methods of fastening himself upon the tribesmen. If the witch doctors can delude a few leaders they are assured a permanent power. There have been cases in which they made themselves agents of chiefs and even divided their income with them. They practice in a crude way the craft that has been used since the beginning of time to hold the ignorant in control and feast off them.

They have initiation ceremonies that are calculated to impress the natives with their power. A part of the rite is as mysterious as those of Eleusis. The chief "ombiasy" gets an ox and has a feast exclusively for the "ombiasys." This is held on the highest mountain and the tribesmen are permitted to view it only from afar. Novitiates are put through secret performances and sent on their way to the top of another high hill, but not so high as the one that belongs to the older

LACE MAKING

conjurors. Here the newly admitted members of the craft plant a banana tree and hang out their shingle, as it were. At these graduation exercises there is an exposure of the witch doctors of other tribes and their skill is pronounced as nothing compared to that of the group present. At the conclusion of the mummeries the people are permitted to appear carrying stones on their heads to build a house for the spirit that gives power to the new practitioners.

Judged by the Binet standards the natives vary widely in intelligence. Many of them have not even attained to the level of children; in fact are not born yet, as the Brahmins say, who declare that there must be several births before one gets to the summit. Their stories are simple and approach the plane of idiocy at times. So they tell of a boy who was working in a manioc patch. He went a distance to get something and as it was very warm he left his lamba over his hoe. When he returned he saw this object in the field and mistook it for a wild beast. The wind was blowing toward it so he fired the grass and moved ahead with the fire, shouting and swinging his arms to drive the thing away. It was too late to save his lamba and hoe when he discovered what a dunce he had been. Another tale recounts the adventure of a half-witted man with an animal called the "tandraka," a kind of tenrec, which makes a hissing sound that is similar to the sentence that in Malagasy means giving clothing to a person. The man heard the "tandraka" making this sound so he at once took off his garments and handed them over to the animal, which thanked him, donned them and became a wise person.

There is a story of a chieftain who had the habit of cracking marrow bones on the bald heads of dinner guests. He liked marrow and disliked baldheads and thus he made both ends of his desire meet. And this story may perhaps take the palm for stupidity: The pestle for grinding rice meal was too short for the mortar in which it was used so two strong men were given the task of stretching it. They pulled at it all night and then thought of cutting down the edges of the mortar, which they did after many hours of patient toil. They never once thought of making a new pestle, a task which would have consumed only a few moments.

The foregoing bits of the folk life and lore are only samples. When all the tales are gathered from over the great island there will be volumes of philosophy added to the world's fund and it will not all be valueless.

CHAPTER XXX
EMBRYOS, SILKWORMS AND LOCUSTS AS FOOD

SOME of the tribes of Madagascar will not eat eggs because they become hard instead of soft in cooking. Almost all of them, however, will eat an egg of any fowl and of the crocodile when it is ripe enough to contain near-hatched life, in which stage it will cook soft. In this respect they are like the Chinese, who prefer an egg with a well-developed chick in it. And we are not so far behind them when we eat squabs that are not much more than hatched, are unformed and differ only from the Malagasy style in that they are removed from the shell or the shell from them.

I have seen Malagasy eggs prepared and when I essayed devouring them found them to be our squabs in consistency and taste. When it came to cracking or breaking the skin of a crocodile egg and tackling a young crocodile I had hard work to conquer my squeamishness. I have eaten embryos of several things and once tackled a Persian lamb that is obtained at the expense of killing the mother sheep or goat and it was no worse than the fœtus of a crocodile or a bird. It is reported there are savages in New Guinea who eat unborn babes.

In Madagascar the gathering of crocodile eggs at their right season is as much of a business as the taking of turtle or tortoise eggs at the Galapagos and even more, because there are more Malagasies than Galapagos natives. One foreigner told me he had seen a Malagasy family take 500 crocodile eggs in a single day.

More wholesome and equally popular for food are grasshoppers and locusts. Of the latter particularly there is no lack. In the summer they come in clouds and are a joy to some and a devastation and a desolation to others. A man who has no crop to lose and wishes to lay in a supply of good food never thinks of the other fellow, but just gathers his supply and stores them away.

Often the locust is more of a scourge in Madagascar than in Argentina, where it is regarded as the child of the devil. They come in such swarms as to leave no green thing on tree or shrub, and rice and manioc and everything else they can devour is done for. They appear like a dense cloud that obscures the sun. The swarm comes to within two feet of the ground and extends upward out of sight. As the approach of the pests is reported—and the news flies even faster than the locusts before the wind—the natives rush hither and yon, some to their gardens and fields and others to fight the enemy. There is a din of shouting and shrieking and striking with cloths and lambas to drive them on to the next place before they alight. The hope of the natives is to keep them going until they pass the fields and finally come down in the uncultivated regions. There they dig shallow holes of great area into which the locusts are swept. Then they take as many as they wish to eat and burn the remainder. If they cannot keep them in flight the locust eaters catch them in large deep baskets woven for the purpose. All they have to do is to thrust the basket into the low flying swarm and it is full in a jiffy. This is done mostly by women and children. There is no such thing as famine in Madagascar. If the crops fail or are eaten the people eat locusts and other insects, worms and wild things. There is no land in the world where there is so little worry over the paramount question of food.

Locusts are prepared for food by cooking them a short time and then removing the wings and legs. In order to preserve them they are half boiled and then dried in the sun. As they are drying they are winnowed often and thus they are not only desiccated evenly but the extremities, which are objectionable, are lost. All forward looking housewives in Madagascar have a goodly supply of dried locusts on hand. They are to be had in the great public markets, whither they are carried in hundreds of huge shallow baskets. When these dried locusts are eaten they are first soaked and then fried in oil in earthen dishes.

The silkworm in the chrysalis stage is as much esteemed for food as the locust and these also are to be found in the markets and in well provisioned homes. I saw more silkworms in the markets of the Betsileo country than elsewhere and especially in the region about Imamo. There was no dearth of them through Imerina, but in most places not so many as in Imamo, for here the tapia edulis is autochthonous and plentiful. This is the food of the Madagascar silkworm and they are to be found in large numbers where it flourishes. Not at all second to the silkworm and the locust and grasshopper is a kind of big, fat, sweet spider. Once I had a delicious stew made from spiders, locusts, silkworms, grasshoppers, fish, manioc meal, rice and suet. When I ate it for the first time I did not know what it was made of, but fuller information did not prevent my enjoyment of the bug and worm stew several times afterwards.

Over the world generally I have eaten and enjoyed the food of the country, although I was disposed to draw the line at eggs ripe with the young bird. When I have done so in company with cosmopolitan natives they invariably take me to task for balking at their fine food and then eating rotten limburger or, worse yet to them, an oyster which they describe as being all belly, guts, and contents. If they ever find out what chitterlings are they will add them to the queer things Americans eat and never wink an eye. Surely intellectual elasticity may be measured by what a person will eat.

CHAPTER XXXI
INFANTICIDE NOT UNCOMMON

THE practice of killing their children is common in Madagascar. This heartless and worse than brutish custom is prevalent in many parts of the world among the tribes low in the scale of civilization. It is shocking to find it prevailing among the Malagasy because they are as civilized in many respects as any people. Nor is it or the kindred crime, abortion, resorted to as a measure of birth control. The Malagasies love children and many of them have large families that are tenderly reared and cared for lovingly. These same people will kill their babes if they happen to be born on days that are considered unlucky. These days are not always the same. They are determined by a set of charlatans called "panandro," or, as nearly as may be translated, astrologers. They decide the destiny or "vintana" of the child soon after it is born.

In fact, the mother does not dare to give rein to her feelings of love until she knows whether the child is to be permitted to live. In case its death is decreed it is much the same as if it never had been born or the mother had not carried it. Strange as this attitude may seem psychologically it is of such ancient origin that there is really no birth according to Malagasy ideas unless it falls on a day that will permit of a favorable augury. The worst of it is that these miserable "panandro" hold out the hope that if there is sufficient material appeasement of the gods the fate of the child may be insured to be lucky. Naturally the result of this is that the murder of babes is much more common among the poor. Inability to pay the "faditra" or reward to the gods, which of course goes to none other than the "panandro" makes it almost certain death for the new-born babe.

There are several very terrible methods of child murder. One way is to fasten the helpless little thing in the entrance of a cattle yard. Then cattle are driven madly through. If the child escapes being trodden to death, which is most unlikely, it is declared that there is some reason superior to the dictates of the evil gods for its salvation and there is great rejoicing. Almost invariably the tender little body is cut to pieces by the sharp cloven hoofs of the beasts. In too many instances the babe is not even given this slender chance. It must die and there must not be a mistake about it. Nor is there. The infant is suffocated. A round rice bowl with one side deeply concave is filled with water. The little one is held face down in this until it is dead. Now and then they cover the mouth of the babe with a piece of cloth to expedite the crime. Yet another way that is even more hellish is to dig a hole in a secluded spot near the village, fill it with warm water, tie a rag over the mouth and stick the babe in head down. Then the earth is filled in hastily and the child is actually buried alive. Within a day or so the murdered infant is buried near the house of the parents, on the south side. This is according to the god devil's decree. Afterwards the parents, who have attended to all these heartless and unnatural acts, rub red earth on their clothing, then dry them and shake them, which removes the evil spirits and cures the sorrow that they might feel otherwise.

Abortion is also resorted to by the poor and by those women who have no visible means of support. It is not frowned upon. Advocates of birth control are not as fair and square as these people who directly and simply resort to the practice of child murder as an admitted convenience to themselves while the cretins of civilization pretend that it is for the good of society. Radama I took humane and practical steps to check child murder in Madagascar, but with his passing there was a return to it in quite as diabolical form as before. This humane prince issued a proclamation to the people prohibiting the killing of any child that the "panandro" decreed must die. In order to make it more effective he declared that all condemned children automatically by their condemnation became the adopted children of the King and that anyone murdering or in any manner making away with a child of the monarch would be executed with torture and without trial.

Thenceforward during the reign of Radama there was no more child killing after actual birth, except in Imamo which, upon surrendering its independence to Radama, stipulated that there must be no interference with the "panandro" and that children born to die in the tragic manner prescribed by those worthies must not be absolved. In Imamo alone

were superstition and the "panandro" who dictated the treaty stronger than loyalty to the country and the ruler. Everywhere else women were glad of an excuse to set the diviners adrift and they were proud to have their children called the King's; indeed they often changed the date of birth from a lucky to an unlucky date.

When the time for the birth of a child approaches the house is prepared for the event by partitioning off a temporary room in the big living apartment of the home. The floor is of mud; so it is easy to dig holes that are required for posts and these are set and fastened so that they will sustain hanging mats and form a place of privacy. A straw pallet is arranged upon the floor. Care is taken to dry the house. This is attended to by those whose duty it is to keep birth fires burning for ten days before the day. The midwife and nurse in well-to-do families take charge a few days before and the mother is purified by both rites and treatment. While this is going on there is feasting and many visitors of both sexes.

The native name for the midwife is "mpampivelona," meaning strictly "those that cause to live." Men are never employed in obstetrics. The native accoucheuses almost never lose a case of confinement. If the birth of a child occurs in a prominent family there is a resort to "androtsy-maty," which is no more than a moratorium in the matter of sex morals. All semblance of marital ties are set aside and there is common sex indulgence even among children for three days. This was so disgusting to a British agent, a Mr. Hastie, that he reported it to his government and was instructed to make a formal remonstrance against it. But the natives paid attention to the remonstrance only until some queen or princess was confined and then there was no staying the insane orgy of lust.

Immediately after a child is born the relatives and friends troop in to felicitate the mother and salute the infant and of course to eat. A tender piece of meat is cut into thin slices and hung on a cord that is stretched across the room. This is a treat for the mother and is called "kitoza."

The story that is told commonly in Madagascar that the children of the Hovas are perfectly fair at birth and only turn olive-hued with age is not true. This is an invention to establish superiority over the other tribes. Hova babies at birth are cute little green things and resemble human olives.

There is a custom of scrambling for food which takes place when there is a first-born babe. Relatives and friends assemble and fat from the hump of a cow is taken and minced fine in a dish. Then it is cooked with a mixture of rice, milk, honey and a kind of grass called "voampamoa." Plenty of hair from the head of the baby is added and the mess is stirred continuously as it cooks. When it is done the dish is held by the youngest girl of the family and all of the women, and women only, scramble for the contents. They sometimes come to blows, for the ones who succeed in getting a hair of the infant are certain soon to become mothers.

Names of children are arbitrarily given and have no relation to the name of either the mother or the father. Several times during a lifetime there may be change of name and this is specially true if there is change in residence and there are others of the same name encountered. It is also very common for the parents to alter their name to that of their son if he becomes rich and powerful.

CHAPTER XXXII
THE BURIAL OF A KING

KING RADAMA was dead. On the forenoon of August 3, 1828, it was officially proclaimed that the monarch "had retired," "had gone to his fathers."

This news was at once followed by a proclamation that all of every age and sex, barring chronic cripples and the bald-headed, must shave their heads. The order went much further and required all women to weep for a week; that no ostentatious clothing nor any jewels should be worn; that perfumes and hair oils should go into the discard during the period of official mourning; that only the lamba of purest and cleanest white should be worn; and that this must not be allowed to trail upon the ground.

Nor was this all. No one of either sex might ride upon an ox or be carried in a filanjana; all work except that necessary to existence had to be discontinued; all persons had to refrain from speaking upon

meeting and should not even salute or ask about each other's health; all musical instruments were to be kept dumb; dancing and singing were not to be engaged in; no bed should be occupied and no sleeping done except upon the ground; no one might sit on a chair or eat at a table and finally, greatest stress was laid upon the injunction not to drink toaka on penalty of being beheaded.

My authority for this remarkable proclamation is William Ellis, a missionary of the London Missionary Society, who gathered the facts of the funeral from other missionaries who were present and wrote down all details. The Ellis account was sent to London in 1830 and published in his history of missionary beginnings in the great island.

The walls of the palace were covered with white cloth and so was the building called Besakana or the house of the kingdom. Over the white background were hung tapestries of rich crimson and purple silk. All the gateways to the royal enclosure were hung with banners of pink and red silk. Brilliant red satin covered the roof of the edifice in which the king "had retired." Richest gold laces and fringes were made use of everywhere to emphasize the gorgeousness. The royal guards were dressed in their most showy uniforms and surrounded the palace grounds. All officials and the members of the royal band wore white lambas over their uniforms, as white is the mourning color in Madagascar. Cannons in all the batteries were fired every half hour and there was an attempt to give the death salvos a smothered effect by discharging the guns into dense piles of thickly matted debris. Queen No. I sent hundreds of cattle to be divided among the masses. The din was kept up until the morning of August 11, when it was increased. Cannon firing and rounds of musketry began at daybreak, and were repeated on the half hour. By 8 o'clock in the morning all the military of the kingdom had assembled at Antananarivo, the capital, and made an imposing array. Tens of thousands had come into the capital during the long period between the time of death and the day set for the funeral. These were massed almost miles deep, but there was no confusion nor disorder. The only spaces anywhere were those narrow pathways through the crowds left for the passage of the

AN ANCIENT TOMB IN THE FOREST

mourners and the officers of burial. Troops made a tunnel from Trano-vola, where the king died, to Besakana, where the body was carried this day to be laid in state.

As the cortege proceeded it was closely hemmed in by the royal bodyguard; an hundred bending, posturing, singing girls mournfully intoned as they repeatedly bowed their heads and touched the ground; another hundred maidens carried funeral fans that are always borne with a royal corpse to the grave.

There were groups of youths of fine appearance, but they apparently did nothing more than serve as contrast to the girls.

By 9 o'clock all was in readiness for the mourners to pass the catafalque for a last glance at the remains. All the wives of the king and bevies of pretty princesses and the wives of the judges wept copiously, some of them hysterically and some sincerely. During the whole ceremony a huge drum was struck dolefully as at military burials. At 11 o'clock the corpse was brought out blanketed in gold and scarlet. Over all was a brilliant canopy supported by youths and the corners of it attached to cords that were held, as an act of honor, by Major General Brady, the English military officer in charge of the army; Coroller, a Frenchman and a Malagasy prince and general; Louis Gros, also French, the royal architect; and Rev. David Jones, a Welsh missionary representing the London Missionary Society.

When the coffin came into public view it was a signal for such moaning and wailing as would only be possible among a people who are temperamental and mercurial. Wherever the remains were borne the pall bearers walked on richest royal blue broadcloth. Just as the body as being borne to the throne, which is done at the funeral of kings, a huge fat bull was slain and the corpse was quickly carried over and suspended for a moment above the bloody and quivering remains. Then it was placed on the throne for a brief time and then carried before the queen No. I, who sat at the door of Maso Andro, the throne room. She tried to appear deeply affected. At another door was the youngest babe of the ruler with its nurse. A bier perfumed with the many fragrant spices and gums the island is famous for had been prepared and upon it was put the coffin, whereupon all retired except the bodyguard. Next morning as soon as the sun shone the obsequies were reopened for conclusion. The intimates of the king's household were permitted again to see the remains and many subjects were allowed to enter the palace yard. Over carpeting of blue broadcloth the coffin was borne to the tomb.

Before it was taken inside the vault seventy-two of the king's finest, sleekest and fattest bulls were killed then and there and the body of Radama was suspended over the pyramid that was formed of the bleeding carcasses.

The singing girls, prostrate on the ground, lined the way to the tomb and would not have budged even if trampled upon. They sang a dirge in a low dismal tone.

The vault was covered by an edifice temporarily erected and surrounded by a balustrade. The canopy was of white satin and there were many pillars ornamented with gold and scarlet bearing purple cords to which were attached the lamps and lustres that peculiarly belonged to the king. The coffin platform within the vault was built of rich woods, including native ebony and mahogany, inlaid with silver and gold. The coffin was of solid silver and massive, eight feet long, four and a half feet high and the same in width. It contained $14,000 worth of metal. Dollars were beaten into silver plates and these were silver riveted. Inside the railing of the tomb the royal mourners gathered and also a throng of young women dressed in white lambas with long black sashes draped effectively. The latter had large fans which they waved gracefully to and fro.

The mausoleum is imposing. It is erected on an artificial tumulus, built of red clay and rough stone. The building that surmounts it really has architectural merit and is strictly Malagasy. There is a suggestion of the barbarous but not baroque, with the refinement of Greece and the mazy weirdness of the Byzantine. There are two stories. On the ground floor is the dais and coffin. Upstairs is a room richly furnished and floridly ornamented. There are two chairs and a table covered with damask. Upon the table the favorite food of the king is kept fresh and a bottle of wine and a carafe of water. There are two glasses and all is kept ready for the spirit of the dead ruler to regale itself whenever it is hungry or thirsty. If it were not for the unusual surroundings one might imagine himself at the tomb of a chief of the Chippewa Indians somewhere in the region tributary to Lake Superior.

Like the Incas the Malagasies follow the custom of burying treasure with the corpse. In this instance enough was sent along with Radama to set him up in business, no matter in which place he wound up. More than a thousand articles went into his "huaco" (tomb).

The following is a partial list of the things buried in the tomb: 49 hats and caps, 155 coats and jackets, 96 waistcoats, 171 pairs of trousers, 53 pairs of gloves, 47 neckties, 54 pairs of socks, 37 shirts, 38 pairs of boots and shoes, 9 pairs of solid gold epaulets, 1 gold vase presented by George IV in 1822, two gold music boxes, 18 gold finger rings, 3 watches, 2 gold watch chains, 1 silver tureen and ladle, 2 large silver fruit and salad dishes, 1 gold spoon, 2 silver plates, 1 silver curry dish, 1 pair silver candlesticks, 4 mahogany writing desks inlaid with pearl, gold and silver, 1 cut glass chandelier, 24 looking-glasses, 1 pair of cut glass decanters, 4 cut glass plates, 1 gold-tipped spear, 2 fine gold sword sashes, 2 braces of pistols inlaid with gold, 10 swords and sabers, 1 shotgun with cleaning and loading tools, 24 muskets inlaid with gold and silver of the finest native workmanship, 1 air gun of gold and silver, 24 silver-mounted spears.

THE TOMB OF THE PRIME MINISTER, RAINIHARO

Six of the king's favorite horses were killed and buried with him. A hogshead of wine was buried immediately outside of the tomb. A brass cannon was loaded to the muzzle and fired and burst and the pieces gathered up and buried with the king. A sum total of 10,300 Spanish dollars was also cached with the dead royal pawn broker. Oxen to the number of 13,952 were distributed to the masses.

It is believed that a portion if not all of this treasure that was negotiable helped to make up the gold and money and plate that were given to Dr. Prince with which to rig out a navy to combat the French, as told in another chapter. Color is lent to this supposition by the fact that the dollars were marked so that they could be identified and it is said that some of the Prince dollars bore the mark of tomb money.

CHAPTER XXXIII
SEPULCHERS OF THE MALAGASIES

No tombs, ancient or modern, are more stately and impressive than those of the Hova kings. It is not easy to determine architectural values. If there was a distinctive sepulchral architecture in the Perso-Iranian period at its best, in the Byzantine period and the Alexandrian, the Mesopotamian and the Carthaginian, if we grant a distinctive quality to the builders of the Mughal tombs from Akbar to the Taj, or of the inlaid mausoleum of Timur, or to the work of the Victorians or even of the builders of today, which is the age of the finest construction the world has known, then the Malagasy sepulcher builders also are entitled to recognition.

The strange fact is that Malagasy architecture stopped with the building of tombs. No other part of their construction has attained to genuine artistic merit. The tombs are for the most part designed to be used by the entire family and that may mean many relatives also. Consequently they are commodious, a fact which gives the architect his opportunity.

As everywhere else in the world, the chief glories of sepulchral architecture are reserved for the royal tombs. No private person, however wealthy or powerful, may occupy a tomb approaching the royal tombs in grandeur.

It is a common belief in Madagascar that the dead like company and do not wish to be forgotten. 'So they bury them in the most public spot that can be found to be suitable. It may be near the home, or in the center of the village or on a sightly eminence or at the intersection of two or more roads. The latter is the preferred position because it is good advertising for the living and offers a chance to the dead persons to see and perhaps speak with the throngs of passers-by. The only secluded graves are those of lepers or of persons who are accursed.

The excavation for the mausoleum is proportioned to the anticipated number of occupants, but in no event is it small. Sometimes it is huge and the labor it involves is staggering when one considers the primitive methods of work. After the hole is dug—and it is more like a reservoir than anything else—it is lined with the greatest slabs of stone that can be handled and in this regard the Malagasy are not far behind the ancient Egyptians. Nor is any distance too great to drag the stones, which again reminds us of those who builded the pyramids and faced them with Abyssinian granite and syenite that were fetched more than a thousand miles.

It is not rare to see stones in a Malagasy tomb twelve feet square. They use all kinds of stone, but prefer granite and marble. They class the beautiful red syenite as granite and work it with artistic skill. In truth they are surpassed by few workers in stone. The stone-walled subterranean room is covered with earth and then stone and then more earth until they have made a stepped pyramid of imposing appearance. It never points up to an apex and sometimes it is stepped only on one side, with a commodious platform at the top. Tombs thus built are sometimes eighty feet long and thirty feet wide. The height is determined by native standards of proportion.

In Madagascar there is a beautiful quartz which may be rose or pink or white and is of great brilliancy. This is used to crown the tomb and may be seen in the sunlight for miles and miles. In form these monuments have counterparts in South America in the Incan and Araucanian epochs and similar ones have been unearthed in the South Sea Islands. I know personally of like tombs in Mexico and Central America and in South America but not in the South Seas, although I have sailed them from one sky to the other.

The Malagasy has known for ages how to fire rock with burning cow dung and then when just right to play on a stream of water from a huge gourd and break the rock in any manner desired. In order to satisfy the witch doctors who must have a part in everything they use their "odys" or rock charms and pretend to think that these do the work. No sooner is a piece quarried than it is bound thickly with straw so that it will not be broken. Then ropes are attached and the stone is hauled out of its place and started for its destination. When they encounter a hill rollers are used and the big burden is edged and pulled and pushed with skill and patience.

It is recorded that more than six hundred men have been engaged in moving a single stone. The foreman rides on the stone and all hands obey him in every detail. The teamwork is perfect. The foreman's function is to sing or grunt or mark time so that they can exert themselves together. He yells all the time, but the workers know the meaning of it all and there are few mistakes. Often the foreman holds a cloth in his hand and waves it in time with his cries. Sacred water is sprinkled on the stone whenever there is a breathing spell and in addition the medicine men follow and chant and rub it with charms.

What with groans and cries and much good medicine, and the most essential of all, elbow grease, the mighty stone is gotten to its place. If it happens that the tomb has not been built until after the occupant has died there is perfect silence so that they may get him in before the gods find out about the neglect. If tombs are not covered with the sparkling quartz they are painted or whitewashed and make a proud showing.

After a burial it is the custom to fasten the heads and horns of the cattle slain for the funeral feast on stout poles and erect them in a circle around the grave. When there is a greater number of horns than usual, indicating wealth, they are also stuck into the ground and built into a horn fence. As many as ten thousand cattle have been killed for a single funeral feast. So important is it to be properly buried and marked that many of the natives begin to construct their tombs early in life and build them as they can afford to do so. These forehanded persons have the best tombs if they are not tempted to sell them to some one who has succeeded better than they. This is a common source of revenue.

To give an idea of a person's economic standing it is quite the thing to say of him that he has a costly tomb under way. The coffin is also an important consideration, but is secondary to the monument. Even lepers may have the satisfaction of a pretentious burial after they have reposed in the ground for a year.

More than one Malagasy will impoverish himself for a tomb because he argues that he will occupy it longer than his house on earth, which is a safer bet than oil stocks.

CHAPTER XXXIV
HUNTING WILD CATTLE

THE spreading plains of the island teem with wild cattle. These fine game cattle also seek the woods at seasons and take to them for hiding as do their kindred, the buffalo of Africa. In fact, as game, they are in a class with the buffalo. When they are wounded or cornered they make deadly rushes and show no sign of timidity. Many a native has been killed and the cattle will fight until they expire in their tracks.

I hunted them with the same weapons and in the same way as I did the African buffalo. The wild cattle of Madagascar are more agile than the buffalo and

like them have a way of lying in wait for the hunter after they are mortally wounded and attacking him from the rear after he has passed and is not likely to be prepared. The only safe way is to be on guard every moment. They are not less keen than the buffalo and are off before one can get in range unless the very best stalking methods are followed.

Sometimes they are driven towards the hunter by a great crowd of beaters. This method does not require much skill, but there is plenty of danger, as no one can say what the beasts will do when in a frenzy of fear. The only thing that makes them easier to hunt is that they are more numerous than buffalo in the best African hunting grounds. When these wild cattle of Madagascar are wounded and charge the hunter they do so with a deep bellowing roar that is more ominous than the roar of a lion. I consider them more dangerous to hunt than the lion and in some respects more dangerous than the African buffalo, which most big game hunters agree in declaring to be the most dangerous beast in Africa and quite equal to the tiger of the north Siberian wilds, the fiercest of all the tigers. The wounded wild bulls of Madagascar will repeatedly charge home and as they are so much more active than the African buffalo with all their stealth and strategy they are bad customers. They are not humped like the native tame cattle of the island and have short, sharp, wicked horns. Wild cattle hunting is the chief sport of the kings and nobles of the island; each petty head of a tribe being designated as a king and his subordinates as chiefs and nobles. The French occupation has not done away with this custom and it will be a long time before it does. In the old monarchial régime the big king was denominated the king of all the island.

Robert Drury, who was a captive for a number of years on the island two hundred years ago, described wild cattle hunting in detail. He went several times with his master. As he was a slave he was not at first permitted to do more than work, carry and look on. Later, when he had won the confidence of his owner, he was permitted to hunt. His description of the hunt is worth quoting.

"The darkest nights are always chosen for the hunt. I begged to be allowed to hunt with the big party. They consented, but first ordered me to bathe myself thoroughly as they had done in order to remove all the human smell and other odors that accumulate on a person in Madagascar. All the best hunters carried two lances, but they would only allow me one as two might rattle in my hand, they said, because I was unaccustomed to carrying lances. The wild cattle feed only at night and if every precaution were not taken we should never come up with them. They are always alert and on guard. We could hear them snorting and bellowing and thus located them and knew there were a great number. The first thing to do was to get the cattle to leeward and then we approached as stealthily as possible. As we approached them we kept pulling grass as nearly like the sound of cattle feeding as we could make. Cropping the top of the grass with our hands, or to be accurate the most expert hunters did this, we soon got to where they heard us. Then there was no more noise from the cattle. They tried to locate the coming danger and seemed to be listening and scenting intently. For a time all the hunters kept a perfect silence except that three or four of the most skillful pulled grass at the tops to make the cattle think it was another bunch of their kind that was near and eating in safety. After a time the cattle continued feeding, which we could plainly hear as they nipped and pulled at the forage. As still as possible we worked nearer to them and at last we were among them and one of the hunted stuck a spear into a cow. She grunted and lunged as if gored by another animal and to this the herd paid no attention, thinking it an occurrence that is common among them. The hunters speared four and then retired to await the light, as it is very dangerous to approach them in the dark when they are wounded. Next morning we followed the wounded ones by the trail of blood and came upon some of them dead and others dying. The latter had concealed themselves in dense cover and one of them charged and wounded a hunter, but not fatally. We also ran into a herd of savage wild hogs and had a fight with them. We killed seven, but not until several of our dogs had been hurt."

The Malagasy also capture the wild bulls in pits and have bull fights; not between a matador and a bull, but between two bulls.

The British' agent, Mr. Hastie, tells in his journal of October 11, 1824, of being with King Radama on an expedition. He said that the supplies for the army of attendants ran low and that they went after wild cattle to replenish them. Two battalions were detailed for the hunting and they went forth in four parties for the purpose of surrounding the cattle. Before the actual attack and when the game was in full view the men were halted and ordered to lay down their guns and spears with their muzzles pointing to the rear until an aged chief might pray for success. This he did in the following eloquent terms:

"O thou great Rangora, master of these superb plains and herds, be it known to thee that the mighty king Radama, attended by a formidable army, is thy visitor. It will only be consistent with thine own dignity and with his exalted rank as governor of the earth, a king unequaled by any other king, that thou shouldst present him with a part of thy superabundant stock, for the use of his attendants. Be it known to thee, O Rangora, that the wants of the mighty king are bounded but that his liberality is without bounds; he is slow in accepting but lavish in bestowing favors. He comes not in hostile array but as thy visitor in amity. O you Kotofotsy and Taihana, guardians of your great master's innumerable flocks, let it be your care to do him honor in the selection of the presents that he may order for the use of this royal visitor so that we, his attendants, may partake of such fare as will induce us to make favorable representations of your attentions to our mighty king and thereby entitle you to his beneficent consideration. We again repeat that we come in amity and claim your hospitable entertainment during our sojourn with you."

All this was recited so loudly that the cattle were frightened away and had to be come up with again. But this was done and the hunters killed and salted down 346 besides wounding many, some of which were caught and slain.

Again, in February, 1825, Mr. Hastie went with Radama on a still bigger hunt. In the former hunt they had gone to the Sakalava Country on the border of Iboina. This time they proceeded to Manerina, 100 miles west of Antananarivo, the capital. It was a vast array of 3,000 soldiers that attended Radama and the sport was carried on after the style of Kublai in the plains of Shanhaikwan. Huge herds resembling the bison of the American prairies when they were at their greatest number were surrounded and more than 500 were slaughtered the first day. Drury tells of his master hunting crocodiles and as he always accompanied his master to do the work of a slave he had a good opportunity to observe how it was done. The weapon was a harpoon with a long staff and a steel point. A rope was fastened to the shank and Drury says it was made fast to both the handle and the point, but those I saw were attached only to the shaft. In a dugout they quietly approach the crocodile that has been sighted, much resembling a floating mass of weeds because a lot of stuff has caught against the body of the saurian and is permitted to remain as a hide. When they get within a short distance of the game but too far to harpoon, the crocodile dives and crawls along the bottom. The hunter keeps track of the quarry by the bubbles that rise to the surface. When these are stationary the pursuit is checked, for the animal will shortly rise for air. Before it can reach the surface they strike where the bubbles indicate the spot and pierce the belly, as the crocodile does not turn until about to expose itself. Thus they are able to make a kill. If the back is hit no impression whatever is made and the crocodile goes lunging away and is lost.

CHAPTER XXXV
SOME MALAGASY GAMES

BULL fighting and bull baiting and cock fighting are favorite sports. Another common sport is throwing for a chicken. The owner of the fowl buries it in the ground up to its neck with only the head protruding. Those who take part in the game throw stones at the head, at a fixed price per throw. If they hit the fowl it is theirs, but otherwise the owner gets the profit and he generally does, although the natives are skillful in both ordinary throwing and with slings.

A game that resembles somewhat one that is in vogue among the French is called "mamely dia manga," which means "striking blue with the sole of the foot." The kick must be backward, whereas the French way is forward. Astonishing skill is developed by the Malagasy in this blind sort of sport. Training begins as soon as a youth is big enough to deliver a kick and is continued until age binds the muscles. They play with such earnestness that ankles and legs are sprained and often broken. The blows are received as well as given by the feet and legs if the participants are skilled kickers. Not infrequently the blow is not parried and serious injury and even death results, but not more frequently than in American football. Armies of hundreds choose sides and engage in "mamely dia manga," which sounds like "maimed and mangled." They rush at each other and turn swiftly and kick backwards.

It reminds one of an early Chinese way of fighting with guns, as described in "Old Canton Days." The Chinese would thrust the gun at the enemy over their shoulders with their back to the foe. Then they would fire and run. The recoil gave them a good start and not much damage was done fore or aft.

Throwing bamboo spears at a target is taught to all youths. They have trials of strength by lifting and there is a game of putting the stone, which is similar to the putting of the shot in modern games.

It is a common thing to seize an unbroken bullock by the hump and mount him and stay on until the rider is thrown or the animal is exhausted and lies down. The bucking broncho has no movement that the Madagascar bull cannot imitate and as like as not go him one better. It reminds one of "dogging" a steer at an American rodeo, only the Madagascar bull is a worse actor.

The natives play a game that is similar to checkers. It is called "katra." Thirty-two square holes are cut in an oblong board. Pebbles or seeds are used as we use checkers. It is an intricate game and is a measure of intellect among the people. If a person is good at "katra" he is graded as able to do other things that involve head work. Often a smooth flat stone near the house is prepared for "katra" and in good weather they play out of doors.

THE VALIHA

CHAPTER XXXVI
MUSICAL INSTRUMENTS AND MUSIC

ALL pigmented peoples are fond of music. Their ears are not all attuned alike, but they are all attuned. Chinese music may be regarded as primitive and barbarous by moderns and it certainly sounds different from ours, unless we include jazz as music. The Celestials assert that it is our music that is elementary and they have as much right to their view as we have to ours. In a way they have the best of the argument, as they have been making sounds according to rule for centuries to our decades.

The buzzing of a bee at summer noontide, the faint vibration of a butterfly's wing, the song of the throstle, the roar of a Mosi O'Tunya or Iguasu, the play of water over the pebbles, all are music, but they are not jazz nor do they follow the rules of the so-called human masters. I have seen a black boy walk for hours naked and barefooted through thorns and under the sun of the equator in Africa twanging a string held between his teeth, in complete oblivion of poisonous snakes and deadly beasts.

Pope stole the saying from Aristotle that discord is music not understood. Whom Aristotle stole this truth from I do not know nor care, for it is a universal possession. Somewhere between the Chinese and the children of Chosen, between the black boy and the modern nocturne the Malagasy comes into the realm of music.

There are three native musical instruments peculiar to the island or perhaps only two that are exclusively theirs, for the drum belongs to the world. Two is a lot. The one that is most popular and that I liked best is the "valiha." I brought one home with me and try to play it, but without much success. It is of bamboo, as long as the distance between the joints of the reed and enough more to hold it with. Eight strips are cut and pried loose from the bark or skin of the bamboo. These are almost as tough as wire and vibrate at a touch. They are made into sizes as are violin strings. Bridges are made of plugs of wood and are arranged to form a scale of sound. The "valiha" is played by strumming, like the guitar and banjo. It makes a more appealing and delicate note than anything of catgut that I have ever heard, but has no such possibilities of range as a violin. The hollow bamboo is its own perfect sounding board. Nearly all natives can and do play on it and sweet music it is, with much variation. It is a far better instrument than the ukulele.

The other instrument that is peculiarly Malagasy is the "lokanga." This is the instrument of slaves and the lower and poorer classes as the "valiha" is the Cremona of the classes. The "lokanga" is made from a calabash and I have seen a similar instrument in the south of the United States made from a gourd by the Negroes. The calabash is the belly and there is a slender, crooked piece of wood attached to it. To the neck thus formed from one to four strings of shredded bamboo are strung. Generally there is but one string. On this one they thrum as did my black boy of the Kalahari. And not much more of a tune can be played than on the one string that the Bushmen once held in their mouths. But it is music and the Malagasies like it.

They are almost as fond of singing as of speaking at "kabaries" and in public. With an orchestra made of "lokanga," a flute as primitive as Pan's, a drum made of a hollow piece of log over which has been stretched a skin, they will make a chorus that has volume and is good to listen to for a short time. I have heard them sing in the mission churches and they do it with their hearts as well as their voices. And I have heard a solitary native humming to himself and women too, and as they did so they would finger their ears, stopping and half filling the aural orifice in order to modulate the volume of sound. Our own children do this very thing and I remember doing and enjoying it myself.

When Malagasies sing in chorus without an instrument they clap their hands to aid in keeping time and it serves to deaden or distract the sound. As a rule they are powerful singers and some of their music has color and dash and emphatic qualities of expression.

Radama had a great choir made up of hundreds of girls. These were trained from childhood. There were also court choirs of boys. Once in a while these sang together. Both accompanied the monarch upon all state journeys and the people would go as far to hear them as to see the sovereign.

They have many songs and a national hymn. They do not know it much better than Americans know the Star-Spangled Banner, so the leader repeats each line of the song before it is sung, as is still done in Negro churches in Georgia and elsewhere. The chorus is as follows:

"Rabodo does not tread upon the ground;
　　(does not walk; is carried)
　The Rabodo of Andrian-Ampoin-Imerina;
Rabodo does not trample on the people;
　　Long live his great life."

"Rabodo" tramples on the people all over the world and he does now in Madagascar more than ever, for he is now a foreigner who is benevolently assimilating them with more emphasis on the assimilation than on the benevolence.

In the evening there is singing and playing on the "valiha" and the "lokanga" in the homes. When it is moonlight and fair many gather ·on the bank of a stream or lake and sing, clap their hands, dance and enjoy themselves. In the country the singing is more common and better than in' the towns.

There are travelling minstrels who go from one end of the land to the other and give entertainment without charge. They are given food and clothing and are very popular and make really fine music. The nearest they come to commercializing their art is to accept rice and a lamba and a bed.

We sell everything. Art has a commercial basis it

LEFT TO RIGHT, STANDING: SODINA (FIFE), KIJEJA (HARP), AMPONGABE (DRUM), ANZOMBONA (SEA SHELL); SEATED: KIMPANTSONA (CYMBALS), VALIHA, LOKANGA (VIOLIN)

it can attain it. Fancy a brown thrasher charging a fee for the sweetest song on earth. In Madagascar the singer will extemporize on any occasion or for any event, whether funeral or wedding. They are also musical mimics. One of my boys would sing so nearly like a bird that for a long time he fooled me. That was partially due, no doubt, to the dullness of my ears.

At a funeral I heard what at first seemed to be a most doleful groaning, but I found that it was a groaning song. They are musical—the Malagasies.

CHAPTER XXXVII
MODES OF TRAVEL & TRANSPORTATION

IT is said that before the conquest by the French there was not a horse on the entire island and certainly there were not many; for there are very few now. The principal way of getting about was to walk, ride an ox or be carried. All who could afford it were carried. There is no palanquin in the world just like the one called a filanjana used by the Malagasies. Even to-day in all the larger towns stout fellows with no covering except a loin cloth will solicit you to be carried. Sometimes they will wear what the South Africanders call shorts, which are exactly the same as athletic running pants. Wearing not even sandals on their feet but with a big and finely woven hat on the head they are a working picture.

In respect to hat and bare feet they are similar to the Mexican, who is always in full dress if he has a good sombrero. These filanjana men are as fine types of native as can be seen in the big island. They will carry one far in a day and on rather scant subsistence. In respect to fueling their bodies they are outclassed by Chinese rickshaw men. Before I had personal experience with the coolie, who runs all day and then all night without food, I was of the opinion that Dr. Smith in his splendid "Chinese Characteristics" had been imposed upon. It was his experience that the coolies would travel for him for almost a week without food because they had board by the week at their point of departure and could get food when they returned without further outlay. I discovered that Dr. Smith was not only well within bounds in this respect, but accurate in all others.

The filanjana, pronounced with accent on the third syllable, and the "j" as an "s," is a very comfortable uncomfortable thing. It has two parallel rails of native teak. These are fastened together by bars that are just as light as they can be and still give required strength. The ends of the bars are flattened so as not to cut the shoulders of the bearer. In the middle between the bars a chair of the same material is slung. It has back and foot rests and is as nearly balanced as may be. These chairs are always made adjustable so that the weight of a very heavy person may be distributed and the strongest bearers may have the share they can handle. If there are three bearers the load is shifted so that the end that has two men will be nearer to the burden. For short journeys two men are sufficient, but for long trips of some hundreds of miles it is better to have a dozen or so in order that they may not play out. However, four men will ordinarily carry a person as far as he wishes to go.

In some parts the filanjana men are loath to go more than a certain distance from home. When they have gone as far as they care to go they insist that others be procured so that they may return to their homes.

When I was first in Madagascar I weighed a little under two hundred pounds. I have had two men trot a considerable distance with me and then drop into a swinging walk and climb very steep hills,

of which there are many in Antananarivo. I never permitted carriers to bear me either in Thibet or Madagascar or elsewhere farther than would give me an opportunity to study them and test them out. In the Himalayas I tried the palanquins as a bearer more than once and after I got accustomed to breathing at the altitudes I was vain enough to think that I could make my living in that way if I had to. Also I found that by aiding the carriers instead of working them to the last notch I got more out of them and enjoyed being with them, for they would tell me the stories of their lives and were never sullen. They were a happy lot. It isn't overwork that is killing the world, but rather the superciliousness of those who arrogate to themselves a human superiority they do not possess; who insist upon taking too much of the increment away from those who work. I have been among the wild peoples of the earth and found them happy as a general rule. If they were not happy it was because some of the adventurous seeds of our so-called civilization had started to sprout in their midst. Can there be wonder that our ways kill savages when they can be depended upon to kill us?

No outright savage tribe has produced an Andrew Carnegie or a type like him. Better far, they say, a Radama or a Dingan Zulu, or a Tchaka, or a Cetawayo or a Lobengula or even a Sitting Bull.

But I must watch or my filanjana will get away from me. One has to get used to riding in it and' when this is once accomplished it is not a bad conveyance. The feet can hang down and one has a choice of many postures. One may foreshorten the body like Noah in Michael Angelo's Last Judgment in the Sistine Chapel, or sit erect and be a man. The filanjana is as comfortable as the terrible tarantass of Persia. When one recalls that Madagascar is a thousand miles long and at places more than four hundred miles wide and that the filanjana was and is now almost the only resort of travelers who cannot or will not walk its importance is obvious.

On journeys of sufficient magnitude to require baggage it is necessary to have men who carry loads on their heads. At this sort of thing the Malagasy is better than the average Swahili, who are used for the same purpose on "safari" in Africa. Streams are crossed in various ways, from a woven suspension bridge made from fibre to swimming and wading.

Noone thinks of traveling where there are many rivers to be forded without providing several "odys" as protection from snakes, of which there are very few that are poisonous, and from biting spiders and crocodiles. The medicine men sell as many of these as of other charms. When the stream to be crossed is entered the "ody" is displayed to the saurian, but great care is taken by the travelers at the same time to make all the noise their lungs are capable of and also to lash the water into a foam with branches of trees and to splash with their hands and legs. This may frighten the crocodiles away and make the "ody" a good charm. If it were not for such assistance given to the "ody" the crocodiles would not realize its magical efficacy and would eat the holder of it.

Once in a big pool in the Lundi river in Africa I shot a huge hippopotamus. It sank and as soon as fermentation set in it floated. When it appeared, after being down less than two hours, myriads of crocodiles had found it and were on the point of devouring it. Inasmuch as I had killed it for my boys and they were hungry and particularly had their appetites up for hippopotamus, they made haste to rescue it from the demon-eyed and hungry throated monsters that surrounded it as completely as a barbed wire entanglement.

My crew had been joined by others and there must have been two hundred in all. Those who wore any clothing at all doffed it and in a jiffy there was a mob of naked blacks in the water. And around the feast was a ring of big beady eyes that glistened in the sunlight. It was a contest of hungry and eager forces. Surely the crocodiles would eat several of the blacks, I thought. Not so; they dived and left the scene, so furious was the human charge. Not one of them, curiously enough, as they were wild negroes, had a charm of any kind except a hungry belly. If they had had an "ody" they would have sworn, as do the poor Malagasies, that it had done the work.

The boats and canoes of Madagascar are not so highly developed as those of most insular peoples and they are in no sense maritime as are tropical islanders generally. The reason for this is that Madagascar is so large that most of the natives do not know it is an island, or at least do not regard it as such.

Along some streams they say it is bad luck to use a canoe. Apparently it was feared that the natives might get away or wander or get beyond control if the canoe habit were formed; hence those who establish laws, customs, and superstitions gave currency to the convenient belief that canoes are unlucky.

Along the coasts there are few harbors and the dhow-like vessels that ply along the shore are clumsy and not suited to long voyages, although they are seaworthy enough.

There is an extended and useful natural coastal canal, called by the natives the Pangalan or Ampanalana, along the east side of the island. On this there is a regular fleet of canal boats. It has more depth and continuity than most waterways of the kind. Formed by an age-old conflict between east coast rivers and the sea, it stretches for miles. When a river has finally broken into the sea and has deserted the lagoon that it had formed, its mouth is again dammed by the insweeping sands driven by the tide and currents of the Indian Ocean. This forces the river to pursue its search for another opening. Several rivers are intercepted in the process and all join to form this coastal canal. Narrow hogback barriers lie between the lagoons, some of which have been cut so as to permit continuous passage. The effect is a valuable natural coastal canal over three hundred miles long, more navigable than any river on the island, not excepting the largest, the Betsiboka. With thirty miles of cuts through barriers half the east coast of Madagascar would be connected by a perfectly protected coastal waterway.

It is safe to say that before the coming of the French the great island was in a more primitive state so far as transportation is concerned than any other populous territory in the world.

The French have started systems of railways and automobile roads that will in time revolutionize transportation, permitting the new rulers to get at the natives with more facility. Compared with what is planned and is necessary very little has been done as yet. When I was on the island the railroad was well on its way from the capital to Fianarantsoa and was completed and running perfectly between Tamatave on the coast and the capital, a total of about two hundred miles. Work on the railway projects was stopped by the World War and is just now again claiming attention.

Colonel Miles Carroll of Antsirabe, wrote to me as follows, of date February 14, 1922:

"The rail to Antsirabe is not yet complete. We are, however, promised the train at the end of this present year. We shall also have electric light this year and water laid in early next year. The town is being boosted and we expect to have quite a lot of visitors on account of the wonderful baths. I send you a few photos of buildings at Antsirabe erected since you left. It is said the rails will be pushed on to Betafo, west of here, and to the south. It will be linked up with either the S.E. or S.W. coast. There are fine openings for trade, but not with America on account of the high duties."

The Paris government, through the Economic Bureau of the French Republic for Madagascar and Dependencies, No. 40 rue Général Foy, reported to me April 3, 1922, the status of the railroad situation in Madagascar as follows:

There exist on the Grande Île (Madagascar) four lines or sections of railway now in operation:

1st. The Tananarive-Tamatave line; length 369 kilometres, in operation the whole length.

2nd. The Tananarive-Antsirabe line; 154 kilometres, only 65 kilometres from Tananarive to Ambatolampy in operation now.

3rd. The tram car line from Moramanga to Lake Alaotra, at present in operation from Moramanga to Anosira, a length of 98 kilometres.

4th. The suburban street car line from Tananarive to Ambohidratrino; a first section of five kilometres of which has recently been put in operation.

CHAPTER XXXVIII
WHAT THEY KNOW OF AMERICA

THERE is an idea generally prevalent in Madagascar that all Americans are Negroes. This comes from the fact that the American consul, Mr. James G. Carter, is a big, capable, handsome Negro. He was the only Yankee representative on the island and when I was there he was stationed at Tamatave on the coast, a deadly place, but the largest town on either seaboard.

Other consular representatives, including the most able of them all, Mr. Thomas P. Porter, recently consul general of Great Britain in America, were at a decided advantage over Mr. Carter. They had headquarters at the capital. When our consul wanted anything he could not get he would resort to Mr. Porter, who was most friendly to the States and skillful as an Allenby, and it would come through.

Consul Carter insisted on being courteous to Mrs. Osborn and me as he does not see Americans often and when he does it is generally a poor lot who need help and want money or some assistance. One of the ways he took to be kind was to give us a state dinner. There were present the consuls of all the nations that have representatives in Madagascar. Of course Mrs. Osborn, who is a pronounced blonde, was escorted to the table by the United States Consul, who is a big yellow buck Negro. No one seemed to notice the situation but myself, so I pretended as thoroughly as I could that I did not. We had a course dinner that would have been creditable in Paris or anywhere. I found Consul Carter to be one of the most capable of the consular officers of America.

Mr. Nathaniel Stewart, of Georgia, as one of the United States supervising consuls, visited Madagascar in 1917 to inspect the service there. It was the first inspection ever made of the American consulate in the island. Now Mr. Stewart is a Southern gentleman. His charming wife was a Cobb, of the flower of the queen state of the South. How generously considerate a Southern gentleman may be is shown by his treatment of the Negro consul in Madagascar. Mr. Stewart was so big and fair that he recommended that Mr. Carter be transferred to Antananarivo, the capital and placed upon a footing of maintenance with the other consuls and that his salary be increased commensurately with the volume of the work so well performed by him. This same attitude and action generally applied in the South might go a long way towards the solution of the black and white problem—or it might not!

One evening at a party at Tamatave there were black French officers with white wives and white French officers with black wives, and they all deported themselves, if anything, with more circumspection than the all whites. The color line is not drawn rigorously by the Germans and not at all by the French, unless possibly the French girls prefer pigmented husbands and lovers; not necessarily both at the same time.

I had a faithful servant who had been trained by the splendid missionaries and he was a rare help. The Malagasy is as quick-witted as the Tagal and much like him, only not so belligerent. Rijes could do anything for me that any one ever thought of doing in his land. He knew the snakes and the insects and the birds. And he was versed in folk tales and music and history. He could cook and draw; indeed, he essayed painting and could turn out a canvas far superior to any I could produce. But he did not know where America is and while he was willing to go home with me he had no sense of what it meant and wished to stipulate that he might return to his wife and children once a week. One day we were catching "grumongs" in the sapphire Indian sea and I tried to make Rijes understand, but it could not be done.

Down at Fort Dauphin there is a sturdy and most worthy American mission from which work is conducted over the island. The members are all Norwegians and as I recall, not one was a citizen of the United States. They all would be creditable as such. One of them had been in America. It is a Lutheran organization supported by this country. As we landed from a little coast trader we were welcomed by the music of the Star-Spangled Banner executed as well as I have sometimes heard it at home. "Executed" is the right word.

It was near Fort Dauphin that I secured a rare egg of the æpyornis. A missionary told me that he knew where there was one, more than a meter in circumference, in a cave. I asked him whether it could be got. He replied that it was worshipped as the source of the world by a considerable following and as the wizards were being discounted because of this fetich he thought it might be stolen or secured in some stealthy manner. In fact, he did not approve

of the "idol" himself and would do his best to find a man who would go to the cave and carry away the god in a shell. It proved to be a perfect specimen and may be seen in the collection of the University of Michigan at Ann Arbor. There are only a few of these gigantic eggs in the world.

In every part of the island I asked about America and very seldom found anyone who knew of such a nation as the United States of America. When I would tell them about our land they would listen with apparent incredulity and invariably asked me if there was really any such place or was I telling them a story just for entertainment? A few of the more highly educated asked interesting and intelligent questions. Even they were surprised when I told them there were more white than colored people in America. Then they would ask which class was in the ascendency and whether they liked each other and were on an equality.

All over the wild world, as in Madagascar, the tribes know next to nothing of America and make no distinction in their minds between the northern and southern continents. Repeatedly in Europe, also, I have been told by persons quite intelligent that they had relatives or friends in Rio or in Buenos Aires and I have been asked if I might know them when their names were told me.

One of the troubles the world has, and it is a major problem, is provincialism. We suffer from it less in America, I think, than elsewhere, but we are worse than all the others in thinking, when we think at all, that we are independent of the world generally, or even worse than that, that we are the most of the world ourselves.

Even our presidents have seldom thought in world terms. Lines of provincial thinking are being stretched all the time, but they are unspeakably local still.

There is a little mixed American blood in Madagascar from the ancient whaling days and some Malagasy blood in the Negroes of America dating from old slavery days, but it has been so completely submerged in the dominant ethnic trend that it is not of the least importance.

CHAPTER XXXIX
MINERALS OF MADAGASCAR

ALL of the useful minerals of the earth are found in some quantity in Madagascar and almost all the gems except the diamond. It is not wholly unreasonable to expect to find diamonds. There are crater chimneys similar to those that produce the diamonds of the greatest Kimberley field and there has been some search for these purest of carbons. Of other gems there are many. Gold is found in paying quantities. There is coal, and while no oil is produced experts find sufficient evidence of it to say that all that needs to be done to put Madagascar on the oil map of the world is to sink wells deep enough in the right places. Graphite of the finest quality is won by crude hand-washing methods and there have been real graphite booms. Iron ore has been found in many parts and has been developed only in a small native way. The natives have made spear points and knives for centuries. They were probably taught the art of working iron by the Arabs.

The first Arabic accounts of Madagascar tell of native furnaces of the most primitive type.

I saw some of these furnaces that were the same as they made them a thousand years ago. They were so similar to primitive forges I saw in Africa as to suggest that some of those who practiced the art of smelting and working iron before the occurrence of the vast subsidence that parted Madagascar from Africa survived the catastrophe and handed down the knowledge to their posterity.

The French policy toward foreigners in mining is most illiberal. It holds back the development of the country, but it also prevents waste of resources. In respect to minerals Madagascar is a little world in itself.

Recently the first two volumes of a comprehensive work on Madagascar mineralogy has been published by Professor Alfred Lacroix (Mineralogie de Madagascar, Vols. I, II, Paris, Auguste Challemel). An excellent review of this work by Mr. George F. Kunz appeared in *Science*, November 9, 1923. The review gives so complete a view of the minerals of Madagascar that, with the generous consent of the author, I reproduce here practically the whole of it:

"Geologically, this vast area contains (1) a region essentially formed of the crystalline schists and eruptive intrusive rocks; (2) a region of sedimentary or volcanic rocks; (3) a small, but interesting zone, forming the eastern side of a narrow border of sediments and sand dunes. The crystalline massif, essentially mountainous, extends for nearly the entire length of the island.

"Of the gems of Madagascar, the author notes that from its discovery the island was reputed to furnish gems, and in 1542 Jean Fonteneau, the second Frenchman to land there, declared that precious stones were to be found, while in 1658 Flacourt speaks of topazes, aquamarines, emeralds, rubies and sapphires, of course from hearsay. However, the mineralogist, Alfred Grandidier, who explored the island extensively in 1870, stated that the Madagascans had no idea of what a precious stone was, and that they only cared for colored glass beads. Indeed, Professor Lacroix says that the actual discovery of gem material hardly dates farther back than thirty years. In 1891, M. Grandidier gave the Museum d'Histoire Naturelle in Paris some fine crystals of rubellite and a few small sapphires and zircons.

"As a result of several years of exploitation it can be said that the beryls are the finest of the Madagascar gems, and they now constitute the chief part of the precious stone product.

Many fine blue beryls have been found, but the choicest are unquestionably the cesium beryls of a peach-blossom pink hue, the type on which the writer of the present notice has bestowed the name 'morganite.' These and others of the beryls of greatest density are found in the sodolithic pegmatites, and since the deposits of Maharitra have become exhausted, the beryls now in commerce come principally from the eluvions of Anjanabonoina. In the British Museum there is a splendid cut beryl from Madagascar, weighing 600 carats, with a density of 2.835, and the American Museum of Natural History in New York owns a magnificent cut example of the morganite type, weighing 57½ carats, the density being 2.827. Professor Lacroix believes that both of these came from Anjanabonoina. He also believes that he was the first to have Madagascar stones cut, at the time the products of the island were exhibited in the Museum d'Histoire Naturelle. These gems were chrysoberyls, garnets, corundums and topazes. Tourmalines occur in great variety (Vol. I, pp. 411-442; Vol. II, pp. 92-95) and of many beautiful hues, the red variety (rubellite) being the most precious. Specimens from Antandrokomby, Ampantsikahitra and other localities have furnished fine gems. Those of a golden-yellow or a lemon-yellow are among the most characteristic; these are found principally in Tsilaizina. A number of exceptionally fine examples of lithia tourmalines are shown on Plate 9, Vol. II. The long list of Madagascar gem stones includes the following: beryl, tourmaline, both in a great variety of colors, kunzite, garnet, spinal, chrysoberyl, zircon, cordierite, diopside, amethyst, smoky-quartz and rock-crystal, opal and also kornerupine, danburite, scapolite and a beautiful ferriferous orthoclase.

"Rock-crystal in remarkably fine specimens, rivalling those from any other source, have been found in Madagascar, which have been splendidly utilized in the ornamental arts. Fine examples of these crystals have been figured in Vol. I, plates 5 and 6. Large crystals have been utilized for several centuries for art objects and ornaments, and many of the artistic cups in our museums have been made from rock-crystal of Madagascar, which rivals that from Brazil in this respect. It is also employed for spheres, seals, boxes, perfume phials and for the pendants of chandeliers (Vol. II, p. II 2).

"The upright stones, called *vatamitsangana* (literally 'standing-stone'), or *vatolsy* ('malestones') in the Androy district of Madagascar (Vol. II, p. 169, Plate 18, opp. p. 166), are granite or gneissic monoliths erected in memory of a relative whose remains do not rest in the tomb of his ancestors. They are sometimes used as altars before which the natives offer prayer, and they anoint the sides of the stones with grease and place quartz pebbles on the summit. In size they vary from an average of two meters (6½ feet) to five meters (nearly 17 feet) in height, with a width of 50 or 60 centimeters (20 to 24 inches) and a thickness of from 25 to 30 centimeters (10 to 12 inches).

"Danburite has been found in the pegmatites of Maharitra and in the eluvions of Imalo, in crystals sufficiently transparent to warrant cutting. They make a gem of madeira yellow of various intensities, possessing properties closely similar to those of the topaz. Professor Lacroix believes some of them have been already sold under that name; he secured from Maharitra a stone weighing over five carats, and in a lot of minerals from Anjanabonoina he came across two fragments of danburite of a magnificent golden-yellow. One of these has been cut and furnished a gem weighing about 13 carats (Vol. II, p. 103).

"The ferriferous orthoclase of Madagascar is sometimes of a magnificent golden yellow and occurs in crystals weighing up to 100 grains; it furnishes cut stones of several grams, which make a very fine effect. The low degree of hardness does not permit the use of these for jewels in constant use, but nevertheless the stone can be utilized by jewelers. Perfectly clear crystals of fine color have sold for from 75 to 500 francs the kilogram (Vol. II, pp. 102, 103).

"The transparent variety of kornerupine (prismatine) was found among some minerals gathered twenty kilometers east of Itrongay. It was in clear, isolated fragments of a deep olive-green, some of them four centimeters long, and was probably derived from a pegmatite rather than a gneiss. They furnish very beautiful cut stones. The polychromism is evident beneath a certain depth, and the tint varies a little according to the direction given to the table. The largest of several weighed 21 carats. The smallest stones, of a clear green, recall certain varieties of beryl and tourmaline (Vol. I, p. 396; Vol. II, p. 102).

"Professor Lacroix notes that among the cut tourmalines from Madagascar he has remarked the following colors (Vol. II, pp. 93, 94):

"Red (rubellite): Magnificent stones varying from blood-red to vinous-red, sometimes with a violet tinge. Certain of them resemble rubies at Antandrokomby, etc.

"Pink: Numerous varieties more or less pale especially vinous-pink, salmon-pink, peach-blow color, recalling the tint of the beryls from the same region and also the burnt topaz. These are the predominant types at Maharitra.

"Amethyst violet: At Anjanabonoina.

"Golden-yellow to orange: These are the richest in manganese and the densest and most characteristic of Madagascar. Found, above all, at Tsilaizina.

"Brown: Dark brown at Tsilaizina; coffee-colored and warm-browns at Anjanabonoina. "Grayish-brown, or smoky: Maharitra, Anjanabonoina.

"Olive-green: Only furnish stones of inferior value. Maharitra, Anjanabonoina; much resemble the Brazilian.

"Pale green: At Vohitrakanga, a variety, the olive hue of which recalls that of kornerupine and some beryls.

"Grass-green: A great range of shades, especially apple-green and grass-green, recalling some of the tourmalines from Maine. At Anjanabonoina, Maharitra. At Ankitsikitsika are some crystals half green and half red.

"Blue: The indicolite variety is the most frequent Maharitra. When very dark blue they have little commercial value.

"Colorless: Madagascar furnishes probably the greatest number of fine, clear, colorless tourmalines, but they are rare. Maharitra, Anjanabonoina.

"The statistics from 1897 to 1921 show that Madagascar yielded quite an amount of gold in that period, the total production being 42,129.95 kilos (1,354,579 ounces). For the past ten years or more there has been a steady falling off, from a maximum of 3,696.87 kilos (118,858 ounces) in 1909 to only 456.24 kilos (14,668 ounces) in 1921. The total value of this gold product was $27,989,147 for the twenty-five years, an average of over a million per year.

"Graphite in considerable quantity has been mined on the island (Vol. II, pp. 148-155), and the exports have been quite important. The deposits occur in a great many localities; indeed, wherever there are gneisses, more or less graphite is to be found. The amount obtained varied much in the several years, reaching a maximum of 35,000 tons in 1917 and falling to about 4,000 tons in 1920. In 1917 the material brought 1,200 francs a ton in Marseilles.

"Of the uraniferous minerals from which radium can be extracted, Madagascar furnishes a number (Vol. II, p. 132), for example, fergusonite, euxenite, samarskite, blomstrandite and three minerals special to the island, namely, betafite, samiresite and ampangabeite. There are also deposits of autonite and uranocircite. Of these the minerals which are economically important are betafite and euxenite, the former being much the most exploited; the largest deposit is that of Ambatofotsy (Vol. I, p. 386). Certain of these betafites have been worth as much as 15,000 francs a metric ton. These ores are sometimes sold according to the radium content, the unity being one milligram per ton, the value of this unit ranging from 100 to 200 francs.

"The fourth section of the work is devoted to the lithology (or petrography) of the island, and Professor Lacroix states that the classification used is that which he has set forth during the past few years in his lectures at the Museum d'Histoire Naturelle. He briefly summarizes it as follows:

"The eruptive rocks are considered, not only from the viewpoint of their mineralogical composition and their structure, as in the classification of Fouqué and Michel-Lévy, but account is taken of the relative quantities of their constituent minerals, and also of their chemical composition, this latter point being especially considered in the present work.

"The rocks are divided into five great classes, based upon the nature of their white minerals (quartz, feldspars, feldspathoides). The first two comprise the rocks rich in quartz; the third class those rocks whose essential white elements are feldspars; the fourth is constituted by rocks in which the feldspars are accompanied by a notable quantity of feldspathoids (nephelines, leucitics), and, finally, the fifth class is reserved to the little group in which the sale white element is a feldspathoid. These divisions correspond to very important chemical properties, the excess of silica above the quantity necessary to enable the aluminum, joined with the requisite quantity of oxides, to form feldspars in the first two groups; the complete or approximate saturation of this silica in the third group, and its lack in the last two classes.

"A very interesting part of the section 'Lithology' is that devoted to comparison of the sodolithic pegmatites of Madagascar with those of other countries (Vol. II, pp. 334-362). This embraces a careful description of these pegmatites in New

England and in California, the greater part of the deposits having been studied in 1888 and in 1913 (pp. 334-346); in the last named year Professor Lacroix was actively engaged in completing the great collection of American gems so generously donated to the Muséum d'Histoire Naturelle in Paris by J. Pierpont Morgan. He was accompanied on several of his excursions by the writer of the present notice and by Mr. Howe. He notes the striking resemblances between the pegmatites of California and those of Madagascar, the association in both regions of lithia tourmalines, notably of rubellite, cesium beryls, kunzite and spessartite, and the existence of native bismuth, of manganocolumbite. On the other hand, mineralogical differences must be noted.

"The special attention here given by Professor Lacroix to these analogous formations in the United States is well worthy of remark in view of the fact that in but too many mineralogical handbooks composed by Europeans rather scant notice is taken of the United States."

CHAPTER XL
ANIMAL LIFE

THE island teems with animal life. There is more life that is autochthonous than in any other territory of like size on the earth. Most of the known species of lemurs are found in Madagascar and a majority of these are found there and not anywhere else. So numerous are the lemurs that Madagascar was once called Lemuria by several French writers. Not all of the species of lemurs that once existed still survive, as is proven by the discoveries of partially calcarified remains in the spring deposits which are common and are best represented, or at least best known, at Antsirabe.

Here have been discovered the remains of flying lemurs, amphibious lemurs and lemurs much larger than any known to-day. There are also found in these spring holes bones of the pigmy hippopotamus; the hippopotamus lemmerlei and the hippopotamus grandidier, and skeletons of the æpyornis titans and æpyornis maximus and other prehistoric beasts and birds.

It was my good fortune to obtain a skeleton of the extinct pigmy hippopotamus and convey it to the University of Michigan with a perfect specimen of a modern hippopotamus that I killed and saved in Africa, to show the difference. There is a mysterious animal in the unexplored jungles that the natives report and fear and use as a bugaboo to frighten their babes. Some question the truth of the tales and others regard them as reasonable and likely.

Snakes are widely distributed and some of them are poisonous. Most of the Madagascar ophidia are not virulent. One of the serpents found on the East Coast is the akoma, which attains a length of more than nine feet and is as thick at the middle as a man's calf. Some of the large snakes I saw were green and others were yellow, black and red. Several large ones had two bony hooks similar to the so-called anal hooks of the boa. The natives say that they strike their prey in the neck with these hooks and drink the blood that flows. This is not credited by observers.

Once in the jungle I saw a big constrictor lying in wait by a wild pig run. Concealing myself, I remained a couple of hours before a pig came sauntering along. The serpent uncoiled, and, dropping on the pig with no suggestion of a strike, enfolded the animal back of the middle of the body. The pig may not have been the one the serpent was looking for or expecting. It was a large boar and its tusks looked as dangerous as any of the armament of the snake.

As the folds tightened around the body of the boar it snorted in terror. Foam issued from its mouth and in a moment there was such a contest going on as was difficult to observe accurately. At first the snake appeared to have the better of it. Then the tables turned and the boar succeeded in penetrating the middle of the boa with its ripping tusks. In a very brief time the snake was uncoiled and prostrate on the ground. The boar seemed to survey it and take a momentary inventory of itself. Then it proceeded calmly to eat the serpent and did not stop until it had finished quite half of its beaten enemy.

Next in size to the akoma are the big harmless species called the lay and the mandotra. Nearly as big as any is the fandrefi-ala or pily which has a reputation not only for deadliness but for belligerency as well. Snakes as a whole are called "kakalava," which translated literally means "long enemy."

As the Sakalava are taller than the other Malagasies and were the most warlike people and were feared and distrusted, it is often asserted that Kakalava and Sakalava are the same and that at one time the Sakalava were thought of only as snakes in the grass.

There is a bad snake called the mantangory whose bite causes great pain and discomfort but is seldom actually fatal. One unknown elsewhere in the world is a slender snake about four feet long which is perfectly white. Big and little, there are enough serpents, but they are not so numerous nor so deadly as in Africa and Asia.

Crocodiles are common and a dangerous pest and are to be found in every water hole. They grow to a great size and can pull down an ox or a man.

Malagasies call the lemur the forest dog; "amboanala." They know their natural history better than most aborigines know the animals that surround them. Not only are they familiar with the common lemurs but with the small and rare ones. They classify these animals under six heads: "babakoto," "simpona," "varika," "gidro," "tsidika," and "tsitsy." The last two are very small, not larger than a common squirrel and even smaller. They live like squirrels in holes in hollow trees and are entirely nocturnal. Lemurs live in the trees and seldom are seen on the ground and this gives rise to the common belief that they can fly. They are omnivorous but prefer a vegetable diet.

Among the carnivora is the fosa, black, clawed like a wolverine, and classed as a viverridæ. To me it seemed to be catlike, and without careful observation I would classify it broadly with the felidæ.

Surely the haihay is a wildcat. It is only to be found with the fosa in the deepest jungles and is nocturnal. The fosa is seen more widely and not infrequently in the day time. The vontsira is like a weasel or a ferret. The fanaloka is much the same as the vontsira only as much larger as a mink or a marten or sable is larger than a weasel.

The bugbear I have referred to elsewhere is called "songomhy." A native said he saw a "songomby" one night as he was getting out of a big wood in which he had been lost. It came out from a big talus at the foot of a lonesome mountain.

Another said he had seen two of them and that they made a noise like the neighing of a horse and were spotted with red. Another story I heard was that they were the size of a donkey and striped with red. It is just possible that there is a relative of the zebra in Madagascar that has not been seen by a trained observer.

If there is a megatherium or a plesiosaurus in Patagonia I see no reason to doubt that there are strange beasts in Madagascar which is less known than Patagonia, because there is no such land on earth now as Patagonia. And no monsters there outside of newspaper mental menageries. (In earlier days writers on South America used to refer to the south quarter of that continent as Patagonia. But now that it has been explored and settled and parceled among the nations there is no part that bears the name Patagonia. Neither Chili nor Argentina, between which ancient Patagonia, the land of big feet, has been divided, had sentiment enough to perpetuate the distinctive name.)

I have referred in another chapter to the wild cattle which are more numerous in Madagascar than anywhere else in the world. Tame cattle are everywhere also. It is not uncommon to find a chief who owns ten thousand and few indeed are there in the cattle country who do not count among their property an hundred head of fine ones. The claim is made that there are more cattle per capita than in any other country. In such riches Madagascar reminded me of Lapland, where I saw one chief who owned twenty thousand reindeer. Those wild forest Bedouins, the Masai of northeast Africa, are not far behind as herdsmen nor are several of the nomadic tribes of Turkestan. When the Masai and the Sarts are on the trek it appears as if they have all the cattle on earth.

In the plains, or open country, as it is called, there are all sorts of tenrecs, but none of them are large. All these little hedgehogs, sora, sokina, and trandraka are good to eat and are much sought. One of them is about the size of a small squirrel with longitudinal stripes of white and brown like a chipmunk. I ate several of these and they were very palatable. Apparently associated with the quilless hedgehogs are a number of species of quilled ones which are the smallest porcupines in the world. Their quills are similar to the finest cambric needles and as they are all serrated they work into the hand with a festering rapidity that is annoying and even may be dangerous.

An interesting animal is the jaboady. It is classified with the cats and has a more pronounced odor than a civet cat and much more pleasant. The natives use it as a perfume and it is more agreeable than much of the cheap scent with which the men and women in civilized lands offend the nostrils. This jaboady is in size between a wildcat and a lynx. In its marking it reminded me of the snow leopard of the Himalayas and it has a long tail that it lashes catlike when it is prowling or angry. The neck is long enough to suggest one of Paul Bunyan's "hodags" and its ears are held erect and pointed forward. It may possibly be a variation of the fosa but Grandidier thinks not.

Wildcats are kept down to some extent by wild hunting dogs that pursue them in preference to any other quarry. These wild dogs are neither the dingo nor the wild dog of Africa and Asia. They appear to be a canine compromise between a coyote, a jackal and a dingo. I saw a pack of them after a cat and as they passed some distance away in full cry I could see that they were fleet runners. The natives say that when they are hungry a pack of them will attack human beings. So far as I could learn this is a story to frighten children.

I heard of a little Madagascar bear, but I failed to get more evidence of it than disconnected reports. It may be a relative of the mythical bear of Uganda.

Two carnivora that Grandidier and Crossley added to those of the world by specimens secured in Madagascar are the bandro, a kind of wildcat, and the famalifivoy or tsidikinizozoro, more like a dog.

Wild guinea fowls were often to be seen if one hunted with enough care. They are even wilder than I found them to be in Rhodesia. The birds are countless. Geese of more than one kind, ducks of infinite variety, herons, egrets, cranes, bittern, snipe, sandpipers, rails, plovers, pigeons of many sizes and beautiful colors, sparrows, numerous falconidæ, sunbirds, humming birds, larks, birds of paradise, lyre birds or some bird suggesting them,

swallows, cormorants, pelicans, gulls, frigate birds, sea chickens and in fact representatives of most of the kinds of birds of the world.

I saw doves and grouse and naturally a number of birds that I did not recognize and could find out nothing more about than what the natives could tell me, which oftentimes was much and interesting. I saw great flocks of fowl that resembled a duck with legs as long as a crane's. They called them tahia and I found true their statement that they were fine food. Unmistakably ducks were other flocks of birds the natives called tsiriry. These were almost as tame as domestic ducks and in the late evening they permitted me to walk near to them and were very slow to take flight, but could fly well when they tried.

Still other birds in big flocks, some aquatic, others not, they told me were vorontsara, sadakely and sama. The latter were migratory. I learned from the statements of the natives that these birds would go away and then return after some time had elapsed. It is likely that their migrations are determined by the food problem. The sama is white with a beautiful crest and is marked with red and reddish brown. They looked like flamingoes to me as they filed along the shore of a lake to feed, but I was not permitted sufficient observation to be certain.

There are arosy which resemble the muscovy duck and a duck they call angaka which means just a duck. The black goose which is not rare there they call vorombemainty. All snipes are kitanotano; divers (grebes) are miombonkomana or vivy; one of these hides behind its wings when it feeds and the natives say it is covering its head so that other birds may not discover its favorite food and steal it. A beautiful small black heron with iridescent feathers on its serpentine neck is the famakisifotra.

The marvellous men of the L.M.S. were ornithologists, geologists, astronomers, zoologists, anthropologists, and in fact covered all the departments of natural science in a thorough manner. Never were men and women better trained to go into a new region and help the natives and at the same time help the world with accurate knowledge not possessed before. As early as a quarter of a century ago they had made fairly complete surveys and knew more about Madagascar than anyone else in the world, not even excepting that great French authority on Madagascar, Grandidier. These missionaries and Grandidier have found and classified sixteen falconidæ, among them some that were previously unknown and that are peculiar to Madagascar, including the serpent eagle, a Madagascar sparrow hawk and the rayed gymnogene (polyboroides Madagascariensis).

Of the striges or owls-there are six known, three of which are peculiar alone to Madagascar. The wonderful bird fauna includes three kinds of parrots; fourteen cuckoos and couas; two kingfishers; one hoopoe and one bee-eater; six ground rollers; one crow; the white-necked; eleven butcher birds and shrikes; the forktailed drongo; fifteen warblers; six thrushes; three bulbuls, two of which are new and all as sweet songsters as the Persian bulbul and the bulbul of the Holy Land; one new tailor bird which has been named orthotomus grandidieri in honor of Grandidier; one nut hatch; one swallow; one martin; three sun birds; one wagtail; two weaver birds; one new Madagascar cardinal; one rice bird; two starlings, one of which is new; one helmet bird (Prevost's); one new lark; two philepitta; two pigeons and two doves, of which one of the pigeons, funingus Madagascariensis, is new; one guinea; one common quail the same as that of the southern United States; one striped partridge; one masked sand grouse; one bustard quail which is more bustard than quail and which should be classified with the little African bustard; ten rails, crakes, coots and water hens, at least two of which gallinula are new; two jacana; one whimbrel and a curlew that is new; fourteen snipes, sand pipers, avocets, pratincoles, turnstones, and godwits,; two mesites; fifteen herons and egrets and bitterns; three storks; four ibis; one flamingo; ten ducks; four geese; one frigate bird; two tropic birds; four pelicans; cormorants, gannets and darters; eleven gulls, six of which are tern and one the Antarctic skua; five petrels; two albatross; two shearwaters; one grebe. This is not a complete list as I know because I saw birds not given, but it furnishes a good idea of the bird life of the island.

For the naturalist there is not a less explored spot on the globe. Beautiful butterflies flit from flower to flower and waste the nectar honey bees seek, only paying their way by their work of cross fertilization.

The beetle life is wide enough to turn an entomologist dizzy and the spiders are everywhere and of infinite variety. It is not to be doubted that many of the lower forms of life that are the fiercest enemies of man are bred in this ideal hotbed.

Man is slowly discovering that his most serious enemies are invisible to any but the eye of the microscope. The life and death contest that has gone on all the time has been between bimana and bacteria and man has only recently come partially to realize the situation. If man is to win he must kill the bacterium in its nest and to do that he must first find the nest.

That he will discover Madagascar to be a first-class battleground is certain. Perhaps also when man learns that the bacteria laugh in glee when he sets out to kill himself off in brutal, senseless wars there will be a new argument for peace on earth, good will to men. Up to the present the smallest animalcule has in more ways than one more sense than man.

CHAPTER XLI
TOPOGRAPHY, SOIL AND CLIMATE OF MADAGASCAR

IN treating of the soil and climate I shall make liberal use of what has been discovered and proven in the agricultural experiment and study stations conducted with skill and thoroughness by the French colonial government.

The first intelligent surveying was done by the men of the L.M.S. and by Grandidier, whose other name might almost be said to be Madagascar.

Travellers have called Madagascar the most fertile and the most barren of islands, depending upon what portion they happened to see. In its entirety it is capable of sustaining many times its present population. Famine has never been known. No part of the world has impressed me as having a greater percentage of productive area than Madagascar. Nor is the island all tropical. It lies between twelve and twenty-six south latitude. The tropic of Capricorn passes Tullear. But as in nearly all tropical regions, the latitude is compensated by altitude and the conditions of all the zones are thus represented. The torrid regions of the coast are hot and deadly; the temperate plains and valleys at five thousand feet are a white man's country. There are frigid altitudes which furnish cool winds, rain and pure atmosphere.

One great range of mountains, the Ankaratra, dominates the island and reaches a height of at least ten thousand feet. There has not been sufficient triangulation to know much more than that the mountains are high enough generally to function as mountains. Their constant erosion and the transportation of the material downward is a natural building and fertilization of the soil. Many of the peaks are volcanic and there are several interesting crater lakes such as Tritriva, which is best known and is one of the most beautiful.

Much of Madagascar that is regarded now as arid will yield to irrigation and to dry farming if the lands are ever needed, just as has been the case with what was once called the American desert. For soil fertility, bright growing sunlight, adequate rains, natural soil food, Madagascar is a favored place.

A considerable area of soil is composed of a red silica-ferruginous clayey material that is deficient in lime. It is called useless but can be made of the best by the application of lime.

The island has an area of about 240,000 square miles. It is roughly one thousand miles in length and about four hundred miles at the widest point. Grandidier, who has written in French ponderous tomes on Madagascar, says that quite two-thirds of the area is unproductive. He was not, however, an agronomist. Those who know more about soil and its possibilities say that quite three-fourths of the area is capable of cultivation and may be practically farmed.

Not a small area of Georgia and Alabama and other sections of the United States have red and yellow ferruginous soil and it has been found to be valuable when treated in the right manner. Grandidier thinks the laterite of India is similar to much of the soil of Madagascar, but it appears to me that he is in error. And he goes on to say that the same soil is to be found in South America, Africa, China and especially Cochin China which, being French, he

knows more about. The fact is that all the soils of the earth have a similar origin. I do not mean that they all have the same source. Some are formed of pure irruptive material, others of sedimentary and organic materials that have gathered many ingredients from the sea or ancient forests and from mollusca and corals and iron bacteria and so on. There is no soil which cannot be rendered productive by proper methods.

Most surprising was the discovery that the deserts were the most fertile, when irrigated.

Gradually the French scientific agriculturists, who for a time had been inclined to accept Grandidier's word as final, have found that he is a better biologist than farmer, and little attention is now paid to his wholesale condemnation of the island as a food producer. The French Agronomic Institute laboratory tests showed that the worst soil that Giandidier had examined contained only 60 to 180 parts of silicious grit in 11 thousand parts of earth. Goodly contents of phosphoric acid, azote, potash and magnesia were found with only lime wanting, and lime can be supplied more easily than most other essential ingredients of fertility.

Because this clayey soil hardens and cracks the natives told Grandidier it was worthless and he accepted their opinion. Intensive tilling has remedied this defect in Madagascar as elsewhere, and the heavy soil that had been condemned has proven already to be of great value.

Madagascar is big enough to show a great diversity in rainfall. On the eastern littoral the rainfall is one hundred and twenty inches a year, while in some other districts it rarely exceeds forty-seven inches. The vapors borne by the winds from the Indian Ocean are condensed when they sink to the mountain ranges near the eastern shore, and the rainfall for a period is as continuous as the Madagascar monsoons. After crossing the mountains the winds are naturally dry, and for several months there is little or no rainfall in the interior. The result is an alternation between wet and dry seasons. But in no part may it be said that there is a deficiency of rain.

In the south central plains, to be sure, there is a limited area which is said to have only seven inches of rainfall a year; even if this is true—and the statistics are meagre—there is an abundance of water in the mountains and there are natural reservoirs which can be practically used for irrigation. There is no water problem such as confronts Australia, where it is necessary to resort to wells whose life is limited, or such as appears in North and South Rhodesia and many other parts of the world.

During the month of January, 1892, the rainfall at Tamatave was thirty-three inches, of which nearly sixteen inches fell in four days. During the same month the rainfall at Antananarivo was thirteen and a half inches and at Fianarantsoa fifteen inches. September, October and November are the dryest months of the year.

The variety of the productions is interesting and valuable. On the road from Andovoranto to Anatananarivo I saw several coffee fazendas, and they are not confined to this limited district. The coffee will take its place in the world's market as of a quality better than the average.

One great aid to agriculture is the vast supply of fertilizer provided by cattle-raising. More rice is produced than is consumed and the island could be placed on a basis of large rice exports in a short time. The same is true of manioc and nearly all of the other products.

The hills and mountains are so disposed as to cut the area into pot holes and valleys and into these humus has been gathered until each is a garden or the making of one.

So corrugated is the surface that, as stated elsewhere, there were no roads on the island before the coming of the French. It is related that in 1867 Queen Rasoherina made a trip from the capital to Tamatave. She and all the nobles and ladies in waiting were carried, but the huge retinue of more than fifty thousand marched. In places they had to march single file. In other places they cut trails through the cane brakes. The queen ordered the master of the count, whose duty it was to report how many had to be fed, also to keep count of the hills they ascended. On the way to the coast he made the total of 4,590 and on the way back he reported 7,435 hills. The discrepancy was noted by the queen, and she called for an explanation. The quick-witted master of the count asked her majesty to remember that it is uphill coming back and was downhill going to the coast. This satisfied the queen and she had the master of the count advanced seven honors in rank for his accuracy and faithfulness.

In the dryer sections there are tamarinds and prickly pears and similar vegetation which supply both food and water. Truly it is a wonderful island.

The inhabitants know about dry farming and apply it in raising peas, beans, potatoes and much other garden truck. The soil is so mellow where it is worked that they do not plow but jab down into it with a wooden shaft weighted with a stone and turn it over as did the first man in the world who planted things.

Grandidier did a huge scientific service to France and the world by his work in Madagascar and then nearly nullified it so far as France was concerned by his pessimistic declarations concerning the soil. One of his chapters is a warning to colonists from France that they may find soil that will be fertile for a time and then play out, which is true of most of the soils of the earth if they are not properly tilled, and true of none of them if they are farmed well. The only drawback to Madagascar is that much of it is in the tropics and is furiously malarial. This drawback can be overcome.

Dr. Gorgas once told me that the tropics would in time come to be the zone of highest development of the human race. All man has to do, said Dr. Gorgas, is to kill off the anopheles and calopus mosquitoes and a few more pests such as the tsetse fly, and the tropics will be ideal for human living. Then the work of the world will be done in an hour a day and mankind will have time to become decent and human. Unless, however, there is a change in the human constitution every fellow who goes into the sun of the equator will still have to wear a spine pad as do always the hardest workers in the tropics, such as the trabadores of Guayaquil and similar laborers along that part of the west coast of South America.

If Theodore Roosevelt had worn a good spine pad during his Amazon trip he would be alive to-day. I warned him at Oyster Bay to do so. He invited me there to discuss his expedition to South America. I reminded him that he had never roughed it in the sea-level tropics. But he scoffed at the idea of its making any difference. After he returned he told me I was right and that he had paid dear for his heedlessness. Bravery, such as he possessed in a supreme degree, does not demand or warrant carelessness at any time or place.

CHAPTER XLII
FLORA OF MADAGASCAR

No region of the world displays a more splendid exuberance of tropical flora than Madagascar. The palm trees and shrubs, all tied together by serpentine lianas, make jungles that can be penetrated only after much chopping with axe and jungle sword.

Not only is there a dizzy wealth of things that are autochthonous, but Madagascar has a way of appropriating anything that comes to it and developing it on a grander scale. I have particularly in mind the poinsettia which is indigenous to Mexico, but which does not know its own possibilities of grandeur in color and size until it is acclimated in Madagascar.

The one Madagascar tree that has won fame for itself all over the world is the beautiful and useful Travellers' Tree, ravenala Madagascariensis. It was first brought to America by Helen Gould and it throve in a way to justify the cost and trouble. I have seen the ravenala, which is said to be native to Madagascar, in the Malay Archipelago, whither it may have been transplanted. It is the urania speciosa and as a musacere looks more like a palm than a plantain. On the plains the stem is about twenty feet high up to the beginning of the striking banana-like leaves. In the forest it drives upward after sunlight until it is more than an hundred feet high. The leaves are twenty to thirty in number, twelve feet long and nearly two feet wide. They grow out from the top of the tree and look exactly like a huge palm-leaf fan. The bole is never more than two feet in diameter. This tree is seldom seen above two thousand feet and is not found in the great central plains at all.

The name Travellers' Tree comes from its usefulness. From its trunk food and fire may be had, its heart is a delicacy; from its leaves a shelter

can be constructed; and no matter how dry the land may be or how poisonous the water supply, good sweet water is to be had in ample quantity by tapping the Travellers' Tree. In many instances houses are built of the tree and floors and mats, are made from it.

Cryptogamous plants, lichens and mosses are found everywhere, but have not been studied and listed. This is true of the flora generally with the exception that thousands of specimens have been sent to Kew Gardens, London and elsewhere for identification and classifying. The only thing that is certainly known is that there is not a richer flora on the earth. More than one hundred and fifty species of ferns alone have been gathered and they have hardly been touched.

Grandidier places the number of kinds of all flora known on the island at more than four thousand and the search has just begun. Tree ferns of vast dimensions cover the lower levels and they are more in the eye than any other one form of vegetation. Without attempting to do more than give a suggestion of the wealth of the flora, I append a partial list of the genera, obtained from Kew: Anonaceæ, ampelideæ, anacardiaceæ, araliaceæ, apocynaceæ, asclepiadaaceæ, ancanthaceæ, amaranthaceæ, aristolochiaceæ, alismaceæ, aroideæ, bixaceæ, begoniaceæ, boraginaceæ, bignoniaceæ, crucifereræ, careophyllaceæ, capparidaneæ, chlenaeceæ, celastraceæ, connaraneæ, crassulaceæ, combretaceæ, cucurbitaeeæ, cactaceæ, compositæ, companulaceæ, cordiaceæ, convolvulaceæ, crescentiaceæ, chenopodiaceæ, casuarinea, commelynaceæ, cyperaceæ, dilleniaceæ, droseraceæ, dioscorea, ceæ, fieoideæ, guttiferæ, geraniaceæ, gentianaceæ, graminaceæ, hyperieaceæ, hippocrataceæ, haloragaceæ, hamamelidaceæ, hypoxidaceæ, hydrocharidaceæ, iridaceæ, juncaceæ, linaceæ, legu. minosæ, lythraceæ, loranthaceæ, loganiaceæ, lentibulariaceæ, liabiatæ, lauraceæ, liliaceæ, lemnaceæ, menispermaceæ, malvaceæ, malphigiaceæ, meliaceæ, melastomaceæ, myrsinaceæ, monimiaceæ, nymphæaceæ, naiadaceæ, ochnaceæ, onagraceæ, oleaceæ, orchidaceæ, polygalaceæ, pittosporaceæ, passifloracaceæ, portulacacæ, pedalineæ, polygonaceæ, proteaceæ, phytolaccaceæ, podostemonaceæ, pandanaceæ, ranunculaceæ, rutaceæ, rhamnaceæ, rosaceæ, rhizophoraceæ, rubianeæ, sterculiaceæ, saxafragaceæ, sampdaceæ, sapotaceæ, solanaceæ, scrophulariaceæ, selanginaceæ, scitamineæ, smilaceæ, tiliaceæ, taccaceæ, unbelliferæ, ulmaceæ, violaceæ, verbenaceæ, xyridaceæ, zygophyllaneæ, zingiberaceæ.

The natives prescribe the juice and the tea of the ranunculus pinnatus for malignant cancerous tumors. Of the menispermaceæ the clematis is the most common. It has medicinal value and is recorded in the American and British pharmacopœia and in the dispensatories of both countries. Hibiscus esculentus, as the name implies, is used in soups like okra and gumbo, and in medicine as a demulcent. There is a new papaya in Madagascar, but it is met with infrequently and has not yet become a food article.

Landolphia vahea Madagascariensis furnishes a superior caoutchouc. Sessamum Indicum is widely cultivated as a food. There are many euphorbias. In many parts they are made into effective hedges and as a fence are all that could be desired.

As early as 1882 quite two thousand wild flowering plants were known and the estimate made then that not more than one-third had been classified is now borne out by the fact that an additional two thousand have been recorded since and the end is far from reached. There is a similarity between the flora of the Seychelles and all the Comoro Islands, Mauritius and Madagascar. The flora of all the tropical zones of the world has a tendency to show no preference for continents, but seems to prefer Madagascar and some other large islands to the continental lands. Inasmuch as the tropical areas cover twenty of the fifty million square miles of the earth it is interesting to note that nearly all the species found anywhere in the tropics appear in the big island and many that are not to be seen elsewhere.

The Philippines and South America are famous for their orchids, but it is claimed that Madagascar has more than both of them together. To take the place of the almost extinct black and red wood of St. Helena there has been found in Madagascar a near relative in the cheirolœna. Much more important

is the discovery of a number of allied cinchonas that yield a good quinine. There is a close affinity between the island flora and that of tropical Africa, which was to be expected in view of the ancient land connection.

A plant called the hydrostachys is believed to be a friend of bulls. It is of the family podostemaceæ. When there is a bull fight all the owners of bulls hunt for this very rare plant and if they find one they give a little of it to their bull to eat and then hold a leaf in their hand and wave it during the fight. If possible they rub the bull if he comes near them in his rushes. One big bull handler told me that his animals never failed to win when he could get this charmed plant for them. As the lowland flora is similar to that of lowland Africa so the Alpine flora of the mountains of Madagascar is very like the flora of the mountains and high reaches of Africa.

The tree xerochlamys pilosa, called by the natives hatsikana, is a dye wood and in tangena ordeals it produces vomiting of blood. A tree called taratana cures fever, so the natives say, if the bark is made into a tea. Ampaly leaves are used as a substitute for sandpaper in the fine polishing of snuff boxes. These leaves have a very fine hard cutting surface. A wild vine called ovinala grows in the jungle and produces an edible tuber as good as a yam. It is much sought and more than once has kept natives lost in the deep forest from starving to death.

The tribesmen all know more or less of the good and bad herbs and they manifest a fine appreciation of the many wonderful flowers. Once I saw them pressing leaves of golden hue bearing long, silvery, hairy tendrils. They had them between hot flat stones and when they had finished the result was a beautiful product.

The hardest wood in Madagascar is called harahara and has been classified as a lignum vitre, but that is erroneous. It has been found to be of the order of santalaceæ.

One of the showiest and most striking orchids is the angræcum sesquipedale. Nectaries of this orchid eleven and a half inches in length have been accurately measured. Another Madagascar orchid has even a longer nectary.

It is worth a voyage to the great island just to see

these and other flowers of indescribable beauty. The so-called rain tree of Madagascar has minute leaves. A watery fluid resembling rain and suggesting a shower drops from the tree continuously. Careful examination proves this rain to be produced by millions of tiny hemipterous insects crowded on the little leaves. They secrete so much of the "rain" that it drops all the time. They multiply as rapidly as they die and there is no discontinuance of the shower from one end of the year to the other.

A fine tree with edible fruit and a beautiful large purple flower is the fotona. Several huge water lilies are as good as taro, the one of which they make the one finger, two finger, three finger poi in Hawaii.

The agy is a nasty climbing thing that is likely to be encountered anywhere in western Madagascar. It flowers the year around and bears a pod that is covered with poisonous needles like a great nettle; it is a near relative of the virulent mucuna pruriens. The agy put real fear into the hearts of the Sakalava when they ran into it and another poisonous plant, a tree called amiana, during an invasion of Ambohimanga. So severely were they poisoned that they fled the country in a terror augmented by superstition.

A missionary traveller named W. Montgomery wrote about an experience he had with the agy in June, 1879. He said: "Journeying towards Mojanga on the northwest coast of Madagascar with my wife and children I had a strange and painful adventure. We were going along the bank of the Ikopa, the river of many crocodiles. The weather was very hot, so when we came to a shady nook we stopped to cook dinner and rest. I made my family comfortable and then started the 'maromita' to work. It was tropical midday, but these bearers had to make a fire to cook food. I pushed into the jungle and in a moment was in great pain and fear. My hands were on fire and my face and head burned as if they were being held against a red-hot stove. The burning increased and was accompanied by severe pain and dizziness. I thought I would die and strove to get back to where I had left my wife and children. My men started when they saw me coming, so great was the agony as indicated by my face. One of them cried out 'he is smitten by an agy' (efa voan ny agy hiano). They

THE TRAVELLER'S TREE

were all activity. Some rushed to the river for water and others went for and brought all the sand and mud they could carry. Then they rubbed all of my exposed parts with mud and sand and water until they had removed the 'lay' or stinging poison hairs. In a brief time the pain and burning ceased and I joined in the rice dinner that was awaiting."

The poison darts of the agy are quite a quarter of an inch long. They are pointed like arrows and are serrated like the quills of a porcupine, and work rapidly into the flesh. In some parts of the island these agy vines are used with the amiana and prickly pear to form a defense that is more impenetrable than a barbed wire entanglement. When the Sakalava ran into them they thought the gods had suddenly turned against them. I have seen the rude castles of feudal nobles and entire towns surrounded by these zarebas of prickly poisonous shafts.

In the agy the prickly shafts are contained in a pod which sheds them in a shower at touch or even in a brisk breeze. The rapidity with which the pods are apparently replenished with ammunition is incredible.

A fibre resembling Brazilian piassava is found in Madagascar. It is produced by a palm and is much in demand for export under the trade name of rofia. The rich brown long fibre when bleached into white or cream is woven into fine and beautiful fabrics. The rofia industry is important and will become more so. The native name of the rofia plant is vonitra. The claim is made that it is finer than the Brazilian fibre. It has been sold, prepared, for as high as two hundred and fifty dollars a ton, and perhaps more.

In another place I have referred to the silk-bearing bush of Madagascar. The natives call it the "voampanory." The manner of bearing is the same as that of the cotton tree—for in South America, where the cotton plant is indigenous, it grows into a tree. The silk-bearing bush has long, pointed, green leaves and a red flower. There is a prickly seed pod that contains smallish seeds wrapped in the silk after the manner of the American milk weed. At ripening the pod bursts and the seeds float upon the first breeze. Of course the natural function of the silken swathing is to effect the dispersion of the plant. No royal babe was ever clad more delicately than the fluffy infants of the silk bush. The manufactured product is as fine as any silk and a few degrees finer than rofia cloth. The fibre is an inch in length and of a lovely yellow. It is commonly used by the natives to stuff the back of the filanjana and for cushions. There is a future for it.

Mahogany, ebony and sandalwood are some of the valuable timbers of Madagascar. During the reign of some of the sovereigns it was necessary to smuggle ebony out of the country, since it was a royal wood reserved to the crown. Under the French, care is being taken to prevent waste, but the wood is, to a limited extent, an object of commerce.

Madagascar sandalwood and ebony were known to the Arabs centuries ago and were sought in exchange for Arabic commodities, mostly rich cloth.

Sandalwood has sold for three hundred dollars a ton in the English market. Rich Hindus import it for the burning of the bodies of their dead and it was and is the wood of the suttee. The latter is still practiced in India despite British interdiction.

Malagasies grind sandalwood, mix it with water and anoint themselves with the mixture, which is by no means a bad perfume. The last price of Madagascar ebony that I have seen quoted was four hundred dollars a ton.

One of the richest parts of the flora of Madagascar consists of the fresh water algæ. One collector in the vicinity of Lake Alaotra obtained in a short time thirty-one genera and one hundred eighty-one species. Of these seventy species were new. The diatoms have not yet been named. The specimens of cosmaria I saw were remarkably perfect.

Elsewhere I have mentioned that Miss Helen Gould imported a Travellers' Tree to America. It cost her thirty-five thousand dollars to do so.

The fertilization of the Travellers' Tree by sunbirds (nectarinia souimanga) is interesting. The sunbird, which is not much bigger than a humming bird, perches on a branch above the blossom and in this position, with bill and head and almost half the body also inserted into the bloom, it sips the nectar. And it pays, for its breast is covered with pollen which it bears to another flower, where it is deposited and the result is a perfect cross-fertilization. Beetles and butterflies seek the nectar also, but they do not get much, and it is an accident if they carry any of the pollen away.

I saw nutmegs and cinnamon and cloves and spices enough to realize that Madagascar is indeed a rare Isle of Spices. Nutmegs resemble horse chestnuts before they are husked.

One could go on writing of the flora of Madagascar for a lifetime and not either finish the subject or satisfy himself. Somehow I pity the institutions that are forever sending scientific expeditions to lands that have been tramped over for centuries and never think of or know of this field which remains comparatively untouched. The day will come when somebody will want to know about Madagascar and then the human sheep will follow in an impetuous herd and Madagascar will become a vogue.

CHAPTER XLIII
MADAGASCAR A COMPLETE WORLD IN MINIATURE

ALL who have seen Madagascar at all—and it is not to be assumed that all who visit the island see it—agree that for its area it has greater variety and more that is peculiar to itself than any other part of the world. The newest rock formations are there beside the oldest, if we are to credit geologic chronology at all, which we must not swallow whole. Madagascar is both very old and also young. Its isolation centuries ago have given it an opportunity to develop forms not known elsewhere.

Its ancient connection with Africa and so with all the continents—for all the continents are in a scientific sense connected—was proved by the discovery of the remains of the steneosaurus Baroni named for a distinguished scientist of the L. M. S. who made the discovery. A majestic fossil dinosaurus was exhumed in the jurassic beds of the northern part of the island. Much more recent were the struthius æpyornis and the testudo Grandidier. The former is the biggest bird and the latter is the largest tortoise that the world has known. Fossil hunters in Madagascar have dug up a lot of things that have not been classified and many for which new orders will have to be arranged. In the brief chapter on the animals I mentioned the felidæ and lemuroids, but I omitted the centetidæ; nor did I allude to that fascinating fossil the megaladapis Madagascariensis, which was a huge lemur, now extinct. Flacourt, who was a French admiral and also employed in governing in Madagascar for ten years, beginning 1650, calls it the tratratratra and describes it as an animal as large as a two-year-old calf, with a round head mostly bone and a man's face; all the feet like those of a monkey, and while it could stand and walk erect it was ungraceful; it had a short tail and curly hair and its ears were like those of some men, small and stingy. In fact it may have been the same thing as the tanache discovered by Ambroise Paré. The one that Flacourt saw was in the neighborhood of Lake Lipomani, where it had a lair. He said they were very scarce—nearly extinct—and that the animal was solitary and was

as afraid of the natives as they were of it so that each ran from the other on sight as fast as they could navigate. Being a French admiral, Flacourt was permitted the license of referring to running on land as "navigation."

In the matter of hot springs Madagascar is second only to the district of hot lakes and springs in the Whakarewarewa and Rotorua regions of New Zealand and the Yellowstone of America and the Valley of Ten Thousand Smokes in Alaska. Not even Iceland equals it.

The crater lakes in their form and beauty and clearness are hardly matched by any others in the world. The natives are awed by them and worship on the banks and keep them as sacred spots where also they bathe for rheumatism and drink the waters. Animals and primitive man know more of the value of just drinking water than most of those who pride themselves on their civilization and culture.

I have visited most of the spas in the world and all that I learned is that all clean water is "medicinal" and will aid in curing anything curable, if it is drunk in sufficient quantities at home or at a health resort. The trouble with moderns is that they do not bathe enough outside and never inside unless they go to French Lick or some other roulette resort. But the Malagasy say that a man is dirtier inside than outside and that the inside dirt is poison. So the conclusion with them is that it is important to wash inside by drinking great quantities of water and let the outside go.

At Roamena I found the medicine wizards to be most clever. They know of the advantage of the naturally hot water. So not only do they order it drunk and bathed in, but pretend that they mysteriously heat it. The native does not bother to think any further than that something or somebody must heat it, so why not the fakir?

There is a noticeable difference in the quality of the water of the hot springs, and also a variation in the degrees of heat and the flow. Those of Antsirabe are of one kind, those of Roamena another and those west of Saloavaratsa, along the Taheza river, are of still another kind. All these springs have their origin in the flow of water from mountains or higher levels over beds of volcanic rocks heated by a smouldering crater. The waters thus heated may flow underground or on the surface or both.

The natives refer to these hot springs all as Andranomay, meaning "at the hot water." The springs of the Ikopa and of the Sarasotra are quite as interesting as those of the other regions.

No complete survey has been made of the hot districts of Madagascar. When they have been surveyed they will prove to be one of the chief attractions of the island. No tourists visit Madagascar now and there are no hotels, but some day this will be changed and the island will be more popular than the shelf-worn South Sea Islands of the Pacific.

I heard accounts of persons being fatally scalded in some of the springs. Others are of perfect temperature for bathing. Professor Waage of the University of Norway, who has given some study to them, says that there are counterparts of Vichy and all the other famous springs. They hold in solution lime, sulphur, magnesia, soda, potash, chlorine, iodine, and sulphuric acid and are often charged with free carbonic acid gas.

The chief discoveries of fossils have been made in the vicinity of these hot springs and close enough to them to be buried in the calcareous deposits from the waters. It is possible that poisonous fumes may have overcome the animals which came near, because small ones are found among the rest. If there were only remains of heavy birds and beasts one might accept the conjecture that they mired and died from starvation.

CHAPTER XLIV
FAREWELL

ONE must stop somewhere while the stopping is good. It is difficult to discontinue writing on Madagascar because the topic is so new and there is so much to say about it that such an ordinary and simple treatment as this book presents cannot be very satisfying nor satisfactory. It is hoped that it will stimulate more study, more writing, and more reading about this island of mystery.

The white race has been largely predatory and epiphytic. The races that are preyed upon and ridden are doing the thing that is natural. They have reached a strength and a subtlety and a ripeness which will serve them when the time comes to make an effort to save themselves. So all over the world the blacks and the browns and the yellows are tugging at the yokes and the chains that a peculiar economy and a selfish forward race have welded on them.

Pan Africanism is taking nourishment in one place; in another Ghandi is leading a struggle for freedom; somewhere else the colors are blending and the white man is just coming to be aware that he cannot hold the tail and that he cannot let go as he might desire.

It does no good for the Lothrop Stoddards to utter jeremiads over the rising tide of color and the menace to the Nordic peoples, whose inherent superiority seemed self-evident to the Kaiser and Treitschke, although the fact is that a Nordic super race never existed. This earth is a sad old raft and those who squirm and fall overboard and climb on again down the river of the ages must learn that if they are to have a place they must grant one. Nearly three-fourths of the peoples of the earth are colored and they are vital and they must be treated right or humanity will pay for it. We must learn justice and practice it and teach it to those from whom we may one day beg it.

Korzybski says man is a superior entity and in a class by himself as a time-binding agency. I like the idea, but the correlative idea is that he must prove himself to be just that.

Other Zeppelin Age Titles

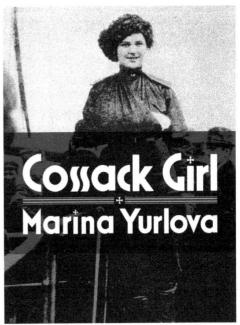

Cossack Girl By Marina Yurlova

HEL5870 • ISBN-10: 1930658702 • ISBN-13: 978-1930658707

arina Yurlova served in uniform as a fighting Cossack, volunteering
1914 at the age of 14. Though repeatedly wounded in combat, she
urned to military service and repeatedly won the St. George's Cross
bravery. Through the war and revolution, Marina encountered Turks,
ds and Reds, drove cars and trucks, fought for the Czech Legion,
ked overland across Siberia, and finally boarded a ship at Vladivostok
ravel to Japan in 1919. Remarkably, whenever asked, Marina never
ied she was a girl.

he distills these five years of her life into a captivating narrative,
d with observations and impressions of places and people Marina
countered in her extensive travels through Russia.

Lester Dent's Zeppelin Tales by Lester Dent

HEL5820 • ISBN-10: 1930658206 •ISBN-13: 978-1930658202

ester Dent penned many pulp adventures before he created Doc
age in 1933 under the house name Kenneth Robeson. Lester Dent's
ppelin Tales collects five airship-themed stories published from 1930
1932, and includes material restored from Dent's original manuscripts!
Zeppelin Bait": Jed Day, American Great War flyer, is framed for spying
a notorious German Zeppelin Captain! Originally published in the
tober 1932 issue of *Sky Birds*.

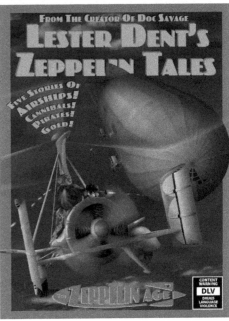

Blackbeard's Spectre": Zeppelin pirates steal the passenger dirigible
y of Oakland before its maiden flight to Japan! One of Dent's first
blished works, it originally appeared as "The Thirteen Million Dollar
bbery" in the March 1930 issue of *The Popular Magazine*.

Peril's Domain": Bill Kirgan battles a pirate band on a Zeppelin en
ite to the Arctic! Originally published under the title "The Frozen
jht" in the February 1931 issue of *Air Stories*.

Helene Was A Cannibal": What menaces the flight of Germany's newest
ppelin, the *Vaterland*? Originally published as "Teeth of Revenge" in
: May 1931 issue of *Scotland Yard*.

A Billion Gold!": A private dick gets mixed up in a Zeppelin-sized
neme in New York City! Originally published as "One Billion-Gold!" in
: June 1931 issue of *Scotland Yard*.

ester Dent's Zeppelin Tales is nearly 100,000 words of pulpy goodness!

Octocalypse! A Zeppelin Age Adventure

HEL5830 • ISBN-10: 1930658303 • ISBN-13: 978-1930658301

Vill Land Octopi doom man's dominion of the earth? Let your players
termine the answer through this role playing game adventure! The
CO game system encourages streamlined fun: creating characters or
ything they encounter is a snap, and resolving the players' actions is
en faster.

Octocalypse! includes everything you need to play (except dice),
cluding all the rules for character, creature, and contraption creation,
aracter sheets, and gear cards. Also included is "The Octopus Cycle"
ginally published in 1927, which served as an inspiration for the
venture.

Where To Find Them

You can find our books in print, PDF, and eBook formats. For more
ormation, see our Buy It! page:

http://www.heliograph.com/buy.shtml

Lightning Source UK Ltd.
Milton Keynes UK
UKHW05f1527260718
326329UK00004B/56/P

9 781930 658714